The Plant Hunter's Garden

The Plant Hunter's Garden

The New Explorers
and
Their Discoveries

Bobby J. Ward

Foreword by Brian Mathew

TIMBER PRESS

Portland • Cambridge

Frontispiece: *Brunsvigia orientalis* PHOTO BY ROD AND RACHEL SAUNDERS

Published in 2004 by
Timber Press, Inc.
The Haseltine Building
133 S.W. Second Avenue, Suite 450
Portland, Oregon 97204-3527, U.S.A.

Timber Press
2 Station Road
Swavesey
Cambridge CB4 5QJ, U.K.

www.timberpress.com

Printed in Hong Kong

Library of Congress Cataloging-in-Publication Data

Ward, Bobby J.
    The plant hunter's garden : the new explorers and their discoveries / Bobby J. Ward ; foreword by Brian Mathew.
       p. cm.
    Includes bibliographical references and index.
    ISBN 0-88192-696-5 (hardcover)
   1. Gardens. 2. Plant collectors. 3. Plant collecting. 4. Plant introduction. 5. Plants, Ornamental. I. Title.
    SB454.W248 2004
    580'.75—dc22
                                                            2004007732
A catalog record for this book is also available from the British Library.

To
Michael E. Chelednik
for first-rate horticultural comradeship
and
Roy C. Dicks
for long-term, supportive partnership

Discoverers of new lands and people, explorers
of unknown rivers and mountains, valleys and plains,
have received fair meed of praise down the centuries.
But he who has explored these regions for their flowers,
their useful and ornamental plants,
remains unsung.

Ernest Wilson, *Smoke That Thunders*, 1927

Contents

Foreword

by Brian Mathew

The exploits of the great plant hunters of former times make fascinating reading, and there is certainly no shortage of literature on the subject. Their journeys were often extremely long and tedious, their living conditions and health risks indescribable by today's standards, and the hazards numerous. Today, as we look upon the array of plants in our gardens bearing tantalizing names such as *forrestii*, *wilsonii*, *douglasii*, and *sieboldii*, we romanticize the whole business and think of it as a glamorous and glorious, though past, golden age.

Nowadays we can travel anywhere in a matter of hours—at most a day or two—and the hardships are more likely to come in the form of the pile of paperwork involved in complying with local and international wildlife laws. So, it is tempting to question whether the day of the intrepid plant hunter is indeed over, existing only on the bookshelf alongside the epic journeys of explorers such as Speke and Grant, Lewis and Clark, and Marco Polo. I think not. The scenario may have changed but the same driving force is still there: that is, to gather information and extend the range of plants available to the ever-growing fraternity of gardeners.

Many of today's collectors are focused plantspeople with particular aims. They may be seeking good or unusual forms of already well-known species, high-altitude variants that are likely to be hardier in less-favored climates, or they may be specialists in a specific genus, striving to push the boundaries of knowledge. This targeted approach is now more acceptable than the "combine harvester" technique of collecting everything in sight to satiate the desires of numerous shareholders, a concept which went unquestioned just a few decades ago.

So who are these contemporary "botanical travelers," to use Sir Joseph Banks's term? There are of course a great many. Bobby Ward has set out to present a personal selection across the spectrum of activities that come under the umbrella term of "plant hunting," and demonstrates eloquently that no longer is it those who "sleep on rocks and drink dew for breakfast" who provide us with innovations for our gardens. Nor is it those whose prime aim is financial gain. Rather it is plantspeople with enthusiasm and inquiring minds, keen to extend the frontiers of their chosen field. Some are geographical specialists, seeking the seeds of a range of unusual plants and special forms within a restricted area.

Others are generic scholars, focusing their attentions on some small facet of the plant world. Obsessive behavior? Of course it is—but we, the plant enthusiasts, are the ultimate beneficiaries.

Bobby Ward's book provides us with an insight into the motivating forces behind the characters he has selected. Unusual for this type of publication it is published while they are extant which gives it a distinct mark of authenticity, much of it being based on interviews with these personalities—before they have joined the ranks of the deceased and romanticized. There is a wealth of interest here for keen gardeners and botanists. Numerous exciting new plants are mentioned and illustrated, their origins and behavior in cultivation are recorded, and the whole is laced entertainingly with many a traveler's anecdote.

Acknowledgments

There are no happier folk than plant-lovers
and none more generous than those who garden.

Ernest Wilson, *Smoke That Thunders*, 1927

Many people have assisted me in the planning, researching, interviewing, and writing of this book. Without advice and support from many friends, both old and new, I could not have written *The Plant Hunter's Garden: The New Explorers and Their Discoveries*. I appreciate the assistance of various persons who helped on this book in so many ways.

Foremost, I owe tremendous gratitude, thanks, and respect to those persons who are profiled in this book and who allowed my intrusion into their lives. All cheerfully responded to me by mail, telephone, fax, and e-mail, and allowed my visits (sometimes repeatedly) between their own travels, speaking engagements, plant hunting trips, and gardening. I particularly appreciate the generosity and hospitality extended me by those who provided meals and lodging in their homes, gave me plants and seeds from their gardens, allowed me to collect seeds with them, and kindly answered numerous questions, often late at night over glasses of wine while the rest of the household was begging for bedtime quiet.

In planning this project, I consulted with several people to get a perspective on contemporary plant and seed collecting. During the early stages of the manuscript, they assisted me in its development. For this, I am indebted to Jim Archibald, Tony Avent, Mike Chelednik, Jack Elliott, John Grimshaw, Panayoti Kelaidis, Neal Maillet, and John Watson.

I am indebted to Mike Chelednik, Roy Dicks, and Mary Kathlyn Ramm who read all draft chapters and gave me valuable critiques, provided salutary discussion and an external, objective eye. Obviously, I am solely responsible for any errors that remain or for any suggestions that I did not heed from them or from others whom I consulted.

Many gardening friends, mostly from the North American Rock Garden Society, the Alpine Garden Society, and the JC Raulston Arboretum, assisted in many ways, including tracking down information on specific plants, supplying magazine and newspaper articles, lending slides, assessing the worthiness of a plant mentioned, critiquing selected chapters, and much more. In addition to those mentioned above, they include Michelle Avent, Jeffery Beam, John and Pat Bender, Bill Burk, Dorothy Chadwell, Betsy Clebsch, Helen Dillon, Richard Dufresne, Jean Elliott, Michael Fay, Marnie Flook, Joyce Fingerut, John Grimshaw, Phyllis Gustafson, Pepa Halda, David Hale, Pamela Harper, Richard Hartlage, Jim Jones, Paul Jones, Josef Jurášek, Jr., Robert Jones, Gwen Kelaidis, Sandra Ladendorf, Roy Lancaster, Todd Lasseigne, Dave Lehmiller, Richard Lighty, John Lonsdale, Robert Lyons, Brian Mathew, Julia and Robert Mackintosh, Jim McClements, Pat McCracken, Jane McGary, Malcolm McGregor, Baldassare Mineo, Jacques Mommens, Phil Normandy, Bob Nold, Graham Nicholls, Sue and Andrew Osyany, John L. (Johnny) Randall, Wade Roitsch, Scott Ross, Loren Russell, Jan Slater, Sandy Snyder, Tom Stuart, Larry Thomas, Sandra Thomas, Judith and Dick Tyler, Jim Waddick, Rannveig Wallis, Andy Wong, and Harvey Wrightman.

To those who helped me but I have inadvertently failed to recall your generosity, I thank George and Georgina Spelvin, in your name.

I received frequent library reference help from Bill Burk (University of North Carolina, Chapel Hill) and Roy Dicks, my in-house librarian. I acknowledge the scores of Web sites maintained on the Internet by plant nurseries, arboreta and botanical gardens, university and academic libraries, and personal sites, which provided ease of accessing (and cross checking) information on plants, plant hunters, plant culture, and biographical and bibliographic information. One source that frequently "Googled" up on my computer screen was the newsletter (*Chronicles*) of the JC Raulston Arboretum, a site chock-full of information on "new," primarily woody plants, including consideration of their horticultural adaptability.

I acknowledge, with appreciation and fondness, Christine Wilton Helms, my freshman botany teacher at East Carolina College, Greenville, North Carolina, who wittingly steered me into the world of botany, where I was later beguiled into horticulture as an avocation. At this writing, she is ninety-seven.

I also acknowledge the staff at Timber Press, particularly the editorial skills of Linda J. Willms.

Finally, I thank Neal Maillet, Timber Press's "prince of a fellow" as well as its executive editor. His enthusiasm, counsel, and assistance in working with authors are, like the plants in this book, without bounds.

BOBBY J. WARD
Raleigh and Goose Bay, North Carolina

Introduction

*Nature is a generous mother and with leaf and flower
has decked the world in loveliness.*

Ernest Wilson, *Smoke That Thunders*, 1927

I garden on a half acre (0.2 ha) in North Carolina, where the summers are hot and humid, and the winters are mild. I grow several hundred perennials, bulbs, and shrubs, and a few annuals. I replace plants that do not tolerate the red clay soil of the Piedmont region or the warm summer nights and July–August rains, the wettest months of the year, and I continually seek new plants for testing against these conditions.

Only ten to fifteen percent of the plants I grow are native to the U.S. Southeast where I live (USDA Zone 7). The remainder are non-native and came to me along myriad paths that included local nurseries, seed exchanges, mail order, my own collecting trips, and gifts from friends. Some of the plants that have adapted best for me originated in other parts of the United States, Mexico, Argentina, Brazil, and the Mediterranean region including Turkey, Greece, Italy, and Spain. There are plants from northern and eastern Europe, the Far East including China, Japan, and Korea, and even a few from South Africa. One raised plant bed measures 8 × 24 feet (2.4 × 7.2 m) and contains 125 rock garden plants from five continents. It sits next to *Musa basjoo*, a hardy banana, native to the subtropical Ryukyu Archipelago between Japan and Taiwan. I grow—though not deliberately—a few invasive plants that are both native (pokeweed, *Phytolacca americana*) and non-native (Japanese stilt-grass, *Microstegium vimineum*).

Gardeners have not always fully appreciated the process by which new plants come into cultivation. We often have scant knowledge of how plants reach the neighborhood nursery. Focusing on making our gardens grow, we rarely have any idea of a plant's origin, its history, or the often charming story of its circuitous pathway to bed and border. Seldom do we ponder over who selected, gathered, cultivated, and put these plants to use in agriculture and horticulture, commerce and industry.

Plant explorers have been the great facilitators of these introductions—some from as far back as three thousand years. Some expeditions have been pleasant and enjoyable, others dangerous and arduous. Plant explorers have endured unbearable weather conditions, witnessed political turmoil, ducked civil war, and suffered imprisonment, all for the sake of collecting new and unusual plants. Many collecting trips have been carried out under difficult circumstances, and the participants have incurred sicknesses, accidents, even loss of life.

For example, the Englishman John Lawson, who surveyed the interior of what is now South Carolina and North Carolina from 1701 to 1711, sent back to London 308 Carolina plants representing about one hundred taxa. His preserved specimens currently reside at the British Museum. In 1711 when he was thirty-six, surveying along the Neuse River (near present-day New Bern, North Carolina), his life was cut short. Searching for a more direct route to Virginia, Lawson was taken by the Tuscarora, a native tribe, and tortured by "sticking him all over with pitch pine splinters before setting him ablaze" while he was still alive (Hudson 1992). In another grisly version of his demise, Lawson "was waylaid [by the Tuscarora] and had his throat cut from ear to ear" by his own razor (Lefler 1967).

The immensely prolific plant hunter David Douglas, of Douglas fir fame, endured arduous travels in the Pacific Northwest. He met his fate in 1834 in the Sandwich Islands (now Hawaiian Islands), gashed and gored by a bull when Douglas either fell accidentally into a hidden cattle trap or was pushed into the trap by convicts who also robbed him (Whittle 1997).

Many gardeners may be familiar with the purple prose of the obsessed plant hunter Reginald Farrer, author of *The English Rock Garden*, who collected plants in Tibet, China, and Burma (now Myanmar). He died in 1920, weakened by a severe chest cold and fever, on a remote, rainy mountaintop in Burma. Farrer was 8000 miles (5000 km) from his home in England, far from medical attention, and he died "for plants and duty" (Shulman 2002).

None of these calamities have stopped the continuing quest by numerous plant hunters around the world. The history of plant hunting is filled with determined individuals driven by commercial, scientific, and personal goals.

As far as we know, Egyptian Queen Hatusu (also called Hatshepsut) sent the earliest recorded plant-hunting expedition to the Land of Punt in northeast Africa (generally the coastal areas of present-day Somalia, eastern Sudan, and the neighboring independent state of Eritrea). Hatusu was one of the few female pharaohs to rule Egypt, first as regent for her nephew (Thutmose III), and later as pharaoh in her own right. In about 1495 BCE, she sent a squadron of five rowing ships down the Nile, by canal to the Gulf of Suez, and through the Red Sea to Punt. Her goal was to improve reliable access to the goods she needed, and thus the expedition was purely commercial. Among her desiderata were living trees and shrubs containing fragrant gums and resins. In particular, Hatusu wanted frankincense, myrrh, and other forms of incense for use in temples, in embalming mixtures, and as ointments, cosmetics, and fumigation for vermin (Edwards 1892).

It appears the expedition was successful. Upon return of the fleet, slave bearers presented the monarch with beads, bracelets, ivory, even an elephant and a giraffe (gifts from the Prince of Punt), precious woods, and thirty-one small trees and shrubs. The botanical identity of the trees is unclear. Contemporary botanists suggest they were frankincense (*Boswellia serrata*), myrrh (*Commiphora myrrha*), or the Ana or sycamore fig (*Ficus sycomorus*). We know about this expedition because it is fully illustrated on Hatusu's temple walls at Deir el-Bahari, near Thebes (now Luxor) in the Valley of the Kings, where the shrubs were planted.

Dioscorides of Anazarbus (40 CE–c. 90 CE), a Greek physician, included approximately five hundred plant descriptions in a five-volume book, written in Greek but now best known in its Latin translation, *De Materia Medica* ("Regarding Medical Matters"), on the therapeutic uses of plants, much of which he learned by traveling extensively as a physician with Nero's armies. These travels gave him the opportunity to study new plants, observe how they grew, and learn their medical properties. Modern scientific pharmacology had its origins with Dioscorides.

Marco Polo (1254–1324), a Venetian, was the first European to cross Asia during a twenty-four-year voyage with his father and uncle. In *The Travels of Marco*

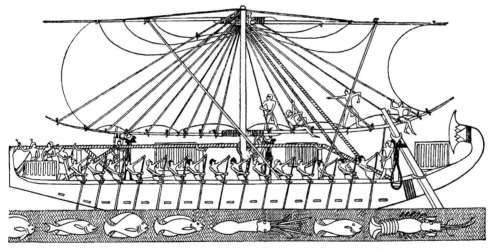

One of Queen Hatusu's ships heading to Punt. From *Deir el-Bahari* (Edwards 1892).

Loading tree saplings on Queen Hatusu's ships. From *Deir el-Bahari* (Edwards 1892).

Measuring the precious gums and resins from Punt. From *Deir el-Bahari* (Edwards 1892).

Polo or a Description of the World, written upon his return, he mentions exotic plants and spices encountered on the trip that carried him from the kingdoms of Ferghana and Sogdiana (now Uzbekistan) to Cathay (now China) and the Gobi Desert, coastal areas along the South China Sea, Sumatra, and back to Italy. He was particularly observant of plants that might have commercial significance. Among those he described were paper mulberry (*Broussonetia papyrifera*), hemp (*Cannabis*), and steppe grass, the latter having been planted by the Kublai Khan in his courtyard as a reminder of his Mongol roots.

The Tradescants introduced many plants from abroad to England in the early to midseventeenth century. John Tradescant traveled to gardens and nurseries in Holland and France, initially for his patron Sir Robert Cecil, and later on other missions to Russia and the Mediterranean, returning with trees, shrubs, and perennials, some of which were new to the British Isles. Tradescant's son (also named John) worked with his father at their horticultural enterprise and their wondrous museum, the Ark, containing "curiosities" of nature at South Lambeth (London). Tradescant the younger made three trips to Virginia beginning in 1637 and returned with many New World plants, including trees and shrubs as well as poison ivy (*Toxicodendron radicans*). John the elder and John the younger were both gardeners to Charles I. The best-known garden plant derived from the Tradescants' garden is *Tradescantia virginica*, collected by John the younger in Virginia and taken to England. The Tradescant family name was honored by Carl Linnaeus in the naming of the genus *Tradescantia*.

The native plants and ethnobotany of present-day Peru and Chile were detailed in the 1780s diary of Hipólito Ruíz, a Spanish explorer under Carlos III (Ruíz 1998). Among the "sundry new plants" that Ruíz observed were *Cinchona* or quinine, vanilla orchid, cocoa, banana, and chili pepper. In all, Ruíz made Europeans aware of about five hundred plants from the New World.

Agriculture, horticulture, and botanical knowledge are beneficiaries of the European discovery, exploration, and occupation of the New World. The Americas have provided horticultural plants, such as dahlia, fuchsia, and sunflower, and important agricultural plants, such as tomato, tobacco, white potato (*Solanum tuberosum*), sweet potato (*Ipomoea batatas*), pumpkin, and squash.

Gathering plants and getting them back as living, growing specimens, however, was a major problem. Ships from the Americas could take months to return to Europe, and sailors had to ration fresh water for themselves, not use it for plant cargoes. If plants did not die from lack of water, the salt water spray would further damage or kill them. Thus on long trips during the sixteenth to eighteenth centuries, explorers brought or sent back seeds, bulbs, tubers, fruit, and rhizomes. A significant breakthrough in plant exploration came with the invention of the Wardian case, a simple glass case that allowed living plants to be "sealed" and shipped thousands of miles, arriving months later at a destination with minimal loss. We know it today as a terrarium. Nathaniel Ward designed the glass cases in the early 1830s, and the face of plant exploration changed forever. Ships became floating gardens.

Modern-day plant hunters have enjoyed relative ease of travel and welcome comforts unimagined by their predecessors. In the latter part of the twentieth century air travel enhanced the opportunity for plant explorers to travel easily and quickly from country to country, a far cry from the lengthy travel by ship even as recently as the early decades of that century. Motor vehicles and good roads, local accommodations, telephones, and satellite geo-positioning have allowed better collection and prompt return, considerably different from the era of the Wardian case in the previous century.

Even with modern conveniences, the twentieth century held difficulties for plant explorers. Political turmoil from the 1940s till the 1970s thwarted and frustrated opportunities for expanded collecting in some areas. From China, for example, few plants were brought into cultivation after the 1930s, with the exception of a short period after World War II, when the newly discovered dawn redwood (*Metasequoia glyptostroboides*) and cultivars of *Camellia reticulata* came to the West (Bartholomew 1997). Other major hindrances included the bamboo curtain (China), the cool relations between Japan and the West following World War II, the Korean conflict, the Cold War between the former Soviet Union and the West, conflicts in Southeast Asia, particularly Vietnam, and more recently, the political isolation of South Africa.

In the last decades of the twentieth century, diplomatic relationships in these areas were rekindled. The unlikely friendship resulting from Ping-Pong games (Ping-Pong Diplomacy) in 1971 and U.S. President Richard Nixon's visit to China in 1972 opened interchange with that country. Benefits to botanists and other scientists began to accrue immediately, but most of the early contacts were between delegations of botanical gardens and arboreta, not nursery owners. From 1978 to 1980 botanists of the Chinese Academy of Sciences and five U.S. botanical gardens participated in an exchange program, the Sino-American Botanical Expedition, the first since the establishment of the People's Republic of China in 1949. As a result of these contacts, "new" seeds, cuttings, and herbarium specimens were sent to participating institutions in the West. While some areas of Asia have re-opened to plant explorations, others unfortunately are now closed or difficult to access, including Tibet, Kashmir, Iran, Iraq, and Afghanistan.

Since the sixteenth century, five great periods of new plant introductions have tremendously affected the way we have gardened, particularly in Europe and in North America (Stuart 2002). The first was the surge of bulbous plants from Turkey and the eastern Mediterranean in the latter part of the sixteenth century. Fritillaries, daffodils, tulips, and cultivated hyacinths began entering gardens in Europe and England. The excitement and awakening of scientific interest in new plants may have helped fuel the Renaissance. During this era, well-maintained topiaries and knot gardens, in vogue at the time, became less favored and were replaced by "open knot" or parterre gardens for display plantings.

The second wave began in the eighteenth century with the introduction of North American plants, such as magnolias, rhododendrons, and kalmias, into the United Kingdom and mainland Europe. The latter part of the century witnessed, though to a lesser extent, the introduction of plants from South Africa, primarily by Francis Masson. Among these were belladonna lily (*Amaryllis belladonna*), *Protea*, carrion flower (*Stapelia*), bird of paradise (*Strelitzia*), calla lily (*Zantedeschia*), and other "porch plants," the most popular of which were the scented geraniums (*Pelargonium*).

The third influx of plants came from South America in the early nineteenth century with new annuals and perennials, bright tropical plants such as orchids and cactus, begonias, ferns, and bulbs. These plants went first to the United Kingdom and Europe, then later to North America. The plants, including those that were half-hardy, became bedding-out plants while tender ones filled Victorian glass (green) houses, conservatories, terrariums, and parlors. During the century, Scotsman David Douglas explored western North America and gardens and nurseries in the New York and Philadelphia areas. His travels introduced many plants to Europe, including selections of fruit trees, Oregon grape (*Mahonia aquifolium*), annuals, numerous conifers, and flowering currant (*Ribes sanguineum*).

The latter part of the nineteenth century and early part of the twentieth century saw the introduction of plants from Asia to the West, first to Europe and then North America. These included Asiatic hydrangea, snowbell (*Styrax*), stewartia, crab apple, flowering cherry, camellia, and the development of hybrid tea roses, derived in part from *Rosa* ×*odorata*, a Chinese species. In addition, important wild collections were made by Ernest Wilson, George Forrest, Reginald Farrer, and Frank Kingdon-Ward.

Now we are enjoying the fruits of a fifth wave of horticultural introductions, the Post–Cold War collecting era. In the last two decades of the twentieth century, a modern plant-hunting renaissance flourished to meet the demands of a public with considerable leisure time for gardening. Ease of travel, along with international political and ideological changes, opened doors to plant hunters, allowing access to collecting locales previously denied for decades.

Contemporary nursery owners–plant hunters as a group have a unique, unifying asset: they do extremely well in introducing plants to horticulture and gardening through their nurseries and mail-order businesses. They have keen eyes for selecting plants with garden potential, resulting in considerable horticultural and commercial successes.

Peter Del Tredici (2000) of the Arnold Arboretum (Harvard University, Boston) has said that botanical gardens and arboreta excel at the pure science and botanical study of plants, while nurseries excel at distribution—and thus the two need to work together. The goals and purposes of botanical gardens and arboreta differ significantly from contemporary entrepreneurial plant hunters. The latter search out horticulturally worthy specimens (the focus and interest of this book), while the former may concentrate on collecting all species of a certain genus or a botanical family and are more interested in taxonomic relationships and herbarium specimens, rather than horticulture. To attract the public and potential financial donations, botanical gardens and arboreta frequently promote their collection of display gardens with new plants as one of the prominent features; however, these institutions are not so motivated to evaluate "new" plants on a short timeline for potential horticulture interest as are nursery owners whose priority is commercial introduction. New plants entering the horticultural trade through botanical gardens, arboreta, and other institutions may take decades, if introduced at all. Nursery owners, after evaluating new plants for garden usefulness, invasive potential, and insect or disease vectors, may offer them in as little as two years.

Richard Lighty, formerly of Mount Cuba Center for Piedmont Studies, studied ornamental plant introductions of the 1990s. He showed that the highest percentage of surviving plants in our gardens from plant-hunting trips made in that decade were from entrepreneurs or nursery owners—*not* the heavily funded expeditions of major botanical gardens and arboreta, or government co-funded consortiums (Lighty 2000). Thus a good-natured rivalry exists between the commercial nursery sector and botanical gardens, or as commonly said, the trade and the academics. Still, as Daniel Hinkley, one of the plant hunters profiled here, says, botanical gardens and university arboreta "are some of my best customers," even buying a share in his plant-hunting expeditions (Klinkenborg 1999).

One issue that has become prominent in the minds of plant hunters and nursery owners, their clientele, and even the general public, is the unintentional introduction of invasive plants. Some worry that "alien" plants introduced into native horticulture may be pestiferous or invasive, capable of out-competing native plants and harming agricultural production. It is a valid concern and I deal with it as a separate chapter.

I should briefly address my definition of "plant explorer." I do not believe the definition should exclude those who do not sleep on rocks and drink dew for breakfast. Many of those profiled in this book, such as the Archibalds, are explorers in the strictest sense—their introductions are almost entirely of those plants they have found in wild places. Others, however, such as Tony Avent, may be just as likely to make their discoveries in gardens and seedbeds as in rain forests. Sean Hogan has introduced several zauschnerias from wild-collected material, but one of the nicer zauschnerias he has found occurred in his mother's backyard. Anyone who finds an unappreciated plant and can see its untapped potential for horticulture is a plant explorer. Most of the plants in this book were "found" by plant explorers in the traditional way, but I ask the reader's indulgence to consider unusual and wonderful plant finds, wherever they happen, as worthy of recognition.

Finally, although it is not the intention of this book to engage in the policy debate concerning the laws and regulations pertaining to plant hunting (this is a book about plants, not politics), it would be impossible to completely avoid addressing some controversies surrounding plant hunting in the wild. The patchwork of international treaties and conventions that concern the collection and importation of plants, as well as their commercial exploitation, has become especially difficult to interpret and understand. Of particular interest is the Rio Convention of 1992—as yet unadopted in the United States—which would more strictly limit the collection of plants and provide for the remuneration of indigenous peoples for the commercial use of plants collected in their homelands. More widely applied (but not without controversies of its own) is the Convention on International Trade in Endangered Species of Wild Fauna and Flora (CITES). This last convention, for example, strictly limits in umbrella fashion the importation of various taxa, such as species in the orchid family, considered to be threatened around the world. Needless to say, responsible collectors will do their utmost to abide by international laws, but the questions and regulations involved are far from simple or clear. I do not wish to argue for or against peculiarities of international law pertaining to plant hunting, but I wish to reassure readers that, to the best of my knowledge, all plants described in this book were collected ethically and legally. Some of the collectors in this book have actually ceased all plant collecting in recent years because of the difficulties in determining the legal landscape.

Thankfully, others persevere, although the research into the intricacies of international law may now take more time than herbarium research. Readers of this book are advised to keep this fact in mind before they begin plant hunting on their own. I can't resist pointing out that increased difficulties put in the way of plant collectors may paradoxically doom many plants in threatened habitats to extinction—these plants can't be saved if seeds or cuttings aren't taken to safe harbors against the sad inevitabilities of habitat destruction.

Ernest "Chinese" Wilson (1927), Anglo-American plant collector and director of the Arnold Arboretum, wrote that "nature is a generous mother and with leaf and flower has decked the world in loveliness." Modern-day plant hunters delight in the love of leaf and flower, a love they share with those in the great fellowship of the garden spade. What follows in this book is an overview of some of the contemporary, entrepreneurial plant hunters and descriptions of significant plant introductions, or the plants that they have widely promoted through their businesses (not all are "new" to botany or horticulture). These individuals have attributes in common: they are obsessed when it comes to plants. They have a nursery or business, or a "green industry" affiliation that facilitates dispersal of plants and seeds to clientele. A few are university-degreed horticulturists or botanists, while many have acquired their considerable skills and knowledge through nontraditional paths. Most important, they are all highly motivated, effective, and efficient in introducing plants to their customers. Except for their own plant catalogs, seed lists, and occasional magazine articles, these plantspeople have been little recognized. When they retire or pass on, their considerable specialized knowledge will be lost. I hope here to preserve a bit of the information on the contributions made by these contemporary plant hunters.

1

What Are Seeds but Dreams in Packets?
Jim & Jenny Archibald

I once spent a long weekend poring over forty years of back issues of Jim and Jenny Archibald's newsletter–seed lists. When I emerged bleary-eyed from my self-imposed incarceration, I felt as if I had seen the history of contemporary plant collecting pass before me. Such is the duration, breadth, and depth of the Archibalds' experience. An additional reason to receive the newsletter–seed list is to experience Jim's acutely distilled, sometimes barbed, commentaries. Whether they are skewering horticultural snobs, botanical academicians, self-proclaimed conservationists, or "waffles of disinformation," they beguile you into agreement by the clarity and lucidity of their arguments. With Jenny's quiet endorsement, no doubt, Jim's iconoclasm and "spontaneous prattle" toss darts at venerable institutions such as the Royal Horticultural Society and the Alpine Garden Society, particularly on the topics of lip-service conservation, bureaucratic high-mindedness, and nomenclatural one-upmanship.

Occasionally the newsletters provide unabashed adulation for the horticultural progenitors on whose shoulders the Archibalds and other contemporary seed collectors stand. The Archibalds' dear tributes to two renowned plantspeople come to mind: remembering bulb collector Paul Furse, who pined for his beloved English strawberry jam while in Iran, and despairing at the funeral service for Jack Drake (Inshriach Alpine Plant Nursery), which was attended by hardly anyone from the plant world.

Jim, a Scot, studied English literature at the University of Edinburgh and during the summers worked at Jack Drake's nursery, where he got his first introduction to the plant nursery industry. After graduating, he and friends made his first collecting trip in 1962 to the Atlas Mountains, where he recorded detailed field notes on living material he observed, and issued his first plant and seed list. In 1964 Jim moved to Dorset at Buckshaw Gardens and there ran The Plantsmen (nursery) with Eric Smith (from 1967 to 1975).

Jenny was born in Weston-super-Mare in southwest England and trained as a teacher for the Women's League of Health and Beauty. She lived in Quebec for a number of years before returning to the United Kingdom and beginning work at The Plantsmen nursery in 1975. When Smith left, Jim and Jenny ran the nursery till 1983. They have operated Jim and Jenny Archibald (seeds) since 1984, moving to Llandysul (Wales) in 1988.

I visited the Archibalds at the peak of strawberry and gooseberry season. What lucky timing that proved to be, for Jenny made me have both strawberries and cream and gooseberry tart. Afterwards, Jim and Jenny guided me around their various gardens and greenhouses, on land that slopes downward behind the house, and to a hillside with grazing sheep. It is a picture-postcard landscape that is quiet and peaceful.

The Archibalds have collected widely, from the earliest trips to Corsica and Morocco in the 1960s to recent trips to central Asia (Kazakhstan and Uzbekistan). In between have been numerous trips to the Mediterranean and Middle East (Spain, Greece, Iran, and Turkey), and collecting expeditions to South America (Colombia, Ecuador, Argentina, and Chile), South Africa, New Zealand, and the U.S. West.

It is a shame that Jim has not continued publishing his travel logs, such as those on Corsica and Morocco, which appeared in 1963 in the *Quarterly Bulletin of the Alpine Garden Society*. His admirable pen-and-ink drawings complement the articles. His daily journal about the love of the land, people, and his freedom to see native plants seems idyllic, an antidote to the urgent seed collecting at hand. Here is a poetic example from "Corsican Spring" (Archibald 1963a):

> Down in the glade by the stream, an ancient *Prunus avium* wore a trousseau of white, with golden-green hellebores as bridesmaids; nearby beneath an equally venerable chestnut, a colony of romuleas grew in the hard clay. Their seeds were ripening well but, brushing away dry leaves, I found two corms still with abortive flowers—so tiny as to be worthless to most gardeners—but how exquisite was their intricacy of shading in white, mauve, and deep-yellow, penciled with violet and green!

Fortunately there have been a few recent writings, including his paean to fellow plantsman and business partner, Eric Smith, where Jim details rather objectively the development, co-management, and problems of The Plantsmen nursery (Archibald 2000). There also is a published transcript of Jim's invited speech at Alpines 1981, Fifth International Rock Garden Plant Conference in Nottingham, on the topic "The Introduction and Maintenance of New Plants" in which he assesses the previous two decades of alpine plant introductions. Contemporary plant explorers would benefit immensely from more of Archibald's commonsense analyses.

When I asked Panayoti Kelaidis of the Denver Botanic Gardens what were the Archibalds' "greatest hits," he said he would "dread to imagine the length of the list," and then quickly rattled off a roll call of plants, and catching his breath said, "Mind you, this does not even touch the bulbs and the cushiony plants that are also noteworthy." Panayoti refers to the Archibalds as the "King and Queen" of contemporary seed collectors. Christopher Grey-Wilson (1999a) wrote that the collections made by Jim Archibald (and others) in the Middle East contributed significantly to the golden age of plant hunting in that region. Will McLewin, the hellebore hound who lives in Manchester (United Kingdom) and who sometimes trades seeds with the Archibalds, says that Jim's writing and knowledge of plants show him to be a "downright genius" and the only one Will knows, with the possible exception of a mathematician who lives in Massachusetts.

Jim and Jenny bring an intellectual approach to the business of contemporary plant hunting. Our gardens and greenhouses are the richer for their introductions, a few of which I describe below.

Carduncellus (Asteraceae) is a plant of the Mediterranean region. It forms a rosette of leaves and produces thistlelike heads of flowers. *Carduncellus pinnatus* has pinnate leaves composed of up to thirty-one leaflets with a hairy midrib and spiny tips. In 1962, Jim collected a stemless form, *C. pinnatus* var. *acaulis*, in the Atlas Mountains of North Africa, where it grows in dry rocky, sunny locations. It produces blue-lavender flowers in spring. Panayoti Kelaidis, who has grown the stemless form, provides this memorable assessment of it, "The waxy foliage in a trim rosette and extraterrestrial, glowing lavender blossoms appeal to even the most devout thistle haters." Jim laughs that he would likely have missed finding this *Carduncellus* had he not picked the exact location where the plant grew to pitch his tent for the night.

Euphorbia niciciana (syn. *E. sequieriana* subsp. *niciciana*) was one of the earliest plants Jim introduced from a collection in 1964 (JCA 521) from Mount

Carduncellus pinnatus var. *acaulis* PHOTO BY JIM AND JENNY ARCHIBALD

Mitschikeli in the Pindus Mountains of northern Greece. A member of the Euphorbiaceae or spurge family, *E. niciciana* comes into flower in late spring with insignificant petals that are yellow. The chartreuse leaves (bracts) surrounding the flower persist till autumn, however, making it a first-rate border plant. In the garden it can form a low, ground-hugging mound about 3 feet (0.9 m) across and 18 inches (45 cm) high. It seems to enjoy poor, dry soil and a sunny aspect. When Jim collected the plant he did not consider it important, but over the years it has become more valued in gardens.

As contemporary plant hunters introduce new plants, one wonders how much information to give the gardener so that the proper conditions can be duplicated for the plant to succeed. It is interesting to read the old description of *Euphorbia niciciana* in the catalog from Buckshaw Gardens Nursery, which Jim was operating at the time. In it he details the collection elevations, soil type, the aspect of the mountain, as well as the plant description. He sets the example by stating his policy for sharing information when he writes:

> We feel that a plant-collecting expedition which fails to provide adequate field-notes on the natural habitats of the plants collected is not only letting much of its own effort go to waste but is also allowing that of its supporters to do so. . . . Most of these notes are by necessity brief and many refer to plants which could only be collected as dried specimens, but we hope that, taken as a whole, they may help to build up a composite impression of the habitats of the collected seeds and bulbs and, in so doing, not only add much to the interest of subscribing but also make the task of cultivating many of these plants much easier.

Dionysus, the Greek name for Bacchus, the Roman god of vine and wine, is the source of the appellation given *Dionysia* by Eduard Fenzl, a nineteenth-century Viennese professor of botany. It is one of the most challenging genera to grow, and according to one reference, "Dionysia are not for the beginner" as they "are mainly difficult alpine house cushion plants" (Bird and Kelly 1994). There are about forty-two species of *Dionysia* (Primulaceae).

Dionysia archibaldii was collected at several high elevations up to 14,000 feet (4200 m) in Iran on Zardeh Kuh Peak in 1966. It forms small gray cushions and has leaves covered in short glandular hairs. The petals are pale pink and notched at the tips. Archibald was aided on the trip in the remote area (at the time) by a local guide, an aristocratic Bakhtiari tribesman, who hunted ibex while Jim collected seed. Per Wendelbo, a Norwegian by birth who worked at the Gothenburg (Goteborg) Botanic Garden in Sweden, published the description of the plant and provided the specific epithet to honor Jim Archibald.

After a tentative start in cultivation—the population may have been down to a single clone—the pinkish-lilac *Dionysia archibaldii* is now contributing its genes to the rapidly expanding ranks of hybrid dionysias. The species remains a challenge, with few growers keeping individual plants more than four years, when

Euphorbia niciciana PHOTO BY JIM AND JENNY ARCHIBALD

they may have made a cushion 4 inches (10 cm) across. Fortunately cuttings allow increase of the plant. Because Dionysus was also associated with agriculture and fertility, perhaps invoking his name when sowing seeds of *Dionysia* will overcome the plant's finickiness.

The Denver Botanic Gardens and the Colorado plant nursery industry chose *Digitalis thapsi* (Scrophulariaceae) and dubbed a selection, Spanish Peaks™ foxglove, for one of its 1999 Plant Select® winners (see chapter 7). The plant was virtually unknown in cultivation prior to its promotion. *Digitalis thapsi* is native to Spain and eastern Portugal in rocky slopes and uncultivated fields, where the Archibalds collected seed in the 1980s and shared them with Panayoti Kelaidis. Spanish Peaks™ has raspberry-rose flowers in midsummer. The plant may reach 15 inches (37.5 cm) high and grow to 12 inches (30 cm) wide. It thrives in various sites and soils. Because of ease of growth in the region, Spanish Peaks™ was well received by gardeners. It is a perennial, unlike typical biennial foxgloves, requiring only low to moderate watering, making it a choice for xeriscape landscaping.

In their newsletter–seedlist of November 1986 the Archibalds describe pulling a caravan (trailer) across Europe to Greece and Turkey earlier that year. The purpose of the caravan was to have a field base camp, the opportunity and flexibility to make trips from as short as a day up to several weeks, and the ability for in-the-field seed-cleaning, drying and organizing herbarium specimens, and a modicum of comfort. The trip yielded a wealth of seeds from several countries, including seed collections of several campanulas (bellflower).

In eastern Turkey the Archibalds found *Campanula troegerae* northwest of Yusufeli (Artvin) growing in crevices of shady, igneous rocky cliffs at an elevation of 2300 feet (700 m). They consider this campanula of great importance to the gardener because it has outstanding leaf and flower characteristics. The leaves are thick textured, gray-green, about 2 to 3 inches (5–7.5 cm) long, and densely pubescent. The funnel-shaped flowers are large and open up to 1.5 inches (3.5 cm) wide by 0.75 inch (2 cm) long. The Archibalds collected seed at the type locality where the plant was first reported ten years earlier in 1976. Regrettably, some of the population will be lost to the planned Yusufeli Dam and Hydroelectric Project in the Çoruh River valley, the only known locality where *C. troegerae* grows.

Campanula choruhensis was offered in the 1986 seed list as *C. betulifolia* because the plant has many characteristics normally found in this latter species and the two species are closely related. *Campanula choruhensis* is from the Çoruh River valley, Turkey, from which the specific epithet is derived. It has large creamy white, open-faced flowers, which are ribbed and slightly pink when in bud, and gray-green toothed leaves. It grows to about 8 inches (20 cm) tall and 4 inches (10 cm) wide.

Campanula hawkinsiana was from a collection near Katara Pass, Greece, growing on classic serpentine scree at an elevation of 5600 feet (1700 m). The natural range of this bellflower is northern Greece to Albania. It has been in cultivation since the 1930s, but not widely grown because it requires serpentine soils. The Archibalds say that it is a wiry, small-leaved plant with wide flowers "of penetrating violet shading to intense electric-blue at the centers [and] a challenge to the cultivator." It grows about 8 inches (20 cm) tall and wide.

Baldassare Mineo, owner of Siskiyou Rare Plant Nursery in Medford, Oregon, has success with it in sun and part shade in scree conditions, but protected from winter wetness. He suggests it is suitable in USDA Zones 6 to 8, based on his regional experience.

Michauxia tchihatchewii (also spelled "tchihatcheffii") is a member of the Campanulaceae. The Archibalds collected it in 1986 at Adana, Turkey, south of Feke, growing on loose shale at an elevation of about 2630 feet (800 m). *Michauxia tchihatchewii* is a monocarpic perennial, sometimes taking several years to reach flowering size, which is ultimately 3 feet (0.9 m) or more. The flower buds are lilac colored and when they open the spectacular white petals reflex backwards, giving a turk's-cap-like appearance to the flower. The plant is not rare in the wild as the Archibalds often found it along road cuts among hills and low mountains of the region. They did not consider it an important plant at the time, but now large international seed companies are widely promoting it. The genus name honors André Michaux (1746–1803), French botanist and explorer, and the specific epithet honors Petr Aleksandrovich Tchihatcheff (1812–1890), a Russian botanist.

Campanula troegerae PHOTO BY JIM AND JENNY ARCHIBALD

Campanula hawkinsiana PHOTO BY JIM AND JENNY ARCHIBALD

Michauxia tchihatchewii PHOTO BY JIM AND JENNY ARCHIBALD

The gardener is often confounded by the myriad forms of *Saxifraga* (Saxifragaceae), or rockfoil. This huge genus is divided into at least six sections. Rockfoils are one of the classic backbone plants of rock and alpine gardening.

Saxifraga wendelboi is native to the Elburz Mountains in northern Iran, where it grows between elevations of approximately 6250 and 9550 feet (1900–2900 m). It is a kabschia saxifrage, or member of section *Porophyllum* (that is, a cushiony, mat-forming plant). The white petals are slightly reflexed, fading to light pink, on both short and long flowering stems. When not in bloom, the plant forms a hard, low dome with lime-green leaves. Jim introduced it in 1966 by way of living material, not by a seed collection as is the case for most of his other plant introductions. Jim says that "cuttings were airmailed from Teheran to Harold Esslemont (an outstanding Scottish amateur grower), Jack Drake, and Will Ingwersen." All of them established plants, but only Jack Drake propagated and listed it. The specific epithet honors Per Wendelbo, who did most of his botanical work in Iran and Afghanistan, beginning in the late 1950s.

Crocus scardicus (Iridaceae) is native to Mount Scardo and the mountainous area on the borders of Serbia, Macedonia, and Albania. It produces flowers in late spring just below snow melt at an elevation of between 5600 and 8200 feet (1700–2500 m). The solitary flowers are pale yellow to deep orange with a white throat. Unlike most crocuses, it grows in a habitat that never really dries out, even at the peak of summer, and therefore in cultivation should not be given a dormant summer period (Mathew 1982). Jim collected *C. scardicus* in August 1963, finding seed heads "popping all around" as it had completed flowering. He re-introduced it through his seed list the following year. The specific epithet recalls Mount Scardo where it was found flowering by Serbian botanist, Nedelyko Košanin. It was published in 1928 as a new species.

Muscari (Hyacinthaceae) comprises thirty to sixty species, depending on the authority cited. Some species formerly grouped with *Muscari* have been moved to allied genera. These bulbous plants range from the Mediterranean and Europe to southwestern Asia. All are spring bloomers (with one exception).

Muscari mcbeathianum was discovered in 1985 by the Archibalds near Tufanbeyli, Turkey (Adana), growing in open sandy areas among pine trees at an eleva-

Crocus scardicus PHOTO BY JIM AND JENNY ARCHIBALD

tion of 3950 feet (1200 m). It is a small plant with ice-blue to white flowers and up to nine slender leaves. On subsequent visits to the site, the Archibalds have failed to relocate the species as trees have been felled and the area is now under grazing.

Muscari mcbeathianum is kin to *M. coeleste*, to which it was tentatively assigned. It is a member of the Pseudomuscari Group, those with bell-shaped flowers without a constricted mouth. Some taxonomists move this group to the genus *Pseudomuscari* (Philippo 2003).

The specific epithet honors Ron McBeath, former assistant curator at Royal Botanic Garden (Edinburgh), who was in charge of the *Muscari* collection. The description was published in 1988 by Kit Tan, one of McBeath's colleagues.

Rosa persica (syn. *Hulthemia persica*) was first raised in 1836 in Luxembourg Gardens (Paris), where it caused a sensation. Dubbed the yellow rose of Persia, it has five vivid yellow petals with a crimson spot at the base, creating an "eye" in the center of the flower, which is about 1.5 inches (4 cm) across. The plant has a lanky, straggly growth habit, usually about 24 inches (60 cm) tall and wide. It is the only rose with simple leaves and for that reason was initially classified in a new genus *Hulthemia* (monotypic), a primitive or proto-rose.

Rosa persica is found in arid regions in Iran eastward to Afghanistan and central Asia. The Archibalds collected seeds on an assignment for Henry Cocker (Cocker Roses, Aberdeen, United Kingdom) in 1966 in Iran, where it was a common plant. Cocker was determined to grow and breed *R. persica*. Jim recalls

Muscari mcbeathianum PHOTO BY JIM AND JENNY ARCHIBALD

spending an entire day cleaning the seeds as the fruit is sticky and covered with painfully sharp spines and hairs.

Many selections resulting from crosses with *Rosa persica* are now entering the nursery trade. The history of the use of this plant in breeding has been summarized in two reports, written in 1977 and 1989, by nurseryman Jack Harkness (Suffolk, United Kingdom), who received seed via Cocker from the Archibalds' collection (Harkness 2003a, 2003b).

In the late 1950s, when plantsman Eric Smith worked at Hillier and Sons nursery (Winchester), he made a cross of a plant labeled "Helleborus colchicus superbus" with a dark flowered *Helleborus torquatus* that grew at the family garden in Southampton. From the cross Eric gave clonal names to five seedlings, including *H. ×hybridus* 'Pluto', which adapted well to culture and proved to be the best (Archibald 1993). 'Pluto' is a dwarf plant growing to 12 inches (30 cm). Its flowers are about 2 inches (5 cm) across and are a dark wine-purple with a blue-gray "bloom."

Seed from 'Pluto' and others, such as 'Ariel', 'Electra', 'Miranda', and 'Sirius', continues to be grown and sold by the Archibalds, from the days of Jim and Eric's business partnership, The Plantsmen. Jim has paid homage to Eric Smith, pointing out his excellent plantsman's skills, including that of hosta breeding, for which Smith has earned great renown (Archibald 2000).

Through their seed lists, the Archibalds re-introduced to cultivation forms of two iris species: *Iris urmiensis* and *I. paradoxa*.

Iris urmiensis PHOTO BY JIM AND JENNY ARCHIBALD

Iris paradoxa f. *mirabilis* PHOTO BY JIM AND JENNY ARCHIBALD

Iris urmiensis (syn. *I. barnumae* f. *urmiensis*) is endemic to the hills south of Salmas in northwest Iran, near the border with Turkey. It grows in an area of stony slopes and montane grassland over rock. Jim collected it in 1966 and again in 2000. It grows about 8 inches (20 cm) tall and has curved, gray-green leaves. The flowers are yellow, unspotted, and unveined and may vary in depth of color. *Iris urmiensis* has "beards of dense orange-yellow hairs above deep-yellow signal-patches on the falls . . . a beautiful and unmistakable iris" and is among the least difficult of the Iranian species of section *Oncocyclus* to cultivate (Archibald 1999). It is a significant plant in that it has provided breeding stock for other iris breeders and nursery owners, to "fuse" the spectacular yellow color from section *Oncocyclus* into the bearded iris hybrids.

Iris urmiensis was originally described in 1900. Brian Mathew and Per Wendelbo much later (1975) described it as a botanical form of *I. barnumae*. The specific epithet derives its name from Lake Urmia in northwest Iran, as the form grows on the west side of the lake. Mathew (1989b) notes the existence of dwarf, compact forms and taller, lankier forms.

Jim laments that more people are not growing irises of section *Oncocyclus*, a capricious and difficult group to grow and maintain. "An enthusiasm for growing [these] wild irises . . . is one of the most esoteric and lonely of horticultural activities," he wrote in "Silken Sad Uncertain Queens" (Archibald 1999). The article won Jim the Clarence Elliott Memorial award from the Alpine Garden Society as the best article published in the *Bulletin* in 1999.

Iris paradoxa f. *mirabilis*, also in section *Oncocyclus*, is a 2000 introduction by the Archibalds from a collection in Iran near Julfa, the site where noted bulb collector Paul Furse searched for the plant in 1966. The form appears to have a limited distribution, found often in barren areas near the border with Azerbaijan. *Iris paradoxa* is distinctive in that it has reduced, stiff horizontal falls compared to the large round standards (Mathew 1989b). Forma *mirabilis* has golden yellow falls, an orange beard, and the palest of blue standards (Archibald 1999). The closely related forma *choschab* has white standards.

With their far-ranging expeditions and amazingly varied seed lists, Jim and Jenny Archibald have been at the forefront of modern-day plant exploration for three decades. They have inspired many individuals profiled in this book.

Jim and Jenny Archibald PHOTO BY BOBBY J. WARD

Jim and Jenny Archibald
Bryn Collen
Ffostrasol
Llandysul SA44 5SB
Wales, United Kingdom
www.jjaseeds.com

Shogun of Plants from the East
Asiatica—Barry Yinger

In downtown Tokyo on Sunday mornings, department stores such as Keio, Daimaru, and Seibu are crowded with families shopping on the one day they have together during the week. Shortly after opening, the stores' elevators, escalators, aisles, and restaurants become occupied to near capacity, mirroring Tokyo's jam-packed streets. These stores all have similar open-air rooftop areas, a dozen floors up, where shoppers flock to snack bars, children's playgrounds, and pet departments.

The rooftops also house well-stocked nurseries, usually off to one side and not crowded. These remarkable oases of calm, unlike any other plant merchandising I have seen, are meticulously clean with healthy-looking plants, free of weeds and debris, constantly maintained by uniformed employees. Each nursery has a staggering number of plants with a wide range of species. Shoppers can find walk-in greenhouses with tropical orchids, succulents, and tender plants; lean-to greenhouses protecting variegated *Clivia* and *Rohdea*; carts of cut flowers, forced bulbs, shrubs, and trees; and tables of perennials and hardy annuals. Westerners may have trouble discerning just how vast the selection is as the plant names are written in Japanese, not Latin or any other language. Luckily, some pots have miniature color photographs of the plants in flower or the plant at mature size, enabling one to identify them as *Aconitum*, *Edgeworthia*, or *Epimedium*, although frequently not the species.

I first learned about these rooftop nurseries from presentations Barry Yinger had given at horticultural conferences and was struck by the numbers and kinds of plants he said were there. When I traveled to Tokyo, Barry kindly provided the names of the department stores and even the subway stops to locate them. His directions were accurate and I spent most of a day seeking out the nurseries and admiring plants. The only limitation was my lack of knowledge of the Japanese language.

Fortunately, Barry, a veteran plant explorer who speaks Japanese, Chinese, and Korean, searches Japan each year for these rooftop nurseries, as well as street-side plant vendors, plant sales at religious festivals, and specialty nurseries. From the bounty in these sources, he has facilitated introductions of plants that would otherwise be unavailable to the Western gardener. Barry's plant hunting is not limited to urban areas, as he also has made collecting trips to remote locations in the wild (Higgins 2000). To date, he has made more than sixty trips to Japan with additional trips to China, Korea, and other Asian locations.

With his business partner Andy Wong, Barry operates Asiatica, a nursery specializing in hardy Japanese and other Asian woodland plants. Barry also works for Hines Horticulture of Irvine, California, a wholesale producer and marketer of plants. At times, he negotiates patent rights with foreign nursery owners or the original breeders to distribute their plants in the United States through Hines's commercial production (Raver 2001). Both Asiatica and Hines are beneficiaries of his collecting. Barry prefers plants that tolerate shade, "in particular, those shade garden plants that will relieve the monotony of traditional overplanting of hostas and simple groundcovers, though I love them both." He points to the many other plants to choose from, *Asarum* and *Arisaema* being two of his current favorites.

Barry lives in central Pennsylvania in a house on the land where he grew up. He credits his interest in plants to his grandmother, in whose garden in Altoona he spent much time and first learned the names of plants such as castor bean and angel's trumpet. He has had varied educational and professional experiences that uniquely qualify him for a career as a plant hunter. These include studies in plant science and Asian languages at the University of Maryland, which afforded him a spring semester in Kyoto in 1974, introducing him to Japanese culture, native flora, temple gardens, horticultural traditions, and nurseries (Darke 1999b). Barry earned a master's degree in the horticulture program between Longwood Gardens (Kennett Square, Pennsylvania) and the University of Delaware, which supported a collecting trip to Japan in 1976, the plants shared between Longwood and the U.S. National Arboretum.

From 1976 to 1982, Barry collected plants on a part-time basis (vacations from education at Longwood), sponsored in part by Brookside Gardens (Wheaton, Maryland) in a program to evaluate and introduce "new" plants from Japan and Korea. From seven trips, he helped Carl Hahn (director of Brookside) design the evaluation program at Brookside and helped push the nursery industry beyond the few tried-and-true plants that were the rule in garden centers at the time. Barry had a stint at the U.S. National Arboretum as curator of the Asian collections, and then at the Chollipo Arboretum (Republic of Korea) working with the late Carl Ferris Miller for two years, giving Barry the opportunity for further travel in Korea and Japan. He also worked as a garden center manager at a nursery in the Washington, D.C., area and in management at public gardens in Missouri and New Jersey. He became a consultant to Hines in 1988, then took a full-time job with that company in 1993 as new plant products manager. He began operating Asiatica with Andy Wong in 1996.

Phil Normandy (plant collections manager at Brookside), who propagated the plants Barry collected for Brookside, says of Barry:

He is perhaps the most successful plant explorer of the late twentieth century from the standpoint of sheer impact on the ornamentals industry . . . [because of] the careful selection of a startling array of cultivars that enrich the diversity of the present-day landscape.

Barry exemplifies the yin and yang of C. P. Snow's "two cultures," having a grounding in both science and the arts. A selection of his introductions follows.

The wild form of *Camellia japonica* (Theaceae), native to Japan and the Ryukyu Islands, Korea, and China, is a small tree growing to 30 feet (9 m). It has glossy, evergreen leaves that are 2–4 inches (5–10 cm) long, and simple red flowers. Japanese and Chinese gardeners had admired this plant as a cultivated ornamental and made many named selections prior to its introduction to the West in the eighteenth century.

Thanks to Barry, we now have a hardy form of *Camellia japonica*, which is able to be grown in USDA Zone 6 and sometimes 5. Barry learned of camellias that could prove hardy when he was in Korea in 1981. There he read an article by a Japanese author (Ueki) describing colonies of *C. japonica* on a mountain island off the west coast of South Korea in the Yellow Sea. Barry was determined to find the island, which is within sight of the North Korean coast, despite military occupation. One midwinter day he and a Korean friend paid a sailor a bottle of Scotch to sneak them onto a restricted ferry. Reaching the island, they located 20-foot (6-m) tall stands of the camellia, prominent against the winter vegetation (Raver 2001). The camellias had bloomed the previous season and dropped seeds on the ground. Barry took back handfuls, evaluating them over the next twenty years. One selection with deep red petals and yellow stamens was named Korean Fire™ and was introduced by Hines Nursery in 2000.

Korean Fire™ produces broad, flat, bright-red flowers in late winter and early spring. The plant matures to 15 feet (4.5 m) tall and 8 feet (2.4 m) wide. So far it has survived temperatures of −12°F (−24°C) without damage and flowered the following spring. Korean Fire™ is considered one of the hardiest camellias.

Japanese (or sometimes Chinese) hydrangea vine is much easier to say than its formal moniker, *Schizophragma hydrangeoides* 'Moonlight'. Barry collected the plant in 1978 on Japan's Kii Peninsula, on a trip for Brookside Gardens. He says, "I literally stumbled over it when I was walking in the mountains in Nara Prefecture . . . and it's one of the finest flowering vines there is" (Raver 2001). Phil Normandy at Brookside took the cuttings that Barry brought back, propagated them, and sent them to gardens and arboreta for evaluation. The plant received such "wow" comments that Normandy had to rush to give it a name. Phil dubbed it 'Moonlight' and it was introduced by Brookside in 1985.

An ornamental climber of the hydrangea family (Hydrangeaceae), 'Moonlight' climbs by aerial roots. The leaves are heart shaped and up to 4 inches (10 cm) across, silvery and glaucous, providing a "shimmering moonlight" effect. The dark veins on the leaves provide dramatic contrast. The plant is slow growing,

Schizophragma hydrangeoides 'Moonlight' PHOTO BY PAMELA HARPER

probably 1.5 feet (0.5 m) per year, and eventually reaches 20 feet (6 m). In mid-summer it produces creamy white hydrangea-like flowers that are large and flat in clusters 10 inches (25 cm) across. 'Moonlight' is put to good use as a wall covering, ground cover, or for tree climber. It is a deciduous, woody-stemmed vine and in the winter the bare stems and branches are striking. The plant prefers sites in part sun to full shade and is cold hardy to −10°F (−23°C), or USDA Zone 6.

About a thousand species comprise *Carex*, a member of the sedge family (Cyperaceae). They look superficially like grasses and have broadly similar uses in the garden, but they are very different morphologically, and in evolutionary terms they are millions of years apart (Grounds 1989). *Carex* is cosmopolitan in distribution, common especially in the temperate regions, and also found in mountain areas of the tropics.

The typical form of *Carex morrowii* var. *morrowii*, known as *kansuge*, is solid green, and it is native to low mountain woods, primarily in the south and central areas of Japan, chiefly on the Pacific side (Ohwi 1965). *Carex morrowii* 'Ice Dance' is a 1996 Hines Nursery introduction through Barry, who obtained it as a selection made by Masato Yakoi in Japan. It is a mounding plant and, although rhizomatous, is not invasive. It has 0.5-inch- (1.25-cm-) wide dark green leaves with a clean, distinctive white-to-cream border. The foliage, thick and somewhat leathery, is upright to arching. 'Ice Dance' grows up to 18 inches (45 cm) tall and attains a spread of 2 to 3 feet (0.6–0.9 m). It serves as an excellent border plant, growing in light shade to part sun. Like most sedges, it will grow in low or wet areas in the garden, including around streams and ponds. 'Ice Dance' produces brownish flowers in the spring, but they are of minor importance and are easily overlooked. Tony Avent, of Plant Delights Nursery, one of the many nurseries selling 'Ice Dance' now, says that it is just like the selection 'Variegata', except that "the rate of spread is just perfect . . . not fast enough to become a problem, but not slow enough to try your patience." 'Ice Dance' is rated as hardy in USDA Zones 5 to 8.

Carex phyllocephala 'Sparkler', another sedge found by Barry, was introduced by Brookside Gardens. It is evergreen with white- and green-striped, whorled, papyrus-like foliage on upright stems that grow to a little more than 12 inches (30 cm) tall. 'Sparkler' is a clump-former with rhizomes, but it is not invasive. Though the plant is native to China, Barry procured it from a nursery in Nagoya (Japan) in 1979 and gave it the selection name. It is recommended for part sun to medium shade and moist garden conditions. Where 'Sparkler' seeds around, it produces a sedge with plain green leaves (Schmid 2002). In my garden I have sited it where it is the last plant I am able to see from my house at dusk after the other plants have "disappeared." It is hardy to USDA Zone 7, and in colder areas with protection.

Loropetalum (Hamamelidaceae) consists of two or three species of shrubs to small trees that are native to Japan, China, and India. *Loropetalum chinense*, the ornamental species from China, has white flowers and is the typical form grown.

I saw my first pink Chinese loropetalum plant at a rock garden chapter meeting in 1993. J. C. Raulston brought a plant that was auctioned off by nurseryman Tony Avent for seventy-five dollars. The selection, named 'Burgundy', had been passed on to him by James Waddick (Kansas City, Missouri) and named by the U.S. National Arboretum. Waddick had acquired it from the in-house nursery at the Shanghai Botanic Garden.

Plum Delight™ is another pink-flowering form of *Loropetalum* that entered the United States at about the same time as 'Burgundy'. Barry obtained Plum Delight™ in 1990 in Kyoto (Japan) from a nursery that had acquired it from China. It grows 6–10 feet (1.8–3 m) tall and about as wide, with "hot pink" flowers and red-purple foliage. Barry says that it was "an important discovery because it has become the standard or benchmark for other varieties for foliage color, flower, and habit." Michael Dirr, professor of horticulture at the University of Georgia, considers *Loropetalum chinense* f. *rubrum* one of the top plant introductions of the 1990s. He points out that Plum Delight™, 'Hines Purpleleaf', 'Hines Burgundy', and Pizzazz™ are the same plant (Dirr 2002). Barry says that all are derived from the single plant he obtained.

Loropetalum chinense f. *rubrum* has rapidly become popular in a short time, especially in the U.S. Southeast. Garden centers and nurseries now carry many selections, as there are numerous flower and leaf color forms. The plant was not even in the United States before 1989 "when it entered by many routes, causing

Carex phyllocephala 'Sparkler' PHOTO BY TONY AVENT

enough confusion that DNA testing was employed to sort out all of the cultivars" (Nyberg 1997).

Hosta yingeri (Hostaceae) is from Taehuksan, Sohuksan, and other islands in the Huksan Archipelago off the southwest coast of Korea. It is found among rocks at the high tide line of the shore and among shady talus slopes and hillsides up to an elevation of about 200 feet (60 m) (Schmid 1991). Its leaves are glossy green with a "polished" appearance to the upper and lower surfaces. In late summer the plant produces spiderlike, light purple flowers on a stalk that may be nearly 24 inches (60 cm) tall. The specific epithet, given by Sam Jones (formerly of the University of Georgia, and owner of Piccadilly Farm in Bishop, Georgia) in 1989, honors Barry, who collected seeds of the hosta in 1985 and provided them to the U.S. National Arboretum and to Jones directly.

Several selections of *Hosta yingeri* are now available. 'Korean Snow' has speckled and streaked leaf patterns, a kind of variegation that is rare in hostas. It was selected by hosta guru Bob Solberg from a seedling crop at Niche Gardens (Chapel Hill, North Carolina). 'Treasure Island' is a selection from the original seed lot by Tony Avent; it has long pointed leaves that are glossy green. Since the initial introduction by Barry, re-introductions of this species have been made, including Dan Hinkley's Taehuksan Form (DJH270), a selection that is smaller than earlier introductions.

Barry's trip in 1985 to Korea also resulted in the discovery of *Hosta laevigata*, closely related to *H. yingeri* and, like it, found on rocky shores on shaded talus slopes. The flowers are larger than those of *H. yingeri* and the leaves are light green, slightly lancelolate, and wavy (Schmid 1991). The specific epithet *laevigata* refers to the smooth, polished surfaces of the upper and undersides of the leaf.

Based on the success of Barry's trip, one of Jones's students returned to the site in 1988 and discovered a third species, *Hosta jonesii*, which honors Sam Jones. One of its characteristics is that some of the flower scapes are branched.

Albizia julibrissin, the silk plant or mimosa, is little regarded in much of the United States as it has become naturalized in waste areas, especially the South. It is the first tree whose name I learned as a child because it grew alongside the well of my grandmother's farmhouse. A summer bloomer, it has pink powder-puff flower heads and finely textured bipinnately compound leaves. It was introduced to the United States by André Michaux at Middleton Plantation, near Charleston, South Carolina.

Albizia julibrissin 'Summer Chocolate' originated from a chance discovery by Japanese horticulturist and variegated plant enthusiast Masato Yokoi, a longtime friend of Barry and professor of horticulture in Angyo (Japan). It had many routes into U.S. horticulture (Lasseigne 2003). One of them was through Barry who got material in 1992 from Yokoi. Barry says, he got the "first plant propagated from the mother plant." This cultivar has velvety chocolate to dark purple leaves and the typical pink flowers. The tree grows to about 20 feet (6 m) tall and 15 feet (4.5 m) wide. Its compound leaves emerge green and then darken as the summer progresses. Todd Lasseigne, assistant director at the JC Raulston Arboretum, notes that the emergence of green leaves is odd in that most purple-leaved plants emerge purple and then fade to green, especially in the heat of the South. The tree is hardy to at least USDA Zone 6.

My grandmother grew bridal wreath spiraea (probably *Spiraea prunifolia*) and, though the old smokehouse beside which it grew is gone, the plant, gangly and overgrown, is still situated where she planted it nearly a century ago. Felder Rushing says it is easy to find long-neglected homesites in the U.S. South by looking for blooming spireas in overgrown woods (Bender and Rushing 1993).

Spiraea (Rosaceae) is a genus of about eighty deciduous shrubs of the Northern Hemisphere. *Spiraea thunbergii*, a native of China, appears to have been introduced from Japan to the West in the early 1860s (Coats 1964). It is the earliest blooming spiraea, producing masses of white flowers on arching branches in late winter. It is commonly called baby's breath spiraea because of its fine texture.

Hosta laevigata PHOTO BY W. GEORGE SCHMID

Albizia julibrissin 'Summer Chocolate' PHOTO BY BOBBY J. WARD

Spiraea thunbergii 'Ogon' PHOTO BY TONY AVENT

The attraction of *Spiraea thunbergii* 'Ogon' Mellow Yellow® is its golden yellow to chartreuse leaves that turn bronze-red in the autumn. Suitable for a site in full sun, this deciduous shrub with arching branches reaches up to 5 feet (1.5 m) tall and wide. 'Ogon' Mellow Yellow® produces small white flowers in the early spring, usually before it fully leafs out. It is hardy in USDA Zones 5 to 9. Barry obtained 'Ogon' Mellow Yellow® from a garden center in Tokyo in 1993.

Acorus gramineus 'Ogon' (Araceae or Acoraceae) is a yellow-striped variegated sweet flag that Barry found in Japan at a Tokyo garden center and introduced in 1976. It is commonly called the golden variegated dwarf sweet flag. Barry does not know its source or breeder, but thinks it is probably an old cultivar. It has become one of the most successfully propagated plants he has introduced. Initially grown at Longwood Gardens, it was passed along to Kurt Bluemel (a grower of ornamental grasses and allied plants in Baldwin, Maryland), and then picked up by Hines for promotion. The foliage grows to about 10 inches (25 cm) high and the plant spreads to 1 foot (0.3 m). It does well in wet or boggy conditions, even water, in sun to part shade. The flower is insignificant. Barry says he introduced this variegated sweet flag at a time when there was little commercial interest in such plants as it was a "collector's plant" (Darke 1999b). "Now it's a mainstream plant with tremendous commercial success," he says.

Acorus gramineus is native to eastern Asia, but *A. calamus*, the sweet flag or sweet calamus, is more commonly known and grown. *Acorus gramineus* has the look of a *Carex* (sedge) and is typically grown as a ground cover, expanding slowly in fans from creeping rhizomes. The specific epithet means "grasslike," for the plant's general resemblance to the true grasses, while the genus name is from classical Greek for "a plant with an aromatic rhizome." The roots and leaves contain the essential oil calamus, which has a licorice taste and fragrance, and is used in gins, beers, and perfumes.

Barry's interest in asarums (wild ginger) and other shade garden and woodland plants goes back to his first trips to Japan in the 1970s. His exuberance had been fueled by seeing a book of Japanese prints at the University of Maryland that contained illustrations of *Asarum* plants. His interest in asarums went from "a slow simmer to a rapid boil" and then to an obsession when he later actually saw the Asian species in Japan (Yinger 1993). As he read more of the Japanese literature, Barry learned that asarums hold a special place in some cultures. For example, in Japan asarums are placed under building eaves to provide protection from storms and earthquakes, and they appear on some family crests. They are also important in traditional Chinese medicines. Barry's interest extends to classical pot culture of *Asarum* cultivars, known as *koten engei*, some having been grown for hundreds of years. His intense interest extended to his master's thesis at Longwood, a monograph on the genus *Asarum*.

Barry's obsession for asarums is such that Asiatica now offers as many as a hundred kinds. *Asarum asperum* is used in temple gardens in Kyoto. It is an evergreen, clump-forming species from central Japan, with patterned leaves up to 3

Acorus gramineus 'Ogon' PHOTO BY TONY AVENT

inches (7.5 cm) long. It has Dutchman's pipe-shaped flowers, a characteristic of some members of the Aristolochiaceae, to which *Asarum* is assigned. Other forms have albino (pale green) flowers. The species is hardy to USDA Zone 6.

Asarum nipponicum and *A. takaoi* are evergreens with extremely variable leaf colors, from solid green to patterned. The latter is also the source of many of the fine classical *Asarum* cultivars grown in Japan. Both are hardy to USDA Zone 5.

Asarum kumageanum is a clump-forming species from Yaku Island of Japan and has a glasslike sheen to the leaves, with yellow-gold mottling. Another Asiatica offering is *A. minamitanianum*, the mouse tail ginger, from Japan's Kyushu Island. Its flowers are variable, from near purple to reddish pink, and have extended starfishlike lobes, often several inches long. Many forms are available.

As a rule the Chinese asarums are not as hardy as the Japanese forms, because they are found in southern China (Yinger 1993). One species for USDA Zone 7 or warmer is *Asarum maximum*, introduced as the "panda bear *Asarum*" because of its 2-inch (5-cm) wide, velvety black flowers with a clean, white interior "eye." It has large evergreen leaves up to 7 inches (17.5 cm) long. Barry believes he was the first to introduce this plant into the United States in 1988.

Osmanthus, a member of the Oleaceae, or the olive family, comprises about thirty species, all evergreen, which range from shrubs to small trees. *Osmanthus heterophyllus* is a cultivated ornamental whose foliage looks superficially like a holly (*Ilex*); however as Dirr (2002) points out, the leaves on *Osmanthus* are opposite, but those on *Ilex* are alternate. The leaves of *O. heterophyllus* are leathery and

Asarum asperum PHOTO BY TONY AVENT

Asarum kumageanum PHOTO BY TONY AVENT

Asarum maximum PHOTO BY TONY AVENT

lustrous, up to 2.5 inches (6 cm) long and about half as wide. They have spines along the margin. The flowers, produced in the autumn, are small, white, and intensely fragrant. The name *Osmanthus* is from Greek for "fragrant flower." The typical form may grow 10 feet (3 m) tall or more.

Osmanthus heterophyllus 'Goshiki' was collected by Barry in 1978 at a nursery in Yokohama (Japan). The cultivar name 'Goshiki' had already been applied by the Japanese grower; it means "multicolored" in Japanese. The new leaf growth of this variegated selection may initially be tinged pink before development of cream, white, and gold markings, which appear in a spattered pattern. It is stable and does not revert. I grow this plant in my garden in a somewhat shady spot near hostas. The contrasting leaf color, texture, and shape give an interesting effect to that corner of the garden during the summer. Phil Normandy (Brookside) reports that the original 'Goshiki' in Brookside has only bloomed once (2002) since planting. The mature plant grows to 6 feet (1.8 m) tall and wide.

Osmanthus heterophyllus 'Goshiki' in the background PHOTO BY TONY AVENT

Osmanthus heterophyllus 'Sasaba' was obtained from the private garden of Yoshimichi Hirose (a Japanese connoisseur of cactus, succulents, and variegated plants) in Tokyo. Barry gave it the cultivar name 'Sasaba', which means "bamboo leaf" in Japanese. It is a tight, upright plant, solid green, with deeply cut starlike evergreen leaves that are extremely spiny.

Both *Osmanthus heterophyllus* 'Goshiki' and 'Sasaba' were collected by Barry under the auspices of the Brookside Gardens program. Regarding the introductions that Barry made with Brookside, Phil Normandy says that *Schizophragma hydrangeoides* 'Moonlight' was the most successful introduction, with *Osmanthus heterophyllus* 'Goshiki' coming in a close second.

Like a modern-day Marco Polo, Barry has helped to once again open our eyes to the wonders of the East. He possesses that rare gift among plant enthusiasts: an eye for both the unusual and the utilitarian. His introductions, especially through his affiliations with Brookside Gardens and Hines Nursery, have reached a market far beyond the rooftop nurseries of Tokyo.

Barry Yinger and Andy Wong PHOTO BY BOBBY J. WARD

Barry Yinger and Andy Wong
Asiatica
P.O. Box 270
Lewisberry, PA 17339
United States
www.asiaticanursery.com

3

Pushing the *Camellia* Hardiness Envelope
Camellia Forest Nursery—Clifford R. Parks

I associate Cliff Parks with Louis S. B. Leakey, the anthropologist who found humanoid fossils at Olduvai Gorge in Tanzania, an association which is not so surprising upon examination. When I was a "green" graduate student at North Carolina State College (now University) in the mid-1960s, my advisor took me to the University of North Carolina (Chapel Hill) to hear Cliff give a talk on cotton (*Gossypium*) pigments, as part of his application for a position on the botany faculty there. A few days later, I returned to the same campus to hear Leakey give a talk on his ground-breaking work. These two trips were memorable because each speaker was a pioneer in his own right, and because students rarely visited the other's campus, except for a sporting event. Cliff got the job and settled in with the botany faculty for a long career, retiring in 2003 as a professor of biology.

A native of upstate New York, Cliff obtained an undergraduate degree in plant science from Cornell University, then went south in the late 1950s to North Carolina State College and obtained master's and doctorate degrees from the genetics department. He studied floral pigmentation in species of cotton, part of an overall large plant breeding program on crop improvement in agronomy and genetics on the Raleigh campus. He took his first job at the Los Angeles State and County Arboretum (LASCA) and while there, from 1962 till 1967, worked on *Camellia* systematics and breeding. At LASCA, Cliff made crosses of camellias using stock from the large collection in Descanso Gardens (in La Cañada, a suburb of Los Angeles) and Huntington Gardens (San Marino). As the climate is mild in Los Angeles, he sent seeds and seedlings to Richard W. Lighty at Longwood Gardens (Kennett Square, Pennsylvania) and to others to test camellias in a colder climate. Longwood had an already established *Camellia* collection and Cliff's interest complemented Lighty's plans to further test hardiness.

Wanting to try a job in academia, Cliff moved to Chapel Hill, North Carolina, in 1967 for the teaching-research job at the University of North Carolina, taking with him hundreds of camellias from LASCA, as interest in *Camellia* breeding had waned there. He continued to make trips back to Los Angeles till 1972 to evaluate the stock and to work with the *Camellia* collections he had left behind. In North Carolina, his botanical interest at the university tended toward vicariance, the study of the separation of organisms by geographical boundaries such as mountain chains and bodies of water, thereby resulting in development of new species or varieties. Cliff studied vicariance at the cellular level, the isoenzyme comparisons between hardwoods, such as different species of *Liriodendron* (tulip poplar) and *Liquidambar* (sweet gum) in eastern Asia and the U.S. Southeast (see also Don Jacobs's similar interest). He says that the last direct DNA "communication" between plant populations of *Liriodendron* and *Liquidambar* in Asia and North America occurred twelve to fifteen million years ago during the Miocene Epoch (other genera have different time parameters).

In the 1980s, Cliff began making trips to China and Japan to study vicariance firsthand and, in doing so, extended his early interest in camellias. On these trips he collected seeds and cuttings of wild forms, and some from nurseries and botanical gardens. By the mid-1980s he had amassed a large collection of camellias at his Chapel Hill woodland garden covering 5 acres (2 ha). Japanese visitors told him that it looked like a *Camellia* forest, so dense was his collection.

In 1985, when the temperature plummeted to −9°F (−23°C) at Camellia Forest, an all-time record low for the area, ninety-eight percent of Cliff's *Camellia* collection was killed to the ground although the roots survived. Among the survivors were the tea-oil camellia (*C. oleifera*) and several selections of *C. japonica*. Taking advantage of the disastrous loss of camellias, he worked on the surviving individuals. After testing, selection, and production, Cliff introduced the 'April' series of spring-blooming *C. japonica* that is hardy to the warmer parts of USDA Zone 6b (Fisher 2002). Camellia Forest Nursery, founded in 1977 by Cliff's spouse, Kai Mei Parks, who runs the nursery with their son, David, has introduced many of these hardier camellias.

Now retired from his university position, Cliff continues an interest in *Camellia* breeding and in writing about camellias. He led an expedition in 2000 to the high mountains of southwest China. The trip, coordinated with the Kunming Institute of Botany, included participants from Longwood Gardens, Descanso Gardens, and Camellia Forest Nursery.

I have visited Cliff several times at his home, the original "camellia forest," and at the nursery, Camellia Forest, now at a separate location. My most recent visit was on a rainy day. I found him peering out at the greenhouse, which had been severely damaged by the previous winter's ice storm, when pine limbs came crashing down on the glass, exposing numerous camellias and other plants to the sudden shock of freezing temperatures. He seemed unmoved by it all, temporarily setting up germination trays of *Primula* (another interest) in his kitchen, waiting to complete the repairs. Much like the winter freeze of 1985 with its benefits of hardier camellias, I suspect something positive will come from Cliff's broken greenhouse.

Camellias are broad-leaved evergreens that are native to subtropical regions of eastern Asia, from Japan through central and southern China and into Indochina. A few additional species occur in the Himalaya and in the Malay Archipelago, but the majority grow in southern China. Altogether there are about two hundred species. The genus name honors Georg Joseph Kamel (1661–1706), a Moravian Jesuit priest, who also studied the plants of the Philippines. In 1753, Linnaeus named the plant *Camellia* (there is no *k* in the Latin alphabet, unless borrowed from Greek), but it is doubtful that Kamel ever saw his eponymous plant.

Members of the tea family (Theaceae), camellias have been cultivated as ornamental plants for centuries in China, Japan, and Korea, where Buddhist monks tended them. Camellias have been also depicted in paintings, literature, and music. In Japan they are known as *tsubaki*, meaning "spring tree," and some plants in cultivation are more than five hundred years old. The first camellia to reach Europe arrived in the early eighteenth century as a dried specimen dubbed the "Japan rose," and the first to bloom was at Thorndon Hall (Essex, United Kingdom) in 1740 (Coats 1964). By the 1840s the Japan rose had become highly popular in France. Apparently its entry into North American gardens was in 1786 through the French explorer André Michaux, who introduced *Camellia japonica* at Middleton Plantation near Charleston, South Carolina.

Camellia japonica, a spring bloomer and the most commonly grown of all camellias, grows in the wild as a small scrubby, understory tree, often in solid stands of individuals up to 30 to 40 feet (9–12 m) tall. The simple flowers have five petals each. In cultivation, hundreds of selections are grown, many with double flowers. Gardeners typically grow camellias and prune them as shrubs, though old plants (and they are long-lived) can grow to 25 feet (7.5 m) or more high and wide. Camellias have traditionally been considered "tender" and "southern" plants—those that thrive best below the U.S. Mason-Dixon line. In the U.S. Southeast, they have become the quintessential winter- and early spring-blooming shrubs, producing masses of large, showy flowers in a range of colors from pure white to deep red.

Another camellia of horticulture is *Camellia reticulata*, a tender Chinese plant that produces large flowers. *Camellia oleifera*, the tea-oil camellia, is a hardy species that is grown primarily for its seed oil and as a breeding partner in *Camellia* hybridization to instill hardiness (Dirr 2002). It is now also being field tested for wider use in horticulture. The tea plant of commerce is *C. sinensis* of which there are a few ornamental forms.

Cold hardiness varies considerably. *Camellia japonica*, *C. cuspidata*, and *C. sasanqua*, a commonly grown fall-blooming species, tolerate 0°F (−18°C) with some wind protection. Some selections of *C. oleifera*, *C. sinensis*, and *C. japonica* and selected hybrids tolerate −10°F (−23°C). Other *Camellia* species are cold hardy from 7° to 32°F (−14° to 0°C).

Richard W. Lighty, formerly at Longwood Gardens and the Mount Cuba Center for the Study of Piedmont Flora (Greenville, Delaware), has looked back at the work that has been done on *Camellia*. He notes that opportunities presented themselves with the severe freezes that William Ackerman's plants experienced at the U.S. National Arboretum and the freeze that Cliff's plants were exposed to in North Carolina some years later. Ackerman's work with the hardiest of the camellias, *C. oleifera*, and Barry Yinger's discovery (see chapter 2) of a wild population of *C. japonica* on a temperate island off Korea added significantly to the choices of camellias for the garden and for hybridization. Lighty says he has been "indebted to Cliff for being willing to cooperate" with the Longwood program that Lighty earlier managed, as each benefited from it, and the relationship helped Longwood fill a gap in its *Camellia* program. He said that all *Camellia* programs need to be tested in a variety of hardiness zones to get a true "reading" on the adaptability of the cultivars being tested.

Cliff told me about several trips abroad collecting numerous plants other than camellias that are also being sold by Camellia Forest. He mentioned *Cinnamomum chekiangense* (hardy camphor tree), *Corylopsis gotoana* (wild seed collected in Hiroshima), *Viburnum atrocyaneum* (wild collected in China), and *Celtis sinensis* 'Green Cascade', a weeping form of hackberry (collected with permission at a Japanese shrine). He recited a few dozen more plants, but they would make an additional chapter on Cliff and his horticultural contributions. I asked him what drives him in his search for new plants. He responded, "Native plants don't have the diversity that gardeners want, so we have to explore for exotic plants."

Some of the camellias introduced by Cliff through Camellia Forest Nursery follow. The April Series of *Camellia japonica* are cultivars recommended for USDA Zone 6b, the coldest areas where camellias can be dependably grown (Parks and Parks 2002). In mild winters with little frost, the spring-blooming April Series will begin flowering in late winter and the last of the blooms will fall by late April.

Camellia 'April Dawn' has a vigorous growth habit and produces a plant with an erect stature. It grows to a height of 6 to 8 feet (1.8–2.4 m) and a spread of 5 to 6 feet (1.5–1.6 m). The blossoms are variegated (non-virused) in shades of pink and white. It is a selection from a cross between *C. japonica* 'Berenice Boddy' and *C. japonica* 'Herme'. ('Herme' is also listed as *C. japonica* 'Hikarugenji'.)

Camellia 'April Rose' is a compact, slow-growing plant with a heavy bud-set and rose-red, double flowers. David Parks, co-proprietor of Camellia Forest, says that of the thousands of japonicas subjected to the severe cold of January 1985, only this selection bloomed to any extent after the freeze. Also, there was no record of cold-induced dieback. 'April Rose' is a cross between *C. japonica* 'Berenice Boddy' and *C. japonica* 'Kumasaka'.

Camellia 'April Remembered' is a vigorous, fast-growing plant with large, cream to pink-shaded, semidouble flowers.

Cliff has also produced hybrids of *Camellia sasanqua* to increase the choices in fall-blooming camellias. His crosses have used *C. oleifera* to introduce more hardiness and *C. reticulata* to introduce larger, showier flowers. *Camellia* 'Survivor' is a selection from *C. sasanqua* 'Narumi-gata' × *C. oleifera*. It produces an abundance of white flowers in the early autumn. It was the lone healthy sasanqua survivor in the garden after the January 1985 freeze. David Parks says that the plant is now 25 feet (7.5 m) tall and reports that a plant of 'Survivor' has bloomed in Ontario, Canada. It is cold hardy to USDA Zone 6B, or 6A with light protection.

Camellia 'Yoimachi' is a hybrid of *C. sasanqua* × *C. fraterna*, the latter parent a white-blooming species from Vietnam. 'Yoimachi' blooms in the autumn, has white petals with pink margins, and is hardy only to USDA Zone 8A.

One of Cliff's favorites is *Camellia sasanqua* 'Midnight Lover', a seedling of *C. sasanqua* 'Crimson King'. It produces the most intense, deep red flowers of all the sasanquas. 'Midnight Lover' bears single flowers in late fall to midwinter. It is vig-

Camellia 'April Remembered' PHOTO BY CLIFF PARKS

Camellia 'Yoimachi' PHOTO BY CLIFF PARKS

Camellia sasanqua 'Midnight Lover' PHOTO BY YVONNE CAVE

orous and erect in habit and grows to a height of 12 to 15 feet (3.6–4.5 m) with a spread of up to 10 feet (3 m). It is cold hardy to USDA Zone 7A and will take full sun to part shade.

Another of the sasanqua hybrids is *Camellia* 'Mason Farm', a selection of *C. sasanqua* × *C. oleifera*. In early autumn, it produces large white flowers whose petals are pink tinged. Cliff named the plant after the large old field, Mason Farm, near the North Carolina Botanical Garden (Chapel Hill), where he planted and grew more than a thousand seedlings for testing. This was the only segregate to survive the coldest weather after thirty years of growth at that location. 'Mason Farm' grows rapidly to 6 to 8 feet (1.8–2.4 m) tall and 4 to 6 feet (1.2–1.8 m) wide. It is cold hardy in USDA Zone 6B, or in 6A and colder with protection.

Among the hybrid camellias introduced by Cliff is *Camellia* 'Crimson Candles', an F_2 (second-generation) cross of *C. reticulata* × *C. fraterna*. It produces bright rose-red, single flowers in February and March, and has bronze-red new foliage. The sepals surrounding the bud are also red and, as the flower matures inside the bud, the elongated flower buds look like red candles. *Camellia* 'Crimson Candles' is cold hardy to USDA Zone 7B, and David reports that it maintains flower color and shape even after nights of 20°F (−7°C). It is a vigorous grower, attaining a height of 10 to 12 feet (3–3.6 m) and a spread of 6 to 8 feet (1.8–2.4 m). *Camellia* 'Japanese Fantasy' is a complex hybrid involving *C. japonica* 'Berenice Boddy', *C. saluenensis*, and *C. rosaeflora*. The result is a fast-growing plant that produces small flowers with pink edges. David writes in his catalog that the profusion of flowers on 'Japanese Fantasy' resembles a Japanese cherry tree in bloom. 'Japanese Fantasy' is cold hardy to USDA Zone 7B.

Camellia 'Crimson Candles' PHOTO BY CLIFF PARKS

Cliff is also developing crosses of the newly described *Camellia tenuivalvis*, discovered in 1990 on Longzhou Mountain in southern Sichuan. It is a high-elevation species, growing at 10,500 feet (3200 m) both in deforested meadows and as a subshrub under a canopy of *Lithocarpus* (Parks 2002). This species does not tolerate the heat and humidity of the eastern United States, but Cliff has successfully grafted it onto other stock and has found that it crosses easily with *C. japonica*. Cliff is also evaluating *C. saluenensis* (syn. *C. pitardii* var. *pitardii*) from Yunnan and Sichuan, and another new species, *C. chekiangoleosa*, a close ally of *C. japonica*.

Cliff's interests include development of a temperate, yellow-flowering camellia. A few yellow species are known in China and Vietnam from subtropical regions, including *Camellia longzhouensis* (south-central China) and *C. nitidissima* (Fangcheng Preserve in Guangxi, near the Vietnam border); however, the yellow floral pigment does not transfer well to hybrids adaptable to cool, temperate areas. "Most potential hybrid combinations have not been attempted," Cliff says, "and hardiness and compatibility assort independently. Available hybrids have not been tested for hardiness." He is also collecting germ plasm from wild collections of higher elevations and more northerly locales to improve *C. reticulata*, a complex grown for its large blossoms, but which adapts poorly to cold winters and high summer humidity (Parks 2002).

Camellia tenuivalvis PHOTO BY CLIFF PARKS

Camellia saluenensis PHOTO BY CLIFF PARKS

Camellia chekiangoleosa PHOTO BY CLIFF PARKS

Camellia nitidissima PHOTO BY CLIFF PARKS

cially since other collectors sometimes misidentify plants in the wild and pass along seeds under an incorrect name, causing gardeners to grow improperly labeled plants and causing potential scientific nomenclatural problems.

Chris has a strong interest in medicinal plants. During 1994 he was a consultant to the Royal Government of Bhutan on traditional medicinal plants of the Himalaya. In India, Nepal, and Bhutan, various government and non-governmental organizations work with traditional Tibetan doctors in growing those Himalayan species whose herbal formulations remain a primary health care feature of the region. There has been no local tradition, Chris tells me, of growing these mountain herbal plants, unlike the commonly grown subtropical and tropical species that are used in Ayurvedic (Indian) medicine. Plant hunters have been sent to the Himalaya and borderlands of Tibet for more than 150 years, searching for plants of ornamental merit, many of which happen also to have medicinal value. Chris says that a good deal of knowledge about the cultivation of these plants comes from rock gardeners, who are helping "put something back into the countries from whence the plants they cultivate came." Individuals like Chris are facilitating the sharing of such useful knowledge, experience, and expertise.

A native of Surrey, Chris grew up in Hertfordshire before studying botany at the University of Southampton. After graduation, he spent a short period as a police officer before working as a field botanist, conducting surveys for conservation organizations in the United Kingdom. He has also traveled to New Zealand, participated on a North American Rock Garden Society Speaker's Tour in North America, and lectured throughout the United Kingdom and Europe. Chris was honored in 1998 for his alpine collections by having *Saxifraga chadwelli* named for him by B. M. Wadhwa.

When I saw Chris's postage stamp–sized garden in Slough (Berkshire), I was amazed at what can be crammed into two 15- by 30-foot (4.5- by 9-m) plots, one in front and the other behind his house, with a bit of additional gardening space on the side of the house, and at the sidewalk. The Chadwell garden is being developed into a miniature botanical garden to commemorate Prem Nath Kohli, founder of P. Kohli and Company and a leading Indian horticulturist who exported Himalayan seeds and bulbs from nurseries in the Kashmir Valley to the West. In October 2003 the Sino-Himalayan Plant Association (cofounded in the early 1990s with economist David White, a former subscriber to Chris's expeditions) announced the Kohli Memorial Gold Medal for persons contributing significantly to Himalayan botany or horticulture. Chris delivered in Delhi the Kohli memorial lecture titled "Flowers Fit for a Maharajah."

I asked Malcolm McGregor, editor of *The Rock Garden*, the publication of the Scottish Rock Garden Club, about Chris's work and he replied:

> Chris is one of the great contemporary seed-collectors going back repeatedly to the same mountains, bringing back collections of Himalayan seed which growers across the world have delighted in. But he also puts back, with real links into the local communities of northwest India, helping pro-

mote the activities of their medicinal plant collectors and gardeners. It's good to know that independent spirits such as Chris are out there . . . and the collections bring a bit of the mountains home to all the subscribers. It is the nearest many people will ever get to the mountains of the Himalaya but at least through Chris they can get within touching distance.

Some of the plants that Chris has collected, introduced, or promoted follow.

Aquilegia is a member of the Ranunculaceae and consists of about seventy species, all distributed in the Northern Hemisphere. In the garden, columbines, as they are commonly called, interbreed freely. According to Bob Nold (Lakewood, Colorado), author of a book on columbines, the taxonomic keys to the genus are "impenetrable: each succeeding treatment seems to contradict the last" (Nold 2003). Some species are difficult to cultivate in the garden, an obstacle probably overstated by Reginald Farrer (1919) in *The English Rock Garden*:

> Though many of the more ordinary sorts are perfectly easy and perennial, it is sadly notorious that in droughty parts of England some of the most lovely queens of this race are correspondingly difficult and miffy in temper—as short-lived as a mid-Victorian heroine, and as resentful of all parched peas or crumpled rose-leaves in their beds as Hans Andersen's Princess.

The fragrant columbine, *Aquilegia fragrans*, is a native of the northwest Himalaya, principally Kashmir. "Columbines are a notoriously promiscuous bunch, so make sure you get the real thing, whether as a specimen from a nursery or when ordering seeds," Chris says (Chadwell 1994b). The best form in his garden is suitable for rock garden conditions, growing 12–18 inches (30–45 cm) tall. Flower colors vary from cream to pure white with pale blue on the outer petals. Each flower stalk bears one to three honeysuckle-scented flowers that are 1.25–2 inches (3–5 cm) wide and long. In the wild, *A. fragrans* inhabits meadows between 8,000 and 12,000 feet (2400–3600 m) according to Polunin and Stainton (1997).

In cultivation, *Aquilegia fragrans* grows well at the lower elevations where most of us garden, either in part shade or full sun on well-drained soils. It blooms in midsummer. In *The Himalayan Garden*, Jim Jermyn (2001) says that *A. fragrans* is one of his two favorite Himalayan columbines (the other is *A. nivalis*, the snow columbine). He recommends a generous planting of it in the rock garden and says that it looks well against the blue form of *Anemone trullifolia*.

The first phlomis I grew a few years ago came to me from a society seed exchange labeled "*Salvia* sp." Only when it bloomed did I realize something was amiss. The mistake gave me the opportunity to grow a new genus in my garden and to appreciate it more fully when I recognized it in a friend's garden. The genus *Phlomis* consists of a hundred or so species in the Lamiaceae (formerly Labiatae), ranging from the Mediterranean and Europe to Central Asia.

According to Chris, *Phlomis cashmeriana* is among the most distinguished Himalayan plants. It grows from Afghanistan to Kashmir, often in wastelands and on open slopes, blooming in the summer. The plant reaches at least 24 inches

(60 cm) tall and produces pale purple to pink flowers, 1 inch (2.5 cm) long, attached as whorls around the stem. Flowers have a large hooded, woolly upper lip; a cluster of unopened buds is striking. The long narrow leaves are wrinkled above and densely woolly-white beneath (Beckett 1933). Chris has grown this species in his garden since 1985. It is also a 2004 Plant Select® introduction, as Cashmere sage. *Phlomis cashmeriana* is hardy in USDA Zones 4b to 8 and is recommended for culture in garden loam, clay, or sandy soil.

I have trouble maintaining tulips from year to year in my garden. Unless I replace the bulbs each year, the quality of the bloom diminishes quickly in succeeding years. Thus I was surprised to read in *Flowers of the Himalaya* (Polunin and Stainton 1997) that *Tulipa clusiana* var. *stellata*, the star tulip, is a weed of cornfields and rocky slopes in Pakistan and Uttar Pradesh (India). There it pops out of the ground in April to May between elevations of 4,900 and 10,900 feet (1500–3300 m). I should be so lucky to find such weeds in my North Carolina garden at elevation 450 feet (140 m).

Chris obtained bulbs of *Tulipa clusiana* var. *stellata* from P. N. Kohli in the early 1980s and his original stock is still growing strong. This is not a new introduction, as Kohli earlier supplied Dutch nurseries with various other Kashmir tulips bulbs from his nurseries. The star tulip produces crimson buds that open into star-shaped white flowers 1.75–2.5 inches (4–6.5 cm) long. When the flower opens, rose-pink to deep red blotches appear on the outside of the petals (Chadwell 1994b). Chris says there is no need to lift or "bake" the bulbs over the summer and that they grow best in light soil and a sunny position in the garden. Best of all, this tulip will seed around.

Tulipa clusiana var. *stellata* (Liliaceae) is listed in some catalogs as *T. stellata*. Others (Beckett 1993) suggest that it should be returned to its specific rank, eliminating the varietal status altogether.

When Chris wrote an article about alpines in the borderlands of western Tibet for *The Rock Garden* (Chadwell 1993), he startled the reader with the opening sentence: "Where did you spend your honeymoon?" If your answer is the Tibetan part of Zanskar, then you are apt to find *Geranium himalayense* (Geraniaceae) just as Chris and his bride, Dorothy, did beside a glacial lake as she washed his socks. A plant raised from seed they gathered at over 14,000 feet (4300 m) still thrives in Chris's Slough garden, "making the honeymoon worthwhile," he says.

Tulipa clusiana var. *stellata*, Pakistan PHOTO BY CHRIS CHADWELL

Geranium himalayense (syn. *G. grandiflorum*) grows mostly on open slopes, though it also frequents moist ground beside irrigated fields, Chris observes. Its ascending stems support masses of purple-blue flowers. It grows from Afghanistan to central Nepal between 7,000 and 14,500 feet (2100–4500 m) elevation. Geraniums, or cranesbills, are highly likely to cross in cultivation and many cultivars are of hybrid origin. Chris says that most of the Himalayan geraniums he has encountered exhibit considerable variation in flower color, and that there may even be a pink-flowering form of *G. himalayense*. Baldassare Mineo (Medford, Oregon) says it grows to 16 inches (40 cm) high and 24 inches (60 cm) wide in a sunny part of his garden that has humus-rich, well-drained soil. He has found that it also spreads by seeds. It is cold hardy in USDA Zones 3 to 8.

Geranium pratense var. *stewartianum*, from Kashmir, produces purplish-pink flowers over a long growing season. In 1986, Chris spotted this form in a nearby meadow while sitting in a long line of vehicles waiting for traffic to move. He says it is rather rampant and tends to sprawl about on itself and other plants. The varietal epithet *stewartianum*, or Stewart's cranesbill, honors R. R. Stewart, an American Presbyterian missionary and college principal in Rawalpindi (Pakistan), who, over a lifetime, produced a thousand-page catalog of the flowers of west Pakistan and Kashmir, which Chris has found invaluable in his work. (Chris's private herbarium at Slough is named the Stewart Memorial Herbarium.)

Geranium himalayense, Pensi La, Zanskar PHOTO BY CHRIS CHADWELL

Geranium pratense var. *stewartianum* PHOTO BY CHRIS CHADWELL

Geranium clarkei 'Kashmir White' is closely kin to *G. pratense*, but is overall a smaller plant, and the flowers on *G. clarkei* tend to face upward. 'Kashmir White' produces showy white flowers.

Geranium wallichianum is best known for the widely cultivated 'Buxton's Variety', which displays bluish flowers with white centers. Peter Yeo (University of Cambridge Botanic Garden) raised a selection from Chris's Kashmir seed of 1983 and then passed it on to geranium specialist Andrew Norton. He named the selection 'Chadwell's Pink'. The Hardy Plant Society (United Kingdom) called 'Chadwell's Pink' a "must have" plant.

Meconopsis (Papaveraceae) comprises about forty-five species primarily from western China and the Himalaya. When I saw an example of *Meconopsis* in NARGS member Ev Whittemore's garden in North Carolina's southern Appalachian Mountains, I became enchanted with the blue flower color. It is a plant not easily forgotten.

Meconopsis aculeata, the west Himalayan blue poppy, flowered for the first time in cultivation at the Royal Botanic Gardens, Kew, in 1864. According to Chris, some forms currently in cultivation listed as *M. aculeata* are hybrids, having resulted from crosses with the beautiful *M. horridula* and rare *M. latifolia*. He says you can tell the true species by its deep and irregular, pinnately lobed leaves and its ovate to oblong seed capsule (Chadwell 1993). The plant grows to 24 inches (60 cm) high and has a somewhat prickly stem. The sky blue flowers have four (sometimes six) petals 2–3 inches (5–7 cm) across. *Meconopsis aculeata* grows from 9,900 to 13,200 feet (3000–4000 m) in its range from Pakistan to Uttar Pradesh (India). It is restricted to rocky slopes and cliffs where boulders shade the rosettes, creating a moist microclimate.

Meconopsis napaulensis and *M. paniculata* are two closely related species. Chris says he has had considerable success in finding and collecting seeds of both species in recent years. *Meconopsis napaulensis* is a robust plant growing to 7 feet (2 m) tall. It is monocarpic and produces reddish-pink flowers, occasionally blue or white. *Meconopsis paniculata* produces a large cluster of yellow, sometimes white, nodding flowers (Polunin and Stainton 1997). Some consider *M. paniculata* to be a yellow-flowered version of *M. napaulensis*, which ranges from Nepal to Assam. Polunin and Stainton describe the occur-

Meconopsis aculeata, Himachal Pradesh PHOTO BY CHRIS CHADWELL

rence of *M. paniculata* in southeast Tibet to Uttar Pradesh (India) as being "gregarious around herdsmen's camping grounds." Yoshida (2002) says that the abundance of *M. paniculata* at these locations results from shrub burning to encourage germination of grasses for the cattle, apparently creating habitat for the *Meconopsis* as well. Because the plant dies after flowering, it grows as a single plant, never clump forming.

Roy Lancaster twice saw the Himalayan musk rose, *Rosa brunonii* (Rosaceae), on his trek in Nepal in 1971. He was impressed by its powerful, scrambling growth reaching up into trees and its ability to overpower less sturdy plants (Lancaster 1995). It grows from Kashmir to southwest China and in Myanmar between elevations of 3900 and 7800 feet (1200–2400 m) (Polunin and Stainton 1997).

Chris says *Rosa brunonii* can clamber up to 50 feet (15 m). It is a sight to see in June and July when it is fully covered in creamy white, heavily scented flowers, 1–1.5 inches (2.5–4 cm) across. He advises (actually warns) to carefully pick your spot to grow it because it is fiercely armed with hooked prickles, a vigorous grower, and stout climber needing a sturdy support. At his Slough garden, it rampantly covered the bulk of the garage roof, requiring a severe cut back. Chris says it grows best where there is plenty of water for it to "drink," its "feet" are in the shade, and its "head" is in the sun (Chadwell 1994b). The specific epithet honors Robert Brown (1773–1858), a Scottish botanist.

Primula involucrata (Primulaceae) was discovered in 1825 in Garwhal (north-

Rosa brunonii, Kohli Memorial Himalayan Garden, Slough, United Kingdom PHOTO BY CHRIS CHADWELL

ern India). It has been a popular plant ever since its first blooming in Europe twenty years later. This species, the Himalayan marsh primula, grows in the Himalaya in marshy meadows, on stream banks, and along springs between 9,900 and 16,500 feet (3000–5000 m) elevation. It is probably the most widespread Sino-Himalayan primula, with a range of 1800 miles (2900 km), and where it occurs, it is often locally common.

The flowers, 0.5–0.75 inch (1.2–2 cm) across, are white to pale purple with a golden yellow eye, sometimes with an overall mauve-to-plum tinge. They are grouped in a lax umbel of two to six flowers and are carried on a slender stem (Polunin and Stainton 1997). The leaves are lanceolate and have a long, slender petiole.

Though *Primula involucrata* grows in marshy, wet areas within its native range, in the garden it will accept drier conditions; however, it needs to grow where it will not be overrun by larger plants. Chris says the flower emits a rich, pleasant scent.

Members of *Primula* section *Minutissimae* have solitary, stemless flowers. According to Chris, the *Minutissimae* as a group have now become much sought-after and have proved difficult in cultivation. *Primula reptans*, one of its members, is found in the western Himalaya between 11,800 and 18,100 feet (3600–5500 m) elevation, where it grows among rocks and open slopes (Polunin and Stainton 1997). It forms mats of rosettes with leaves smaller than the blue-purple flowers. The creeping primula, as it is known, has been a source of frustration for Chris, who says that he has been rarely able to locate ripe seed capsules. It grows in locations where the snow lies longest. When its companion plants have bloomed and produced seeds, *P. reptans*, often remains in full bloom, only to be covered by an early snowfall. The blooming period is June to August, or later at higher elevations.

In his travels, Chris has developed an interest in *Lilium* (Liliaceae). Currently, there are six recognized species in the Himalayan region. *Lilium polyphyllum* is a tall, robust plant, producing yellow-greenish to greenish-white flowers with rose-purple speckles and streaks inside. In bud it is ivory colored. The plant grows up to 4 feet (1.2 m) tall and inhabits open forest and shrubby areas from Kashmir to Kumaon (northern India) at the 6900- to 9900-foot (2100- to 3000-m) elevation (Chadwell 2001b). In *The Gardener's Guide to Growing Lilies*, Jefferson-Brown and Howland (1995) said that *L. polyphyllum* has not yet made a

Primula involucrata, Himachal Pradesh PHOTO BY CHRIS CHADWELL

Primula reptans, Himachal Pradesh PHOTO BY CHRIS CHADWELL

strong presence in the garden and suggested that if strong clones could be found, it would be desirable and attractive.

Chris has seen *Lilium polyphyllum* in the wild twice, first during his Kashmir Botanical Expedition in 1983. His team found a small colony on an island in the Lidder River (Pahalgam Valley) and two months later went back to collect ripened seeds. On a return trip two years later, a bridge had been constructed, allowing vehicles and grazing goats access to the island, and, regrettably, the demise of the colony.

Lilium nanum (syn. *Nomocharis nana*), the dwarf Himalayan lily, grows in the Himalaya to western China, usually on alpine slopes among small shrubs, between 10,900 and 14,100 feet (3300–4300 m) elevation. Chris's introduction to this species was in 1994 in Bhutan, where he was a consultant to the Royal Government of Bhutan on the cultivation of medicinal plants for the Traditional Medicine Project. The species is known as *a-bi-kha* to Tibetan doctors, who use it traditionally as a detoxicant and "to join the parts of a broken skull" (Chadwell 2001b). It is a small plant growing 4–10 inches (10–25 cm) tall, producing a bell-shaped, drooping flower. The flower is usually solitary and ranges from white to purple.

Euphorbia wallichii (Euphorbiaceae), Wallich's spurge, grows on open slopes and grazing grounds up to an elevation of 11,800 feet (3600 m) from Afghanistan to southwest China. It forms an erect cluster of stems 12–24 inches (30–60 cm) high and produces a flower head with golden- to yellow-lime bracts (Polunin and Stainton 1997). The flowers themselves are small and inconspicuous. Chris says it is much sought after by spurge aficionados and, with about sixteen hundred species in the genus, they have a lot of choices. Unfortunately, at times, nurseries have distributed the wrong species and thus impostors are being grown as *E. wallichii*.

Roy Lancaster, however, has seen the real McCoy. In *Garden Plants for Connoisseurs* (1987), he describes *Euphorbia wallichii* in alpine pastures and high plateaus above Gulmarg ("the flower-filled meadow") in the Vale of Kashmir as "one of the most striking and desirable of all herbaceous perennials for the garden." He said it flourishes as far as the eye can see "despite the attentions of the ubiquitous goats and other grazing animals who each spring, following the receding snow, climb the steep slopes devouring all before them" except the euphorbias, which contain caustic white juice. The specific epithet honors Nathaniel Wallich, director of the Calcutta Botanic Garden from 1814 to 1841.

"Quaint, intriguing and beautiful are all adjectives for this genus and there must be very few not worth at least trying." The quotation is from the *Corydalis* entry in the *Encyclopaedia of Alpines* (Beckett 1993), an unusual bit of gushiness in otherwise just-the-facts, clinical descriptions of alpines. Altogether, there are about three hundred *Corydalis* species in the Papaveraceae (some classify the genus in the Fumariaceae), a sufficient number to include many praiseworthy plants.

Corydalis thyrsiflora is from the high slopes and wet areas from Pakistan to Kashmir, growing at elevation of 9,900 to 14,100 feet (3000–4300 m). It produces bright yellow flowers on robust stems up to 16 inches (40 cm) high.

Chris first collected *Corydalis crassissima* on the 1983 expedition to Kashmir, where it grows in barren alpine scree at 11,800 to 14,800 feet (3600–4500 m). The large flowers, which are violet to pinkish white, develop large, globular, inflated

Corydalis crassissima, Kashmir PHOTO BY CHRIS CHADWELL

capsules. Chris says it is a striking plant whose leaves are conspicuously glaucous and succulent; however, it has proved a challenge to maintain in the garden.

Around forty species of *Ephedra* (Ephedraceae), all evergreen shrublets and shrubs, occur in the Mediterranean and eastward to China and in the Americas (Beckett 1993). Male and female flowers are borne on separate plants. Some species have medicinal properties, and are the source of ephedrine and pseudo-ephedrine, stimulants on the central nervous system and ingredients in over-the-counter asthma and cold medications, and dietary supplements for weight loss. In North America, species are called Mormon tea and squaw tea, *ma huang* to the Chinese herbalists, and joint-pines because of their primitive conifer look. The stems are usually thin and flexible, sometimes trailing, and leaves are reduced to scales that form a joint, or sheath, around the stem, an adaptation to xerophytic conditions to prevent water loss.

Ephedra gerardiana grows on dry, stony slopes and terraces between 8,200 and 16,400 feet (2500–5000 m) from Afghanistan to Bhutan. It grows from 12 to 24 inches (30–60 cm) high. Chris says that in Ladakh, the stems are used as toothbrushes and are ground to make a snuff. The stems also are a winter food for yaks and goats. *Ephedra gerardiana* is closely related to *E. intermedia* and is sometimes

Ephedra intermedia, Zanskar PHOTO BY CHRIS CHADWELL

confused with it; however, the stems of *E. intermedia* are more glaucous and narrower than those of *E. gerardiana*.

Lancaster (1995) also reported *Ephedra gerardiana* var. *sikkimensis* in Nepal and noted that "this is a most acceptable subject for the rock garden, especially when bearing its bright red currant-like berries." Unfortunately, once in cultivation it often waxes fat in the fertile soil, under benign conditions, and grows into a course mound up to 2 feet (0.6 m) high.

Androsace mucronifolia (Primulaceae) is a common plant on mountaintops and high passes in Kashmir. Here at 11,500 to 14,100 feet (3500–4300 m) it flowers in midsummer, producing pink, and occasionally white, flowers. It is a lax, mat-forming plant (Chadwell 1986).

Androsace muscoidea is a mound-forming plant, also from Kashmir. Its flowers are white with a greenish eye. One selection, *A. muscoidea* 'Millenium Dome', is slightly larger, woollier, and more silver haired. It won the Alpine Garden Society's Award of Merit in Edinburgh in 1999.Both are introductions by Chris (collected on expeditions in 1983 and 1985) and have earned honors at Alpine Garden Society shows.

My introduction to *Arisaema* was the native plant I knew as a child as jack-

Androsace mucronifolia PHOTO BY CHRIS CHADWELL

Androsace muscoidea, Kashmir. Collection from which 'Millenium Dome' was raised PHOTO BY CHRIS CHADWELL

in-the-pulpit. At the time, I did not know its Latin name, *A. triphyllum*, nor even that such nomenclature existed. My knowledge of the "jacks" has improved in the last few years and gardeners' interest has increased as a the result of more available information. Deni Bown's book on aroids, the common name for the plant family Araceae, is now in its second edition (2002). Guy and Liliane Gusman's book (2002) on the genus *Arisaema* has helped fuel further interest, as has U. C. Pradhan's book (1997) on Himalayan cobra-lilies, the common name for *Arisaema* in the region.

About seventeen species of cobra-lilies occur along the Himalaya, so called because the shape of the plant looks like the head of a cobra about to strike. Chris's introduction to Himalayan cobra-lilies came in Kashmir, where he first saw *Arisaema propinquum* (earlier called *A. wallichianum*). It grows up to 32 inches

(80 cm) tall and 20 inches (50 cm) wide. The inflorescence forms just below the leaves and emerges before the leaves unfold (Gusman and Gusman 2002). The inflorescence includes a dark purple spathe with light green to white stripes. *Arisaema propinquum* flowers in May to June and the red fruit ripens in August to September. The Gusmans report it growing at elevations of 7,900 to 13,800 feet (2400–4200 m). Chris has observed it growing in humus-rich coniferous forests.

Arisaema jacquemontii attains about the same height and width as *A. propinquum* but flowers and fruits later in the growing season (Gusman and Gusman 2002). Eastern and western Himalayan forms exist, those at higher elevations being smaller. Chris says that the cobra-lilies of the eastern Himalaya are more tender as they grow at modest elevations in moist, shady forests. *Arisaema jacquemontii* is found at higher elevations and can cope with less shade than that needed for *A. propinquum*.

For at least a decade, Chris Chadwell has been the highest-profiled plant explorer in the Himalayan region. Many of his introductions are now firmly in cultivation, and his seed subscription service remains popular with many British and North American plant enthusiasts.

Chris Chadwell
Chadwell Plant Seed and
Sino-Himalayan Plant Association
81 Parlaunt Road
Slough
Berkshire SL3 8BE
England

Chris Chadwell, Himachal Pradesh PHOTO BY
BOBBY J. WARD

Plant Geeks

Cistus Nursery—Sean Hogan & Parker Sanderson

D riving along the tree-lined neighborhood in Portland, Oregon, in search of Sean Hogan and Parker Sanderson's house, it is difficult to determine where their garden ends and another begins. You gradually realize that there has been an expansion into a neighbor's backyard, over to another's front yard, a leap across the street to another, and so forth. Sean and Parker practice the art of neighborhood street-gardening—spilling your garden up and down the street onto your neighbors' property (with approval from the neighbors, of course).

I once asked Sean what his favorite plant was and he responded without a moment's hesitation, but with a sly grin: "The plant that is in front of me at the moment." That is probably a rehearsed answer from a confirmed "plant geek," an endearing term bestowed on Sean and Parker by their friends and by professionals in the nursery industry. Sean and Parker are *into* "extreme plants" (the odd, the unusual plant) and "zonal denial" (stretching limits by testing a plant's adaptability to horticultural hardiness zones outside its range), a term they coined.

A native of Portland, Oregon, Sean studied biology in college in California. From 1988 till 1995, he worked as a horticulturist at the University of California (Berkeley) Botanical Garden where he managed the New World, Australia/New Zealand, Africa, and California cultivar plant collections. Parker is a native of Wales and spent time in Hawaii. He has a botany degree from the University of California at Davis and worked for the Davis campus arboretum for seven years.

Sean spent time as director of collections of Portland's Hoyt Arboretum, renowned for the extensive conifer collection, and he and Parker were co-curators and planting designers of the Classical Chinese Garden, a garden of tranquillity and beauty walled away from Portland's busy streets. Both of them volunteer with numerous plant and horticultural organizations, write about plants, lecture, and travel to see plants in gardens and arboreta and in the field, both domestically and abroad. They have a commingling expertise in plants: for example, Parker is an authority on the *Brodiaea* alliance of *Allium*-like bulbous plants and Sean on *Lewisia*, native plants of western North America. The *Lewisia* interest extended to assisting in completion of LeRoy Davidson's book, *Lewisias*, and in sorting out taxonomic problems and the range of *L. cantelovii*, including the recognition of three botanical varieties (Davidson 2000).

Sean and Parker founded Cistus Design in Portland in 1995, specializing in the design and creation of private and public gardens. The business was expanded to include a nursery, now carrying about twelve thousand selections of plants and specializing in hardy tropical plants, broadleaf evergreens, Mediterranean, and Southern Hemisphere plants. Their tastes in plants are catholic. Sean and Parker's great skill is in facilitating the introduction of "new" plants—not necessarily plants that they have collected themselves, but the found, neglected, overlooked, and unpromoted plants. Sean says:

> There is such a candy store of plants available now and so many that are "new" that the market demand for plants is growing. Folks are not interested just solely in a few bold, or even native plants, for the garden. They want everything. There is a horticultural agenda afoot!

Sean continues, tongue in cheek, "Parker and I tend to promote plants that are appropriate to our climate and any plants that we can force the climate to accommodate!"

Helen Dillon (Dublin, Ireland), gardener, lecturer, and writer, has frequently visited the United States, including Portland. She says of Sean and Parker:

> One of the most extraordinary plant experiences of my life was a visit to Sean and Parker's plant collection when it was all housed, higgledy-piggledy, in a series of damp greenhouses. Crammed together, leaf on leaf, peering out of the gloom, were thousands of enticing plants. The most exciting bit was that many were hitherto unknown to me.

I know well the old cramped greenhouses Dillon is speaking about. On a visit there with Sean, he led me over, around, under, and literally through plants. It was, in the kindest possible meaning, a jungle. Still, I came away with a box full of plants, stunned by the botanical inventory there. Now Cistus Nursery has new facilities and site renovations on Sauvie Island, about fifteen minutes from downtown Portland. Sean and Parker have now expanded to mail-order sales. Some of the plants that Sean and Parker have introduced or promoted follow.

In *My First Summer in the Sierra* (1911) John Muir wrote in chapter four ("To the High Mountains") of crossing Crane Flat, which drains into the Merced River, marveling at a meadow "bright" with a multitude of small plants, including lilies, columbines, and the "brilliant zauschneria." Later in *The Yosemite* (1912), he wrote in chapter four ("Snow Banners") of seeing delicate herbaceous plants such as zauschneria "soothing and coloring . . . wild rugged slopes with gardens and groves."

Zauschneria (Onagraceae) is commonly called California fuchsia or hummingbird flower. It is a genus of four species native to the western United States and Mexico. Several species were briefly transferred to *Epilobium* by some authorities and others consider certain forms to be subspecies of *Z. californica*.

Plants are heat and drought tolerant and hardy to USDA Zone 7. Flowers are tubular shaped, red-orange, and typically produced late in the summer. They usually spread by underground stems, sending up shoots in the spring.

Sean and Parker found *Zauschneria* 'Merced' as a seedling in Sean's mother's garden in Merced (California). Sean believes that it is a hybrid of *Z. arizonica* and *Z. californica* 'Catalina'. It is luxuriant, he says, growing to about 18 inches (45 cm) tall, with silver-gray foliage and "lipstick-orangey" flowers. (Sean is entirely imaginative when it comes to providing adjectives to describe the plants he grows.)

Zauschneria septentrionalis 'Fiddler Silver' is a plant Sean and Parker found in the Siskiyous in southern Oregon and took cuttings of. It is mat forming, growing to 8 inches (20 cm) high, and has large (for its size) orange-red flowers.

Zauschneria arizonica 'La Peña Blanca' is an evergreen Sean and Parker found in southern Arizona in the La Peña Blanca canyon, an area receiving summer rain. As most *Zauschneria* species do not need summer moisture, this selection does well in areas receiving more rain, making it an excellent summer garden plant, Sean told me. The flowers, which are produced earlier than those of other species, are "very deep-dark orange-red." The genus honors Johann Baptist Zauschner (1737–1799), a Prague botanist and medical professor.

Lapageria rosea (Philesiaceae), the Chilean bellflower, is the national flower of Chile. The only species in the genus, it is native to Chile and Argentina to about latitude 4 degrees south (Phillips and Rix 1997). This evergreen vine climbs 10–12 feet (3–4 m) and has leaves that are simple, glossy, and leathery with prominent veins. Known as *copihue* in the Amerind Araucanian language, *L. rosea* produces pendulous, bell-shaped, red to rose-colored flowers that are waxy, 2–4 inches (5–10 cm) long; they are produced in the late summer into winter. There is a white-flowered form, var. *albiflora*, and several cultivars. The plant is tender, 15° to 20°F (−9° to −7°C), at USDA Zone 8.

Sean and Parker have promoted this plant for some time. They were not the first to introduce it, but they are promoting various color forms by growing plants from seed batches received from Chilean nurseries. So far, they have flowers that are pink, white, salmon-colored and picotee.

In *Flora Silvestre de Chile: Zona Araucana*, Hoffmann (1982) said that the

Zauschneria californica PHOTO BY MARK TURNER

fleshy, elongated fruit (berry) is sweet and edible and that the roots are used in traditional medicine for treatment of gout, rheumatism, and venereal disease. The genus honors Empress Josephine of France (1763–1814), wife (née Tascher de la Pagerie) of Napoleon Bonaparte and patroness of botany.

Phormium, the New Zealand flax, consists of two evergreen members of the Phormiaceae (formerly Agavaceae) from New Zealand. *Phormium tenax*, the larger of the two, forms basal, fan-shaped, moderately stiff leaves that may reach 10 feet (3 m) long but only 6 inches (15 cm) wide. The typical leaf color is a dull, olive green. The branched flower stalk, soaring to 15 feet (4.5 m) high, produces dull to rusty red, 2.5-inch (6-cm) long flowers, which attract nectar-feeding birds. The flowers appear in the summer from the center of the clump. There are many leaf color forms, some with native Maori names, in cultivation. The leaf color varies from near black to coffee to pink and variegated.

Phormium 'Good Sport' is a hybrid of *P. cookianum* and *P. tenax*. It has leaves that are 4 inches (10 cm) wide and arch upward to 3 to 4 feet (0.9–1.2 m) tall. They are deep olive green with maroon stripes. 'Good Sport' appeared in Sean and Parker's Portland garden as each of the parents blooms there. Sean says it is a very vigorous, tough plant. It is cold hardy to USDA Zone 8.

The fibers of New Zealand flax are no longer used commercially for cordage, except in native Maori craftweaving. The genus name is from Greek for "mat," alluding to the use of its fiber.

Fremontodendron mexicanum, the Mexican flannelbush, is a member of the cacao family (Sterculiaceae) found in southern California and northern Baja California (Mexico). It is a rare species with declining populations, known only from a few sites. This treelike shrub is found in coniferous forests and mixed chaparral, including the Otay Mountain region in San Diego County, California. The maplelike, evergreen leaves are five lobed, 1–2 inches (2.5–5 cm) wide, and thick and leathery, green above and white below. Flowers, produced from spring till late summer, consist of five orange-yellow petal-like sepals and are 2 inches (5 cm) across. Plant height reaches 15–20 feet (4.5–6. m) tall. Young twigs are densely woolly.

Fremontodendron californicum, an evergreen shrub between 6 and 30 feet (2–9 m) tall, is native from Arizona to California and to Baja California. It is similar to *F. mexicanum* but has leaves with three lobes and smaller flowers. 'Ken Taylor' is a selection, possibly hybrid, of *F. californicum* and *F. decumbens*, which forms a spreading shrub to 4 feet (1.2 m) tall and up to 12 feet (3.6 m) wide. It is a tough garden plant, Sean says. The selection is named for a great Monterey area horticulturist, Ken Taylor. The Mexican flannelbush is cold hardy to USDA Zone 8.

The former genus name, *Fremontia*, was named in honor of Major General John Charles Frémont (1813–1890) who explored the U.S. Far West during the 1840s and discovered many shrubs and trees, which were sent to John Torrey (Columbia) and Asa Gray (Harvard).

Fremontodendron mexicanum PHOTO FROM GLOBAL BOOK PUBLISHING PHOTO LIBRARY

Heimia salicifolia (Lythraceae) is a shrub native from Texas southward to Argentina. It has small, willow-like leaves and grows to 10 feet (3 m) tall. The flowers are yellow, solitary, and small at 0.75 inch (1.9 cm) across. It was called *sinicuichi* by the Aztecs who used it during rituals to induce hallucinatory or trancelike visions and increased auditory sensitivity. In Brazilian Portuguese, it is known as *abre-o-sol* or "sun opener," an allusion to the experience of "golden visions" produced when partaking its fermented leaves. Also, it contains chemicals with anti-inflammatory properties. It is cold hardy to USDA Zone 8.

Sean and Parker collected a new species in Argentina in 2002 on a plant hunting trip that included Tony Avent, Bob McCartney, and Carl Schoenfeld—all also profiled in this book. The "new" *Heimia* has large, rich creamy yellow flowers on an 8-foot (2.4-m) trunk with golden flaky bark. Sean and Parker have begun propagating it and releasing it through Cistus Nursery under its collection number.

Abutilon, or flowering maple, a member of the mallow family (Malvaceae), consists of about a hundred species, mostly shrubs and robust perennials. They are found in tropical and subtropical regions, mostly in South America. Abutilons have pendent, bell-shaped flowers consisting of brightly colored petals and a calyx (usually of a different color). They are also commonly called Chinese lanterns, an allusion to the hanging flowers resembling paper lanterns. They tend to have a long flowering season with only a short rest period in midwinter.

Heimia salicifolia PHOTO FROM GLOBAL BOOK PUBLISHING PHOTO LIBRARY

Parker comments that "they bloom forever" and that even in a colder year in Portland the plants will flower up till Thanksgiving and start again by Valentine's Day (Jaeger 2003). The abutilons that Sean and Parker work with are hardy to USDA Zone 8. Just in case the "big freeze" comes to Portland, they take cuttings to overwinter and start new plants in the spring.

Numerous hybrids and selections of *Abutilon* ×*hybridum* are in cultivation, many involving *A. megapotamicum* from Brazil and southern Uruguay. Cistus Nursery offers about seventy-five selections. *Abutilon* 'Furious Yellow' is a complicated cross that Sean made (my eyes glassed over when he rattled off its genetic lineage). He says 'Furious Yellow' is an "open bell," bright yellow and very floriferous. The plant has black stems. Sean says that is such an exciting plant that "it makes you look ten years younger—and thinner—when you admire it."

Abutilon 'Tiffany Sconce' grows 6 feet (1.8 m) tall and looks "just like a Tiffany lamp shade," according to Sean. The flower color is "warm tangerine, pink-red veined," also on dark stems. Though it blooms year-round, it tends to produce more flowers in autumn than any other time.

Abutilon 'Moonshade' grows 2–3 feet (0.6–0.9 m) tall and has felted leaves and open flowers that are flat like an hibiscus. They are creamy yellow and 4 inches (10 cm) across.

The common name "flowering maple" derives from the superficial resemblance of the leaves of *Abutilon* to maple leaves. The genus name derives from the Arabic word for a mallow-like plant.

Delosperma nubigenum (Aizoaceae) is one of about 130 species of this genus of succulent plants native to South Africa and Madagascar. Delospermas and other succulent members of the Aizoaceae are sometimes placed in their own separate family, the Mesembryanthemaceae (Smith et al. 1998). *Delosperma nubigenum* forms a mat about 12 inches (30 cm) across and produces yellow flowers about 0.75 inch (2 cm) across and 4 inches (10 cm) high. It is native to the southern part of the Eastern Cape province, growing among rocks to an elevation of 10,500 feet (3200 m). A closely related plant with yellow flowers is sometimes sold as *D.* cf. *nubigenum* 'Lesotho'. It is the *D. nubigenum* "of commerce." Sean collected this on trips to South Africa in 1991 and 1993.

Sean also collected *Delosperma congestum* 'Gold Nugget', another hardy ice plant, in South Africa. It has proved immensely popular, particularly in a rocky setting in the garden. 'Gold Nugget' has yellow, daisylike flowers with a small white "eye" surrounding the disk flowers. They are produced over a long period, from early to late summer. 'Gold Nugget' grows about 2 inches (5 cm) tall and 30 inches (75 cm) across. Its succulent leaves turn maroon-red in the winter. It grows best in full sun in a well-drained, sandy soil.

The genus name *Delosperma* derives from Greek for "visible seed," an allusion to the fact that capsules have no membrane covering. The specific epithet

Delosperma cf. *nubigenum* 'Lesotho' PHOTO BY BALDASSARE MINEO

nubigenum means "born above the clouds," a reference to the plant's high elevation occurrence, and *congestum* means "arranged close together," a reference to the foliage growth habit.

Begonia boliviensis (Begoniaceae) develops from large, tuberous corms, producing showy, red-orange pendulous flowers. They are produced in profusion over the entire growing season. The plant develops erect, robust stems, 18–24 inches (45–60 cm) high, which die back in the winter, even in a greenhouse. In warm conditions, the stems may be lax or drooping, making them ideal for a hanging basket. The leaves are narrow and dentate. The Bolivian begonia originates from montane cloud forests on the eastern side of the Andes in Argentina and Bolivia. It is found typically among rock crevices and slopes near streams, where the overall plant competition is low (Halloy 2003).

This species first reached Europe in the mid-nineteenth century and is one of the species from which tuberous hybrid begonias have derived. Recent collections include hardier forms and various color selections. Sean, who initially collected it in Argentina in 1990 near Tucumán and Jujuy, and again in 2002, was one of the first nursery owners to promote it widely. Though the original plant he collected is still unnamed as a selection, he thinks it is the best form. The genus honors Michel Bégon (1638–1710), governor of French Canada and patron of botany.

Tetrapanax papyrifer (Araliaceae), the rice-paper plant, is a large shrub to small tree that normally grows to 12 feet (3.6 m) tall. Native to southern China,

Begonia boliviensis PHOTO BY BALDASSARE MINEO

including Taiwan, it is the only known species in the genus. It has large, umbrella-like, lobed leaves that are up to 3 feet (0.9 m) wide. In my North Carolina garden, it blooms in mid-November, just about frost time. The creamy white flowers, produced in a panicle above the plant, emerge from striking brown, woolly buds. *Tetrapanax papyrifer* is fast growing and tends to sucker around in the garden by underground stolons, as I have new plants appearing 10 feet (3 m) from the mother plant. A fine rice paper is made from the stem pith, which is easily pushed and rolled out.

Sean obtained *Tetrapanax papyrifer* 'Steroidal Giant' through Ed Carmen (San Jose), who had kept the plant in a pot for few years. Ed had gotten it via Hawaii from Japan. A piece of it was given to Roger Warner (Camellia Mountain, Sea Range, California), who passed it along, in the pass-along plant tradition, to Sean. Because the plant soared to 25 feet (7.5 m) tall in his garden, Sean called it 'Steroidal Giant'.

Sean and Parker's interest in plants reaches to the Cactaceae. In 1991 Sean traveled to Argentina to benefit the University of California (Berkeley) Botanical Garden and concentrated on dryland plants. From that trip some eight hundred plant and seed accessions were made. Most of the plants reside at the University of California at Berkeley, but they represent yet another type of plant, indicative of Sean and Parker's broad interests.

Species of *Tephrocactus*, a genus formerly assigned to *Opuntia*, are found in Argentina. *Tephrocactus alexanderi* var. *geometricus* (syn. *Opuntia alexanderi*) is

Tetrapanax papyrifer 'Steroidal Giant' PHOTO BY BOBBY J. WARD

small, erect cactus with large white to rose-colored flowers. The globose stem segments are up to 2 inches (5 cm) long with stout spines up to 1.75 inches (4 cm) long (Anderson 2001). It is found in northwest Argentina in the state of La Salta, southward to Tucumán and La Rioja.

Pterocactus species are dwarf, nearly geophytic plants with tuberous roots and underground stems (Anderson 2001). They are distributed throughout Patagonia and northward to La Salta.

Maihueniopsis bonnieae (syn. *Puna bonnieae*) is a cactus from several areas in Argentina. It is a small geophyte about 6 inches (15 cm) in diameter with thick, branched taproots (Anderson 2001). Flowers are light pink.

Echinopsis bonnieae (syn. *Lobivia bonnieae*) is also from Argentina. Its flowers are small, 1.25–2 inches (3–5 cm) wide, and yellow-brown.

Trachelospermum (Apocynaceae) consists of about twenty evergreen climbing shrubs native from India to Japan and in the U.S. Southeast. The plants form star-shaped flowers, which are fragrant, and are commonly referred to as star jasmine. *Trachelospermum asiaticum* 'Theta' is a selection Sean and Parker made from a batch of seed they received from China. It has narrow, lance-shaped leaves on dark stems. It forms a ground cover of 12 to 18 inches (30–45 cm) tall, but it does not flower, nor does it develop the more typical adult or rounded leaves, instead maintaining juvenile leaves. 'Theta' is named for Sean's mother.

Philadelphus mexicanus (Hydrangeaceae), the Mexican mock orange, is found from Guatemala to Mexico. It is a large shrub to small tree growing to 15 feet (4.5 m) tall and 8 feet (2.4 m) wide and is an evergreen with a vinelike growth habit. *Philadelphus mexicanus* 'Rosemary Brown' is a collection Sean made in Coahuila (northern Mexico) at an elevation of 7000 feet (2130 m). It has arching branches, leaves with a silver sheen, and fragrant white flowers. A friend of Sean's has grown it in the Oregon coastal range where 'Rosemary Brown' was exposed to 10°F (−12°C) without damage. The selection is named for a gardener neighbor of Sean and Parker.

Sean has told me of still other "new" plants he and Parker are adding to their catalog. *Oxalis oregana* 'Klamath Ruby' (Oxalidaceae), the wood sorrel that is native to the Siskiyou range, has maroon leaves and pale flowers. "It's a beauty," Sean says.

Oxalis oregana PHOTO BY MARK TURNER

Arctostaphylos viscida PHOTO BY MARK TURNER

Pittosporum tenuifolium 'Ruffles' (Pittosporaceae), which Sean describes in one breath, is "upright with black stems, apple-green ruffled leaves with a silver overlay, and did I mention black petioles." It's a seedling that mysteriously appeared in the garden. The species is a New Zealand native and 'Ruffles' is "an upper Zone 8 plant," Sean says.

A couple of manzanitas or bearberries are also noteworthy. *Arctostaphylos viscida* 'Silver Dollar' (Ericaceae) from the Illinois Valley of southern Oregon has "round leaves and shell pink flowers." *Arctostaphylos hispidula* 'Serpentine Wings' has long leaves and pink flowers. Sean found it at high elevation in the Siskiyous, "growing in the shade of *Arbutus*."

With their peripatetic travels and eyes for new, exciting plants, Sean and Parker are a force to be reckoned with in the plant exploration arena. With such wide-ranging interests between them, their combined enthusiasms encompass nearly the entire plant kingdom.

Sean Hogan and Parker Sanderson PHOTO BY
BOBBY J. WARD

Sean Hogan and Parker Sanderson
Cistus Nursery
22711 NW Gillihan Road
Sauvie Island, OR 97231
United States
www.cistus.com

From Snowdonia to *Stauntonia*

Crûg Farm Plants—Bleddyn & Sue Wynn-Jones

It is hard to imagine a more bucolic setting than Crûg Farm in northern Wales. On a visit there, I could gaze at the serene panorama of the Snowdon massif and hear the intermittent bleat of calves and sheep. It is in this idyllic location that Sue and Bleddyn (pronounced *ble-thin*) Wynn-Jones operate Crûg Farm Plants, a nursery specializing in woodland plants from the Far East. The word *crûg* (pronounced *creeg*) means "look out" or "high point" in Welsh, a reference to "The Mound," an elevated area of the gardens presumed to have been used by the Romans.

Originating from old, long-established North Wales families with strong maritime connections, Bleddyn and Sue knew each other as young children. While Sue was educated in Caernarfon, Bleddyn attended primary school in nearby Bangor and later went to a boarding school in Derbyshire (England). Neither followed an academic career. Sue trained as a fashion buyer in the West End of London, moving to Switzerland and the United States until a family crisis brought her home in 1974. Meanwhile Bleddyn trained on the family farm and soon started his own family, establishing his own garden in his spare time. After Bleddyn's first marriage broke up, he and Sue met up again and have hardly spent a day apart since (1975).

Sue and Bleddyn raised beef cattle and sheep as their main livelihood at the 200-acre (80-ha) Crûg Farm from 1974, when they took over the farm, until 1990, when economic conditions in the beef industry, and later the "mad cow disease" scare, forced them to consider alternatives. For them, gardening and horticulture had been primarily an avocation (they grew their own vegetables and some strawberries for local sales), but when confronted with the need for an expensive slurry tank, they quickly decided instead to invest in less-expensive polytunnel plastic greenhouses, concluding it would be the chance to prove their green thumb. Initially they grew plants for wholesaling. The barns and stockyards were gradually converted to production facilities (for one customer, Crûg Farm produced ten thousand plants of *Tropaeolum speciosum* in one season). The Wynn-Joneses quickly gained the courage to begin on-site retail sales and continued to wind down the beef cattle operation. The nursery opened for retail sales in 1991, and the last of their cattle went to market in 1992.

top of a short peduncle (hence the varietal epithet *brevipedunculatum*). *Arisaema taiwanense* f. *cinereum* boasts ashen-gray leaflets. The spadix in all three forms is similar: broad, cream-colored to dark, and spongy, surrounded by the sinister-looking hooded spathe, which accounts for one of its vernacular names, the cobra-lily. *Arisaema taiwanense* tends to produce immense fruit heads.

Actaea (some species were formerly in the genus *Cimicifuga*) is a member of the Ranunculaceae. Sue and Bleddyn made collections of this genus in South Korea near the demilitarized zone where they found tall seed spikes of *A. dahurica* under a tree canopy. This dioecious species produces flower stems rising to a height of about 6 feet (1.8 m) and large ternately compound leaves, which can be 2 feet (0.6 m) across. The male plants produce the more showy flowers.

In the same area on Mount Sorak, in northeastern South Korea, they found *Actaea heracleifolia* var. *bifida*, a rare form that grows to 3 feet (1 m) tall and produces late-summer white plumes; it has only three leaflets and flower petals with notched apices. On the slopes of Mount Hallasan on the island of Cheju, they found a diminutive form of *A. japonica* in flower at 4 inches (10 cm); it has upright flowers that are somewhat scented. Seed from *A. simplex* var. *simplex* (the continental or mainland form) was collected by the Wynn-Joneses and Dan Hinkley in South Korea and they each grew it as *A. ramosa*, an invalid name. Incidentally, this is the taxon that gave rise to the seedling cultivar 'Atropurpurea' with purple leaves.

Arisaema taiwanense PHOTO BY TONY AVENT

Actaea japonica PHOTO BY BLEDDYN AND SUE WYNN-JONES

In the fall of 1992, Sue and Bleddyn found a related plant, later described as *Actaea taiwanensis* (BSWJ3413). Hailing from the high mountains in southern Taiwan, this species has upright branching stems to about 5 feet (1.5 m) and scented white flowers in bottle brush–like "spikes" or racemes.

The genus name is derived from the Greek *aktea*, the name for the baneberry or cohosh. In the vernacular, cimicifugas are bugbanes and snakeroots, the racemes of which are typically ill scented. The word *cimicifuga* in Latin means "to drive or chase away bugs," a reference to the ability of some species to thwart vermin (vermifuge), as they contain a resinous principle, the powdered form of which was applied to bed ticks (covers) and mattresses. Actaeas arise from creeping rhizomes and most tolerate part shade. They are hardy in USDA Zones 3 to 8.

The genus has recently undergone taxonomic revision by James Compton of the University of Reading (United Kingdom); he has absorbed *Cimicifuga* into the genus *Actaea*. Compton collected actaeas in Korea in 1993 with Dan Hinkley, who was later joined by the Wynn-Joneses.

The genus *Tripterospermum* (Gentianaceae) is relatively rare in Western cultivation. It is kin to the genus *Gentiana* and was at one time so classified; Dan Hinkley refers to it as the "vining gentian." Although Ohwi's *Flora of Japan*, the bible for English-speaking botanists working in Japan, was published in the English translation in 1965, it listed only *T. japonicum*. In *A Plantsman in Nepal*, Roy Lancaster (1995) reported finding *T. volubile* in 1971 twining among large bushes and small trees.

The Wynn-Joneses have found three additional species in the high mountains of Taiwan. *Tripterospermum cordifolium* and *T. lanceolatum* have evergreen leaves that are purple on the underside; they are small plants that twine to 3 feet (0.9 m). *Tripterospermum taiwanense* is relatively rare and produces large whitish-green, gentian-like flowers with dark stripes. It has semi-evergreen leaves. All three Taiwanese species produce shiny purple fruit pods that contain small black, three-winged seeds.

In 1999 the Wynn-Joneses went to Vietnam, where they were joined by Dan Hinkley. They were quickly immersed into the botanical treats of northern Vietnam near the Red River border with Yunnan (China), and a marvelous view of the Fan Xi Pan (also Fansipan) mountain range with Vietnam's tallest peak at 10,339

Tripterospermum japonicum PHOTO BY BLEDDYN AND SUE WYNN-JONES

feet (3143 m). On the slopes of Fan Xi Pan, they described a deforested native hill-side, now recolonized in *Hedychium coronarium*, as "an ocean of large white-scented flowers."

Here they stumbled upon *Disporum* aff. *tonkinense* (Convallariaceae), known in the West as fairy bells, one of about forty species in the genus and closely kin to the genus *Polygonatum*. It grows to about 3 feet (0.9 m) with one or two arched stems, and produces a terminal cluster of white flowers that develop into clusters of blue fruit in the autumn. What really entranced them was an unusual feature: the plant was producing new plants from the top of the old plant, a phenomenon known as vivipary, in which bulbils or seeds germinate while still attached to the parent plant. The genus name *Disporum*, from the Greek *dis* and *spora*, is an allu-sion to two ovules in each carpel chamber of the fruit.

One of Bleddyn's botanical passions is the genus *Polygonatum* whose Latin name means "many kneed," alluding to the plant's jointed stems. Except for a few species, this group of woodland plants, commonly called Solomon's seal, is gen-erally not known by gardeners and is certainly under-utilized. Bleddyn aims to change that as evidenced by his listing of more than thirty species or forms in his catalog. He has doubled the number of plants in the U.K. National Collection of polygonatums, largely via collecting trips that he and Sue have taken.

An introduction they consider among their best is *Polygonatum cyrtonema* from the mountains of northern Taiwan at Taroko. Strong stemmed and arching, it may attain a height of 7 feet (2.1 m) and is considered by them as "the most stately of all the Solomon's seals." It displays an impressive show of flowers, which are tubular shaped and white with green tips. Some horticulturists confuse *P. cyrtonema* and *Disporopsis pernyi*, as the latter was first misnamed *P. cyrtonema*. The flower of *Disporopsis pernyi* has a corolla and the plant itself is much smaller.

Polygonatum kingianum is a yellow-flowering form that Sue and Bleddyn found in northern Thailand near the border with Myanmar. Compared to some of the better-known North American diminutive forms of *Polygonatum*, this spe-cies is tall, with stems that rise up to 14 feet (4.3 m) from a stout rhizome. The yel-low, sometimes bright, pendent flowers with light green tips occur in clusters of nine or more.

Although most species of *Polygonatum* are terrestrial, a few species including *P. punctatum* and *P. oppositifolium* can be epiphytic. The Wynn-Joneses found the latter in Sikkim, growing on *Rhododendron arboreum*; it formed rhizomes that produced stems up to 3 feet (0.9 m). Unlike most species in the genus with alter-nate leaves, this one has evergreen leaves that are opposite each other. *Polygona-tum altelobatum*, a rare species collected in northern Taiwan, has waxy, bright green leaves and a slightly arching habit.

Syneilesis aconitifolia is a member of the daisy family (Asteraceae) and is closely akin to *Ligularia*. Its fascination and allure derive from the silky, shaggy foliage that emerges parasol-like in the spring; by the summer when flower heads develop and the sheen has disappeared from the aconitum-like leaves, it still

Polygonatum cyrtonema PHOTO BY BLEDDYN AND SUE WYNN-JONES

Polygonatum oppositifolium PHOTO BY BLEDDYN AND SUE WYNN-JONES

Syneilesis aconitifolia PHOTO BY TONY AVENT

remains attractive. In South Korea, Bleddyn collected another species, *S. palmata*, whose expanding leaves were like a giant pulsatilla. Still another introduced species is *S. subglabrata* (considered by some to be *S. intermedia*) from the central mountains of Taiwan.

One of Crûg Farm's specialties is geraniums and the nursery has offered an intimidating inventory of at least 230 taxa, the result of an extensive breeding program for hardier forms and new additions from collecting trips. Most of the cultivars that originated at the nursery have "Crûg" in the plant's name.

Geranium 'Bertie Crûg' is a hybrid named for the Wynn-Joneses' Jack Russell terrier, which stalks squirrels in the garden. It is a low-growing geranium with deep pink flowers. *Geranium* 'Rosie Crûg', another hybrid from the Crûg strain (*G.* ×*antipodeum*) and *G. lambertii*, has large pink-veined flowers. *Geranium* 'Dusky Crûg' is a chance nursery seedling, one of whose parents is *G.* ×*oxonianum*. It sports rounded, velvetlike, dusky-colored leaves. One of the best forms developed is *G.* 'Sue Crûg', a plant bearing large flowers, the deep pink petals of which have alternating dark and light areas. The catalog describes it winsomely as "combining the long flowering season (May to frost) and toughness of *G.* ×*oxonianum* with the charm of *G.* 'Salome'."

Geraniums are members of the Geraniaceae; the name is from Greek *geranos* for "crane," alluding to the beaklike fruits.

Geranium 'Sue Crûg' PHOTO BY BLEDDYN AND SUE WYNN-JONES

Many additional plants are available from Crûg Farm. For example, a wide array of hydrangeas (more than seventy-five forms) is shown in the on-line catalog. *Cardiandra formosana*, "appearing like moths fluttering in the gloomy shade," is an herbaceous member of the Hydrangeaceae from Taiwan. It has hairy leaves and lace-cap flowers that are pale purple.

Crûg Farm has introduced new species of *Disporopsis* (Convallariaceae), plants with evergreen stems and spreading rhizomes. *Disporopsis arisanensis* was found in the mountains of Taiwan, and a newly described species, *D. luzoniensis*, came from North Luzon in the Philippines.

Crûg Farm also offers plants of the genus *Chloranthus* (Chloranthaceae), a perennial with spikes of white flowers and attractive foliage. *Chloranthus oldhamii*, an evergreen ground cover from Taiwan, is generally unknown outside Asia.

The show-stopping species from China, *Thalictrum delavayi* var. *decorum* (Ranunculaceae) has long-lasting pink flowers with recurving tips. Blooming in July to September, flowers are held on terminal branching cymes. Stems may be 5 feet (1.5 m) tall. The plant may grow to 16 feet (5 m), according to Bleddyn, if sited in soil that is humus rich but lime-free.

The flower illustrated on the Crûg Farm Plants logo, *Tropaeolum speciosum* (Tropaeolaceae), is a climbing perennial and one of six forms for sale. It produces scarlet flowers in summer followed by blue fruit.

Thalictrum delavayi var. *decorum* PHOTO BY BLEDDYN AND SUE WYNN-JONES

Tropaeolum speciosum PHOTO BY BLEDDYN AND SUE WYNN-JONES

Bleddyn and Sue Wynn-Jones, though relative newcomers to the game, have made some important discoveries since their travels in East and Southeast Asia began. Their extensive expeditions have produced a dazzling number of shrubs, vines, and perennials, mostly for the shady and not-so-shady garden.

(on-site sales only)
Crûg Farm Plants
Bleddyn and Sue Wynn-Jones
Griffith's Crossing
Caernarfon
Gwynedd LL55 1TU
Wales, United Kingdom
www.crug-farm.co.uk

Bleddyn and Sue Wynn-Jones PHOTO BY BLEDDYN AND SUE WYNN-JONES

Polymath Rock Star

Denver Botanic Gardens & Plant Select®—Panayoti Kelaidis

I remember one late-evening talk with Panayoti Kelaidis, after the rest of his household had long since gone to bed, my jet-lagged body and mind were still several time zones away. I am sure I contributed little to that conversation and he must have noticed my leaden eyes. My notes from that conversation say that Panayoti told me, "You know, Bobby, all plants are hardy till you find out otherwise." That comment would only come home to me when I accompanied him on his workplace rounds.

You might assume that someone who manages one million pounds (450,000 kg) of rock on a one-acre (0.4-ha) plot is a professional geologist, speleologist, or rock climber. Not in this case. Panayoti is the designer of the plantings at the rock alpine garden in the Denver Botanic Gardens (DBG) in Denver, Colorado, considered by many as the finest public rock garden in the United States.

Panayoti Kelaidis fully embodies the attributes introduced in C. P. Snow's *The Two Cultures and the Scientific Revolution* (1959)—the melding of science and art—being both a Vladimir Nabokov devotee and Chinese literature scholar as well as a horticulturist. He lectures and writes with graceful words, so lucid you wonder if the left side of his brain has an embedded electronic silicon chip arranging, editing, and parsing the narrative that sallies forth so effortlessly. He is as likely to spit out allusions to Antigone or classical Chinese literature as he is to *Delosperma* (the ice plant) and the Madrean montane forests of southern Colorado.

The DBG's rocky outcroppings, laden with more than four thousand plant species, each "cuter than a bug's ear," is Panayoti's workaday Zen. At the garden I was hard pressed to keep up with this self-taught plantsman who can recite the provenance of each plant while he arabesques and glissades among ledges and crevices of the garden, crammed with South African and Asian plants as well as the indigenous flora from Colorado and the intermountain basin. The plants must persevere in the Rocky Mountain's continental steppe, a climate of low overall rainfall, cold dry winters, and searingly hot (low humidity) summers.

Panayoti's philosophy for determining the hardiness of plants is simple and direct: "Grow them in as many locales as possible and do not believe what the textbooks tell you. . . Don't garden in your head; garden in the ground to prove what will grow in your area or won't grow."

Many of the plants he tests in the DBG rock garden have come from his collecting trips to various countries including South Africa, Pakistan, Chile, Argentina, and Spain. Panayoti's first horticultural "high" was his trip in 1978 with Paul
Maslin to Chihuahua, Mexico, to collect seed of Mexican phloxes, including the
yellow phlox, *Phlox lutea* (syn. *P. mesoleuca*). It was an experience that turned
Panayoti forever to horticulture. Gardeners have been the richer for his explorations, especially his South African travels, which resulted in the introduction of
hardy delospermas and many other plants unknown in North American gardens
prior to his visits.

Phlox lutea PHOTO BY PANAYOTI KELAIDIS

Panayoti has introduced "new" plants from his tests in the DBG rock garden in a unique, successful partnership with Colorado State University (Fort Collins) and the "green" industry (the nursery and landscape industry) of Colorado and other Rocky Mountain and Plains states. Plant Select®, as the program is known, aids in the introduction and evaluation of perennials, annuals, trees, and shrubs that adapt particularly well to the Colorado Front Range—plants that have low water requirements and can survive in the region's cold winters and hot summers.

A native of Oak Creek in western Colorado, Panayoti grew up in Boulder, Colorado. He studied Chinese in Cornell University's doctoral program in the mid-1970s, but was drawn back to Colorado where he had begun gardening and taking an interest in native plants and rock gardening. In 1977 he helped create the DBG rock alpine garden and took a job as a curator, where he has remained in various capacities.

Gwen, his spouse, is a native of New York, near Schenectady. She became interested in plants through her mother, a passionate gardener. Gwen moved to Wisconsin and earned undergraduate and master's degrees in biology and science education at the University of Wisconsin (Madison) and stayed on there as curator of the herbarium. She met Panayoti in 1986, while she was chair of the Illinois-Wisconsin Chapter of the North American Rock Garden Society, and they were married the same year.

Both Panayoti and Gwen have been prominent in introducing native flora through a business, Rocky Mountain Rare Plants, they operated from 1987 till 1996. It was a mail-order native seed nursery, an unusual specialty as there were few others focusing on intermountain, western flora. They found an eager market and were the first to introduce to gardens certain species of western native plants. They sold the business so they could spend more time developing their own gardens and it continues to operate under new owners.

Joyce Fingerut (Stonington, Connecticut), past president of the North American Rock Garden Society, has known Panayoti for a number of years through the society. She says of him:

> Panayoti is a person both receptive and giving. He is open to a wide range
> of new experiences and ideas with people and plants. These are always fol-
> lowed by a great generosity in sharing those experiences and the knowledge
> gained, embracing with enthusiasm and admiration those plants and people
> he has encountered. As a much-sought-after lecturer, he doesn't teach or
> preach, so much as shares, assuming others as equals in enthusiasm, elevat-
> ing his listeners to colleagues. He acts on an audience as both inspiration
> and spur, expanding horticultural horizons, exploding myths, and generat-
> ing plain old plant lust. He and Gwen are among the all-stars when it comes
> to donating seed to society seed exchanges, whether from their own garden,
> wild collected in the West, or from overseas travels.

Some of the introductions through Plant Select® and Rocky Mountain Rare Plants are described below.

When Panayoti and Gwen operated Rocky Mountain Rare Plants, one of their introductions in 1989 was *Aquilegia scopulorum* (Ranunculaceae), the seeds of which were collected in Utah on the Aquarius Plateau, near Bryce Canyon. It also grows in Nevada on limestone scree. *Aquilegia scopulorum* has showy, long-spurred flowers that are near sky blue. The glaucous leaves are tufted or congested and short. It grows to a maximum height of 8 inches (20 cm) in flower and about 6 inches (15 cm) wide. Though introduced initially in the 1950s by Carleton Worth, by the 1960s the species had disappeared in cultivation or had become hybridized with other columbines. Graham Nicholls (2002) finds that he can grow this species in Somerset (United Kingdom) in a trough or scree bed, but it does not like winter moisture, as its native habitat is typically winter-dry. Panayoti says that the characters that distinguish the species are the silvery, overlapping leaves and the upfacing, true blue flowers with long spurs, and it is "maahvelous." The Kelaidis form has persisted in cultivation thus far.

Prunus besseyi (Rosaceae) is the Colorado native sand cherry, which typically grows 4–6 feet (1.2–1.8 m) tall. Cuttings from a dwarf form were collected by Panayoti during a trip in the early 1980s with Jim Borland, who at the time was a plant propagator at the DBG. Upon finding this plant, they debated whether the dwarfness resulted from genetics or from localized environmental factors. The form was given the selection name 'Pawnee Buttes' when they realized it was a unique form with stable characteristics. It has become useful as a ground cover because it attains a height of no more than 18 inches (45 cm) and a width of about 6 feet (1.8 m). It has white flowers in the spring and a crop of black edible cherries in the summer. As autumn approaches, the lustrous, deciduous green leaves change to a stunning bright red and purple. It is an unfussy plant that accepts full sun to partial shade, sandy or clay soils, and even dry conditions. The dwarf sand cherry is hardy in USDA Zones 3 to 8, up to an elevation of about 9000 feet (2740 m). As a result of the Plant Select® 2000 introduction, 'Pawnee Buttes' has been widely propagated and sold throughout the United States and Canada.

Aquilegia scopulorum PHOTO BY PANAYOTI KELAIDIS

Another introduction from Rocky Mountain Rare Plants is *Salvia dorrii*. Commonly called the Great Basin purple sage or desert sage, it is fairly widespread and native to many of the western U.S. deserts. It is a subshrub with silver-grayish, evergreen foliage that is intensely aromatic. It produces showy, deep blue to purple flowers over a long season from spring to early summer. *Salvia dorrii* (Lamiaceae) makes a compact shrub growing from 1 to 3 feet (0.3–0.9 m) tall and wide. Unfortunately it is not yet widely cultivated, "but has become a standard in sophisticated western gardens," Panayoti says.

Betsy Clebsch, a salvia grower in La Honda, California, and author of a book on salvias, has found it a bit of a challenge for her area in northern California:

> The very pretty and perky *Salvia dorrii* is a challenge to get established in a garden setting . . . its evergreen silver-gray foliage enhances the small and sparkling lavender-blue flowers. Because of its wide distribution in California and the west, I feel sure that a particular clone will in time come my way and find a suitable home in my rocky garden.

"Redbirds in a tree" is the poetic name given *Scrophularia macrantha* (Scrophulariaceae) by High Country Gardens nursery of Santa Fe, New Mexico, which introduced this plant in the early 1990s and credits Panayoti, who collected a

Salvia dorrii PHOTO BY PANAYOTI KELAIDIS   *Scrophularia macrantha* PHOTO BY PANAYOTI KELAIDIS

few capsules of its seed at about 7200 feet (2190 m) on Cookes Peak, a pine-covered summit overlooking the great Chihuahuan desert near Deming (Luna County), New Mexico. It is considered the showiest plant in the genus. A penstemon relative, also called Mimbres figwort, it is described as having "long wands of white-lipped cherry-red flowers" and dark green, angular foliage. Tolerating drought, it blooms throughout the spring into autumn, attracting hummingbirds as pollinators. It grows as an erect plant 2–3 feet (0.6–0.9 m) tall and may spread to 1.5 feet (0.5 m).

Approximately fifty species of *Zaluzianskya* (Scrophulariaceae) occur in southern Africa mainly in the Western Cape province and the Drakensberg. *Zaluzianskya ovata* is distributed by Silverhill Seeds as well as by Panayoti, who collected it on a 1994 trip. It has white flowers that are marked reddish on the reverse. The plant grows to about 6 inches (15 cm) high and spreads to about 12 inches (30 cm). In the Drakensberg, it grows on shady ledges on south-facing cliffs.

Panayoti recalls that when he began his career in horticulture in the 1980s, South Africa had been ignored by gardeners, horticulturists, and botanical gardens, largely for political reasons (McCormick and Leccese 1995). Among the plants overlooked in cultivation were the diascias or twinspurs. In 1980 they were hardly known in North American gardens, nor even in Europe. He credits U.S. botanist Kim Steiner (who studied the genus in South Africa at Kirstenbosch), Hector Harrison (British hybidizer), and Olive Hilliard and Bill Burtt (South African and Scottish botanists who introduced many species and hybrids and revised the taxonomy of the group) for raising the interest level in this plant. The result was a flood of plants into garden centers in Europe and North America from the late 1980s through the present day. In all there are about seventy species of *Diascia* (Scrophulariaceae) native to southern Africa. Today they have become popular bedding and hanging-basket plants around the world, generally used as annuals or short-lived perennials, Panayoti says. In general, diascias are sensitive to dryness and require some irrigation.

From the Drakensberg of South Africa's Eastern Cape comes *Diascia integerrima* 'Coral Canyon', hardy in USDA Zones 5 to 9. Panayoti says, "It is the first diascia that has proved durable in a range of garden soils and settings because it thrives in many garden soils that are not heavily amended." The introduction by Plant Select® in 2000 offers a plant that is heat tolerant and can be grown in full sun to part shade. 'Coral Canyon' is a compact plant growing to about 15 inches (37.5 cm) and produces rose to salmon pink flowers from May to August, and longer if deadheaded. Panayoti says emphatically, "It has the constitution of a garden plant, rather than the delicate habit of most other plants in the genus, and it is by far the toughest performer in the genus."

Panayoti remembers that ice plants (*Delosperma*) were generally not a feature of colder gardens until the "big two" were introduced: *D. cooperi* and *D.* cf. *nubigenum* 'Lesotho', the latter long known as "Mesembryanthemum from Basutoland." These resulted in excitement and interest and demand for more hardy

Zaluzianskya ovata PHOTO BY PANAYOTI KELAIDIS

Diascia integerrima 'Coral Canyon' PHOTO BY PANAYOTI KELAIDIS

ice plants, the result of which has been the scores of hybrids, selections, and species crowding today's market.

His first selection was *Delosperma floribundum* Starburst™ (Aizoaceae), which Panayoti collected in 1994 in South Africa's Free State near Springfontein. Unlike other ice plants, Starburst™ is a clumping plant, shrubby in habit, that grows to 4 inches (10 cm) tall and 10 inches (25 cm) wide, requiring full sun in moderate to dry soil. It is a long bloomer, from June to autumn, with brilliant "metallic" pink flowers containing white centers and cream-colored "eyes," making it easy to distinguish from the other delospermas. Starburst™ was a Plant Select® introduction in 1998.

The old 'Lesotho' selection has been widely distributed and cultivated, but it appears to be a sterile triploid, rather than the true species, *Delosperma nubigenum*. On Panayoti's four trips to South Africa he has recollected *D. nubigenum* in the wild in numerous locations from Sani Pass (in the Drakensberg on the border of Lesotho and South Africa) to Mont-aux-Sources (the highest mountain in South Africa in the Drakensberg at elevation 10,822 feet [3290 m]). These collections have produced a fertile, smaller plant that is different from the 'Lesotho' form in cultivation. Panayoti says, "This wild form I introduced to cultivation is quite charming and a much better rock garden plant due to its smaller size." The wild form has yellow flowers—*not* orange-red as has been published in nursery catalogs, Panayoti told me—just like 'Lesotho'.

Among the ice plants I grow in my garden is *Delosperma* 'Kelaidis' Mesa Verde™. It is a sport of a dwarf form of *D. cooperi* found growing at the DBG. It

Delosperma floribundum PHOTO BY PANAYOTI KELAIDIS

is iridescent salmon-pink, but takes on a hint of straw color in the summer sun in my garden. It grows to 2 inches (5 cm) tall and about 10 inches (25 cm) wide and produces many flowers. At a spring picnic in my garden, it was the one dwarf plant that rock gardeners flocked to for close inspection. It appropriately honors Panayoti and his contributions to horticulture and was introduced by Plant Select® in 2002.

Dierama robustum (Iridaceae) is from central and southern Africa. It goes by the winsome appellations of angel's fishing rod and fairy wand. *Dierama* species have grasslike leaves and pendent, bell-shaped flowers that are attached to slender stalks, which are arching and graceful. The flower stalks may soar from 3 to 6 feet (0.9–1.8 m). Many members of this genus are not hardy below USDA Zone 7; however this one is, even in Colorado. Panayoti brought back seeds of *D. robustum* in 1996 and 1998, and the plant has now become established in gardens in North America as cold as USDA Zone 5.

The purple mountain sun daisy, *Osteospermum barberae* var. *compactum* 'Purple Mountain' (Asteraceae), is another Plant Select® introduction whose seed Panayoti collected from near the summits of South Africa's Drakensberg. The

Dierama robustum PHOTO BY PANAYOTI KELAIDIS

bright purple ray flowers rise on stems to 10 inches (25 cm) and the plant will spread about 12 inches (30 cm). It flowers from April to midsummer in the Northern Hemisphere and longer if deadheaded. 'Purple Mountain' is a full sun plant and very hardy from USDA Zones 4 to 9.

Panayoti says that 'Purple Mountain' is the darkest purple form of this plant. The species was first introduced by Helen Milford, a gardener from Gloucestershire (United Kingdom), in the 1930s from a northern Natal (Drakensberg) collection. Panayoti first saw the plant in the United Kingdom in 1991 and brought plants back to the DBG. Later, in 1994, in the Drakensberg, he saw a form with dark purple-magenta flowers, and he collected seeds. He thinks the garden form is a paler shade than the color he has observed in the wild, which is extremely variable in depth of color, perhaps due to the intensity of light in Drakensberg versus that of Colorado.

Osteospermum 'Lavender Mist' is a 1998 Plant Select® introduction. It is a clump-forming sun daisy, growing to a height of 12 inches (30 cm) and a width of 15 inches (37.5 cm). The flower heads open white and turn a soft lavender-purple as they age. 'Lavender Mist' is a full sun to light shade plant, also from South Africa.

Osteospermum barberae var. *compactum* 'Purple Mountain' PHOTO BY PANAYOTI KELAIDIS

Osteospermum 'Lavender Mist' PHOTO BY PANAYOTI KELAIDIS

Gazania linearis PHOTO BY PANAYOTI KELAIDIS

Panayoti became entranced with the hardy gazanias when he obtained seed in the early 1980s from the Woodbank Nursery in Longley, Tasmania. He lost the plants after a few seasons but made it a point to collect seeds in the wild on subsequent trips to South Africa, where they are native. *Gazania linearis* 'Colorado Gold' (Asteraceae), a hardy, perennial daisy, has shiny, golden ray flowers that respond to sunny weather and close under cloudy skies and at night. It is a cold hardy (USDA Zones 4–8) botanical relative of the familiar (but tender) bedding gazania, *G. rigens*. Its leaves are glossy green, somewhat straplike, and the plant reaches a height of 3 inches (7.5 cm).

John Grimshaw (Colesbourne, Gloucestershire) knows the plant and observes: "A pretty composite well suited to dry, lean gardens; in rich soil it becomes too leafy and the brilliant flowers do not show to their full advantage. It is very quick to flower from seed." The plant was initially offered by High Country Gardens and from Plant Select® in 1998. 'Colorado Gold' is a reliably perennial gazania and is now widely sold throughout North America and Europe.

Panayoti's charisma and formidable intelligence have made him a master at finding, promoting, and writing about new plants. His selections from the intermountain U.S. West and the Drakensberg of South Africa are especially notable.

Panayoti Kelaidis PHOTO BY BOBBY J. WARD

Panayoti Kelaidis
Denver Botanic Gardens
909 York Street
Denver, CO 80206
United States
www.botanicgardens.org

Plant Select® Program
Colorado State University
Department of Horticulture and
Landscape Architecture
Fort Collins, CO 80523
United States
www.plantselect.org

From China With Love
Eco-Gardens—Don Jacobs

I vividly remember a lecture Don Jacobs gave in North Carolina on the ecology of native woodland plants. As the formal part of the program ended and the lights were raised, he crossed his arms, much like a university professor, and took questions for half an hour, often turning his answer into another question. Some of the questions related to "what is a species," which led to a discourse on scientific observation, methodology, and conventional wisdom, using as an illustration an *Asarum* he pulled from the plant sales table. It was a Socratic dialog of teacher and students, a depth of discussion to which our gardening group had rarely plumbed in meetings, and one I have not forgotten.

Don Jacobs has been a pioneer in understanding the ecology of native flora of the U.S. Southeast. His training in ecology, his years of teaching at the University of Georgia (Athens), and his experimental garden (Eco-Gardens) near Atlanta, Georgia, have given him the opportunity to select, grow, and understand the adaptability of plants suitable for the Southeast. His intense interest in the flora of this area inspired an interest in the corresponding climatic region of eastern Asia. He made trips to that area much earlier than most of the featured collectors in this book, and his collections have had more time to prove their horticultural worth. The floristic affinity between eastern Asia and eastern North America has been widely studied. Botanists estimate that 120 genera in sixty families have disjunct populations in temperate North America and eastern Asia (Flora of China Project 2003).

A relationship between flora of the broad-leaf deciduous forests in eastern Asia and that of eastern North America was established in a series of papers beginning in the 1840s by naturalist Asa Gray of Harvard University. He suggested that there was once a great Northern Hemisphere forest, which extended from eastern North America, into the Arctic, over the Bering Strait, and into eastern Asia. Plants of eastern Asia and eastern North America were commingled during the mid-Tertiary Period, when this flora reached its maximum extension. Subsequent geological and climatic changes, including glacial ice sheets, separated the two areas. A large number of primarily woody flowering plants began to evolve separately in the two geographical regions having similar topography, climate, and rainfall, and covering about the same latitudes (Zhang and Lasseigne

1998). Gray's notion attracted the attention of Charles Darwin who corresponded with Gray on the subject of the disjunct plant populations and the foundations of plant geography were laid (Dupree 1968; Sargent 1969).

Beginning in the early 1980s, Don made three collecting trips to Asia, visiting China, Japan, eastern Mongolia, Thailand, Singapore, and Taiwan (Copeland and Armitage 2001). He collected numerous plants on his trip to Sichuan's Mount Emei in 1983 including *Impatiens omeiana* and *Lysimachia congestiflora*, both of which have become widely known and grown. His rate of plant introductions from abroad, as well as from his extensive North American travels, has been high, with most plants bearing the appellation of "Eco-" in the cultivar name.

Don's interests and occupations have always been biological. He first operated a business selling aquarium fish and aquatic plants, then developed an interest in herpetology and wrote numerous professional articles on the subject. In the late 1970s, he started Eco-Gardens, whose mission is to research, display, and sell native and exotic plants suitable for the piedmont of the U.S. Southeast. One of his specialties from that area is *Trillium*. With his son, Rob, Don co-authored *American Treasures: Trilliums in Woodland and Garden*. Don's work at Eco-Gardens continues to garner recognition.

Tony Avent, owner of Plant Delights Nursery (Raleigh), says of Don:

> He has long been a legend among plant collectors for his work in the exploration, selection, and propagation of new plants. His work, focused on Southeast U.S natives and their Asian counterparts, bridged the gap between the plant explorers of the past while serving as a catalyst for the next generation who have since picked up the torch. I can think of few others with a botanical background and horticultural eye that have made the significant contributions of garden-worthy selections as Don and his work at Eco-Gardens.

Don is proud of his many introductions. He says that there are other worthy plants available "that have been ignored as garden plants, because no one has taken the time to find them and determine their utility in the garden. We too often want the exotic plant, when many natives serve a useful purpose." Some of the plants, both native and exotic, that Don has promoted are presented below.

In 1983 Don collected *Impatiens omeiana* (Basalminaceae) on Mount Emei's upper slopes at about 8000 feet (2430 m), growing in a forest of Sichuan fir (*Abies sutchuenensis*). In the cloud-shrouded forest, he found it among yellow-flowered *Rhododendron chengshienianum*, *Tiarella polyphylla*, *Lysimachia congestiflora*, and ferns (Jacobs 1993). The leaves on *I. omeiana* are a marbled dark green with a white stripe down the center. For me this hardy impatiens grows carpetlike, about 12 inches (30 cm) tall, though I have seen it a few inches taller. It is grown for its foliage, not flowers, which are orange-yellow, but not showy, appearing in leaf axils in the early fall. Unlike many garden impatiens (or "busy lizzies" as they are known in the United Kingdom), *I. omeiana* is a hardy, herbaceous perennial. I grow it in light shade along a border in front of *Carex phyllocephala* 'Sparkler'. As dusk fades, these are the last two plants I am able to see in the garden from the deck of my house.

In July 1983, when Don visited the Plant Science Building at Sichuan University in Chengdu, he met Dr. Won-Pei Fang and his son Ming-Yuan, both of whom allowed Don to look at herbarium specimens as they discussed the flora of Mount Emei. Inquiring about a begonia Don had seen and collected there earlier, Dr. Fang responded that there are many begonias on Mount Emei (Jacobs 1993). Don eventually identified the specimen as *Begonia limprichtii* (Begoniaceae), a "semi-hardy, rhizomatous species with near-round, bright, glossy green leaves with erect red hairs, and groups of white flowers." Don, who has found the plant is winter dormant and hardy to about 20°F (−7°C), was the first to introduce it into the West.

Although Mount Emei is known for its many shrines, it has botanical treasures as well. One such treasure is *Lysimachia congestiflora* 'Eco Dark Satin' (Primulaceae), which has become one of Don's most popular introductions. It is a prostrate, non-invasive loosestrife with bell-shaped, golden flowers that bloom over several months, from about May till September. The throat or eye of the flowers is reddish brown to orange-red. 'Eco Dark Satin' is a rambling plant that grows to about 4 inches (10 cm) tall. Its leaves are dark green with a satin sheen. The original plant that Don brought back to Georgia died, but seven seeds germinated.

Impatiens omeiana PHOTO BY DON JACOBS

Out of those seven seedlings, Don spotted one with excellent foliage having a "ruddy glow" and named the selection 'Eco Dark Satin' for its satin sheen (Jacobs 1985). Don's examination revealed that the bristle hairs that covered the leaves in the other six plants were absent on 'Eco Dark Satin'. Even though this mat-forming, stoloniferous plant is suitable for a lightly shaded garden, I have seen it growing and flowering prolifically in a garden of marl-sandy soil at Beaufort, near the North Carolina coast, easily accepting the heat of the full summer sun without flagging. It is cold hardy to USDA Zone 7, but is a popular bedding plant and is grown as an annual in colder areas.

Several additional plants introduced by Don from China are now in distribution. From a shaded ledge on a sandstone cliff near Mount Emei, he collected a rela-

Begonia limprichtii PHOTO BY DON JACOBS

Lysimachia congestiflora 'Eco Dark Satin' PHOTO BY DON JACOBS

tive of the African violet, *Petrocosmea flaccida* (Gesneriaceae). Called the Mount Emei cliff violet, it was previously unknown outside China, but is now admired in Europe and the United States because of its deep blue-purple flowers. The leaves are flat green with small hairs. It can be propagated by seeds or leaf cuttings.

Don also collected on Mount Emei two ferns, *Woodwardia japonica* (Blechnaceae), the chain fern, and *Lepisorus bicolor* (Polypodiaceae), the Sichuan ribbon fern. The latter, known to occur in four provinces in China, grows typically between elevations of 3,300 and 11,000 feet (1000–3300 m). It is a rhizomatous fern with long, simple, leathery leaves, growing to about 2 feet (0.6 m).

Another collection on Mount Emei was *Ardisia bicolor* (Myrsinaceae), a low groundcover, up to 12 inches (30 cm), which spreads by rhizomes. It is a plant for the shady part of the garden.

From the Karst mountains near Guilin (China), Don found *Cheilanthes argentea* (Adiantaceae), the lip fern, a small deciduous plant that grows in dry, rocky areas, attaining a height of no more than 6 inches (15 cm).

Ruffled evergreen leaves are the outstanding feature of *Tupistra* sp. 'Eco China Ruffles' (Convallariaceae). Don collected it on Mount Emei, thinking it was a remarkable form of *Rohdea* and he even distributed it as *Rohdea* 'Eco China Ruffles' until scientists at the Smithsonian Institution suggested it was really an aberrant form of *T. chinensis*. Don says that it produces no seed when pollinated

Petrocosmea flaccida PHOTO BY DON JACOBS

Cheilanthes argentea PHOTO BY DON JACOBS

Tupistra sp. 'Eco China Ruffles' PHOTO BY DON JACOBS

with typical *T. chinensis* and is self sterile. For this reason he calls it *Tupistra* sp. 'Eco China Ruffles'. The plant, looking like a hybrid between a hosta and a rohdea, has long, strap-shaped leaves that are strongly puckered like seersucker fabric. Flowers are crowded in a dense cone, like those of *Rohdea*, about 5 inches (12.5 cm) tall. I grow 'Eco China Ruffles', now a small clump, near a rampant population of *Asarum splendens*, the pairing giving a peculiar, other-worldly look to that corner of the shady garden.

At least seventy-five species of *Pellaea*, mostly small clump-forming ferns, occur in the cool tropics and temperate regions. *Pellaea viridis*, the green cliff brake, is a native of southern and eastern Africa, possibly Madagascar, and the West Indies.

Don obtained several forms of this fern from Africa and Puerto Rico in 1974 and 1975 and introduced them into a south-facing rock garden at his home in Decatur, Georgia (Jacobs 1995). The fern, shaded at noon by a large southern red oak (*Quercus falcata*), has persisted and naturalized around rocks and in crevices for nearly thirty years. Despite its assumed tenderness and use only as a house or conservatory plant that can stand low light and low humidity, the Puerto Rican clone has survived low temperatures of −8°F (−22°C) without mulch or other protection. Its rich green, deciduous fronds (leaves) may grow up to 2 feet (0.6 m) long. The pinnae (leaflets) are dark lustrous green, nearly leather-like, and the stipes (petioles), wiry and dark.

Don believes that natural selection of the clones has taken place (with the less hardy ones dying), resulting in a form he calls 'Eco-Gardens'. The form is hardy to USDA Zones 6 and 7. As a garden plant it has been ignored far too long, he thinks. Fern taxonomists disagree on the family assignment of *Pellaea*; currently Adiantaceae or Sinopteridaceae are being used.

One of the stalwarts of the shade garden is *Heuchera americana* (Saxifragaceae) or coral bells (sometimes called alum root), a species of eastern North America. Despite its reputation for loving shade, it will tolerate some sun if there is good soil moisture and drainage. I know of a thriving population growing in full sun on a roadside ditch in eastern North Carolina's Nash County. From time to time plants are badly mangled by Department of Transportation mowing equipment, but I have managed to salvage a couple of divisions. Now they are living in deep shade in my garden, though the bright leaf markings they had in full sun have faded.

Most people grow coral bells for the attractive leaf pattern, not the small flowers that are tan to buff colored. Don found a selection of coral bells near Weaverville in Buncombe County, North Carolina, in the state's western mountains, which he dubbed *Heuchera* 'Eco Magnififolia' for its silvery white leaves and medium green veins. I admire this selection because it is showy, yet in a very natural, understated way. It competes equally well with the more flamboyant, currently popular selections whose foliage may be a burnished orange, chocolate, or plum.

Pellaea viridis, at left PHOTO BY DON JACOBS

Heuchera 'Eco Magnififolia' PHOTO BY DON JACOBS

Asarums, the wild ginger or heartleaf, belong to a family of plants with the tongue-tripping name of Aristolochiaceae, the birthworts. *Asarum* is a genus of woodland plants of both the Old and New Worlds, with about a dozen species in eastern North America. Some American botanists continue to classify asarums, particularly those in the U.S. Southeast, as members of *Hexastylis*. When I moved to Wake County, North Carolina, a generous population of *A. arifolium* was growing on the property. I have since divided it and moved it around, but despite my attempts to build paths throughout the garden, individuals continue to make a comeback in unexpected places, tenaciously pushing up through wood shavings and gravel in paths. I now zigzag around them as these are not plants that I wish to eliminate.

Asarum naniflorum is a Southeast native that grows in a rather limited range in a dozen or so counties in the Carolinas and Virginia, primarily on acid, sandy loam on bluffs and ravines in deciduous forests. It is often associated with *Kalmia latifolia* (Weakley 1997). Because of its infrequent occurrence, the dwarf-flowered heartleaf is a U.S. threatened species, meaning that it is a taxon likely to become endangered and therefore extinct in a portion of its natural range.

Asarum naniflorum 'Eco Decor' is a selection that Don found near Spartanburg, South Carolina. It has small, round to heart-shaped evergreen leaves about 2 inches (5 cm) wide, which are dark green and glossy with silver markings around the veins. The selection has been tissue cultured and is sold now by the thousands in garden centers. I placed 'Eco Decor' at the edge of a woodland path where I can easily admire it.

Iris cristata (Iridaceae), the dwarf crested iris, is a native of moist deciduous woodlands from the mid-Atlantic states to the upper Southeast, and westward across the Appalachians and the Ozarks to eastern Oklahoma. It thrives in light shade, producing its flowers in the spring before trees leaf out. The specific epithet *cristata* means "crested," a reference to the crest or parallel ridges on the falls (sepals) of the flower. The falls are bluish to violet with a distinct crest of golden yellow to white bands. The upright or erect standards (petals) are narrower than the falls and usually a uniform color.

Don has made several selections of *Iris cristata* and has widely promoted it as a choice plant for the spring woodland garden. 'Eco Little Bluebird' is a compact, colony-forming plant with overall smaller flowers. 'Eco Royal Ruffles' has unusually prominent white ruffles or crests while 'Eco Purple Pomp' has deep purple flowers with yellow-orange crests. Both of the latter two have large flowers to just over 2 inches (5 cm) across with leaves of about 1 inch (2.5 cm) wide. Don named all three of these in 1993. 'Judy's Roulette' consists of a wheel of six equal sized falls and standards (signals), which are violet colored with gold and white crests. Gardener Judy Springer discovered it in her Virginia garden and passed it along to Don.

I grow *Iris cristata* in a raised bed of rock garden plants. It spread rapidly in a single growing season, forming a dense colony that expanded to about 1 foot (0.3 m) across and about 6 inches (15 cm) high in a few months.

Now often overshadowed in the arena of plant exploration, Don Jacobs has made some important contributions. His collections in China in the early 1980s far pre-dated the rush in the 1990s, and many of his selections of U.S. Southeast woodland natives have proved extremely garden-worthy.

Don Jacobs
Eco-Gardens
P.O. Box 1227
Decatur, GA 30031
United States

Don Jacobs PHOTO BY BOBBY J. WARD

Beware the *Jaborosa*, My Son!

Flores & Watson Seeds—John Watson & Anita Flores de Watson

On clear days from their garden in Los Andes, Chile, John Watson and Anita Flores de Watson can gaze at the snowy summit of Mount Aconcagua breaking on the distant horizon. It is the tallest mountain in the Western Hemisphere at an elevation of nearly 23,000 feet (7000 m), sitting just inside Argentina, near its border with Chile. Aconcagua is at once their backyard sentinel and a constant reminder of the Andean *altiplano* (high plain) flora of Anita's native land and John's adopted home.

In Los Andes, huddled in the foothills about 2000 feet (610 m) above sea level and an hour's drive north of Santiago, John and Anita operate Flores and Watson Seeds, which they relocated from Kent (England) in 1996. Anita is John's spouse, business partner, and collecting companion. From 1991, when Anita joined the business, until 1996, they divided their time between England and Chile, the latter becoming a base of operation for seed-collecting trips.

The couple now concentrate entirely in South America, primarily Chile and Argentina. In Chile, the Atacama Desert collecting areas are to the north of Santiago (latitude 32 degrees south), while true alpine plant collections are made in the uplift areas to the south, around the volcanoes in central Chile and Argentina. Patagonia is east of the Andes, to the south primarily in Argentina, beginning at about latitude 40 degrees south.

John was born in Catford (London), England, and became interested in plants at age five when he recalls vividly "a bewitching orange Dutch crocus transplanted from a derelict bomb site during the war." His parents had a limestone rock garden, allowing him to develop an interest that would eventually become a career. He remembers going with his father to Robinsons' Hardy Plants nursery to restock the family rock garden. There the addiction to alpine plants became firmly cemented. He worked part-time at the nursery, then a short while at Whiteleggs Nursery and G. Renthe. John studied horticulture for a year in the Royal Horticultural Society program at Wisley. After that he taught himself taxonomy.

Note: The chapter title is John Watson's jocular paraphrase of "Beware the Jabberwock" from Lewis Carroll's *Jabberwocky*.

As a teenager John became interested in plants, primarily alpines and bulbs, but he did not begin serious plant exploration till after 1962 when he founded Watson Seeds. From 1966 onward, seeds were offered from trips that John made to Turkey and Lebanon either alone or with other British plant hunters, often Martyn Cheese, and at other times Sydney Albury, Ken Beckett, and Tony Mitchell. On the final Turkish trip in 1977, his travel companion was James MacPhail (Vancouver, British Columbia). In the 1970s, the relatively unknown flora of the Andes Mountains had begun drawing Watson's attention.

Anita was born in Chuquicarnata, Chile, near the Bolivian border. She remembers a strong El Niño weather event in 1971 and 1972 that resulted in a huge wealth of flowers. Anita read an article about a native plant conference, which she attended. There she learned more about the desert flora in bloom at the time. She studied biology at the University of Chile (La Serena), taught school for several years, and did research at the University of Chile (Santiago). She met John in 1988 and later they formed Flores and Watson Seeds.

Interest in Andean flora, once thought impossible to grow in the Northern Hemisphere, is increasing, as evidenced by the Alpine Garden Society's (AGS) devoting the entire September 1994 issue of its *Quarterly Bulletin* to South American alpine species. The articles, half of which John wrote, address problems associated with germination, propagation, hardiness, and nagging questions on taxonomy. In one article, Peter Erskine describes the AGS tours that John led to the temperate Andes in 1991 and to Patagonia in 1992. Erskine recalls sharing a room with John, who often stayed up well after midnight to identify yet another species of *Nassauvia* (Asteraceae) using *Flora Patagonica*. This dedication to mastering Andean plant taxonomy, according to Erskine, is one of Watson's "great strengths and a major contribution to our understanding of the Andean flora."

The bulk of the AGS publication is a survey of significant, cultivation-worthy genera of the Andes and surrounding region, in which John whets the appetite with striking photographs of Patagonian oxalis, flamboyant ourisias and calceolarias, cushion-forming asters, and tongue-tripping bulbous genera such as *Tecophilaea*, *Tropaeolum*, and *Conanthera*. He does not overlook the rosulate violets or the wonderful flora of Chile's Torres del Paine National Park.

For John, mastering the identification of Andean flora has been a challenge since the first trip he made to the region with Martyn Cheese and Ken Beckett in September 1971. On that trip, which ended in April of the following year, they had their taxonomic work cut out for them as there were few botanical references or resources at their disposal. Over four years beginning in 1974, John published a diary of this six-month expedition in the *Quarterly Bulletin of the Alpine Garden Society* in an extensive, incomparable, fifteen-part series simply titled "Andes, 1971 and 1972." This series notably advanced horticultural knowledge of Andean flora, and many alpine gardeners consider it a milestone. Building on this substantial scholarship, John would later contribute chapters to the *Alpine Garden Society's Encyclopaedia of Alpines*. John's long-established connections continue today as Martyn Cheese in the United Kingdom is John and Anita's worldwide seed distributor.

The winds in Patagonia can be relentless, often with snow in the air in mid-summer at the southernmost latitudes. John and Anita, too, have been relentless in pursuit of botanical knowledge of Andean flora. At the time of this writing, they are preparing several scientific papers detailing new species and the range extension of others. John has been honored by Peter Davis, editor of *The Flora of Turkey*, with *Thlaspi watsonii* (Brassicaceae) from Kurdistan. John and Anita have made plant specimen deposits to herbaria in Chile and the United Kingdom. The total accessions for all trips currently exceeds nine thousand. A few of the plants they have made available through their seed lists follows.

Asperula sintenisii (Rubiaceae) is one of about a hundred species in the genus *Asperula*. John found the species in the Kaz Dağ (mountains) in northwest Turkey (at an elevation of 5300 feet [1600 m]) in 1966 with Martyn Cheese and Sydney Albury, and he collected it again in 1977 with Jim MacPhail. It was originally identified as *A. nitida* subsp. *puberula* by copying the same mistaken identity from a specimen at an institutional herbarium. *Asperula sintenisii*, one of the woodruffs, boasts pink flowers, which are paired or solitary, about 0.5 inch (1 cm) long. It has small, glaucous leaves and the stems may not reach more than 0.75 inch (2 cm) long.

John considers this a choice plant and it has been given an Award of Garden Merit by the Royal Horticultural Society. The genus name is from the Latin *asper* meaning "rough," alluding to rough hairy stems, characteristic of most species.

Mimulus naiandinus (Scrophulariaceae), probably better known to gardeners as *M.* 'Andean Nymph', is a species of monkey flower found by Martyn Cheese and John in the Chilean Andes, where they collected it on damp rock faces by a small waterfall. The cream-colored flower has light purple staining on the floral tubes and upper two lobes; the lower lobes are a pale yellow with yellow hairs and are dappled in purplish dots—the overall effect is a pinkish flower. John says that, although potentially very perennial, it is usually a short-lived summer bloomer, easy to grow from seed. It "went commercial" in 1974 and has become widely available in seed catalogs and even supermarkets, and has lent its genes to a variety of *Mimulus* hybrids. John formally described the species in *Curtis's Botanical Magazine* (Watson and von Bohlen 2000).

Seed-collecting trips to Turkey in 1967 and 1977 provided an important intro-duction of *Origanum rotundifolium* (Lamiaceae), an oregano or marjoram. It grows to about 12 inches (30 cm) tall with round gray leaves and tiny pale pink flowers, which are supported by pale green bracts that may be up to nearly 1 inch (2.5 cm) wide. Two cultivars, 'Barbara Tingey' and 'Kent Beauty', have been selected from chance hybrids between *O. rotundifolium* and the hybrid of *O. tournefortii* and *O. scabrum* respectively. 'Kent Beauty' is an excellent seedling that arose at Wash-field Nursery in Kent. The two hybrids are easy to root from shoot cuttings if taken in the spring when the stems begin to elongate.

Asperula sintenisii PHOTO BY JOHN WATSON

Mimulus naiandinus PHOTO BY JOHN WATSON

Veronica liwanensis (Scrophulariaceae) is a creeping perennial also collected in Turkey. When John found the plant, it had passed its peak flowering, but he saw potential in it and twice made a seed collection "on spec." Returning to England, John included it in the selection of seed he passed along to Jack Elliott, former AGS president, who grew it in his Kent garden and adored it. Seed eventually reached Panayoti Kelaidis of the Denver Botanic Gardens, in Colorado, who found that it performed well there. Panayoti saw commercial value in the plant and introduced it more widely through the Plant Select® program. *Veronica liwanensis* is a late spring bloomer, carrying blue flowers 0.75 inch (1.9 cm) across, clustered in groups. In Turkey and the Caucasus, it grows in high grasslands, rocky fissures and ledges, and spruce forest edges.

On his 1966 trip to Turkey, John collected two dwarf forms of *Dianthus* (Caryophyllaceae) from the summit area of Kaz Dağ or Mount Ida. These dianthus were "target plants" for that expedition. *Dianthus erinaceus* var. *alpinus* is "painfully prickly," according to John's description. It has wide, bluntish, squared-off, pink petals. It flowers more reluctantly than *D. anatolicus* var. *alpinus*, which flowers freely and has narrow petals that are round at the tips and somewhat *Silene*-like. *Dianthus anatolicus* var. *alpinus* forms a domelike hummock and has non-vicious foliage and small, pale pink flowers. Both forms prefer dry conditions and are sensitive to winter rainfall. They were collected at about 6000 feet (1800 m).

John considers the choicest alpine produced from the 1971–1972 Andes trip

Dianthus anatolicus var. *alpinus* PHOTO BY JOHN WATSON

to be *Ourisia microphylla* (Scrophulariaceae), despite its having been collected before in the 1920s by H. F. Comber (it appears to have died out in cultivation). The small, neat shrublet, with basally branched stems and dense leaves, produces solitary flowers about 0.5 inch (1.25 cm) across, most often pink but rarely white. It grows from the central *cordilleras* (mountain ranges) in Argentina and Chile southward, up to 6000 feet (1800 m), where it is a profuse summer bloomer. Skilled growers find that it does well in alpine houses or cold frames but that it is still prone to dieback, especially from winter drought (it should be kept wet in winter). John recalls that the Royal Botanic Gardens, Kew, once displayed six plants of *O. microphylla*, all of which were stolen, so perhaps the thefts suggest the high desirability of the plant.

Perhaps the most spectacular ourisia, collected on trips made with Anita Flores in 1994 and 1995, was *Ourisia polyantha*, a plant John had searched for often and fruitlessly since 1971. He knew it only from a single herbarium specimen at the Royal Botanic Gardens, Kew, where it was labeled "from southern Chile." Finding this species in the wild had become an obsession with John that was finally achieved, ironically on an AGS expedition, through an encounter with a solitary plant. *Ourisia polyantha* grows to the south of Santiago, Chile, with velvety, orange-scarlet flowers, slightly longer and larger than those of *O. microphylla*, which it resembles quite closely in foliage.

David Hale (Portland, Oregon), an aficionado of Andean alpines, observes:

> Both species are easily propagated if the foliage is allowed to drape over the sides of the containers onto the plunge medium. In this way the stems root into the medium and are easily detached. *Ourisia polyantha* is much easier for me as I rarely lose a plant.

Ourisia microphylla has a 0.3-inch (8-mm) long perianth tube, which is nearly obscured by the light pink corolla lobes as they reflex slightly. In contrast, *O. polyantha* has a 0.75-inch (1.9-cm) long perianth tube which is prominent and not covered by the perianth lobes. *Ourisia* honors General Ouris (d. 1773), governor of the Falkland Islands, where the genus was first found.

Anarthrophyllum desideratum, the Patagonian scarlet gorse, is a cushion shrublet of southern Patagonia that grows in desert or semiarid steppe at elevations from near sea level to 300 feet (90 m). About fifteen species of gorselike *Anarthrophyllum* (Fabaceae) are known, all from South America. The modified leaves have developed into spinelike structures subtended by equally sharp, paired stipules.

Anarthrophyllum desideratum is strikingly handsome in the wild, a 4- to 24-inch (10- to 60-cm) tall shrub, producing its scarlet-orange flowers in mass and often found squatting on the ground in front of snow-capped mountains that drape the distant landscape. Both yellow and orange forms exist. Ruth Tweedie, an English expatriate living on a ranch at Stag River in Argentine Patagonia, introduced this species in the 1950s. It proved difficult to grow and soon disappeared from cultivation; it is easily overwatered and must have bright sun and good air circulation.

Ourisia polyantha PHOTO BY JOHN WATSON

John and Anita say that the plant is "legendary," because tales of its beauty caused many alpine gardeners to seek it, even long after the plant had died out in cultivation. In brief, it was desirable, as its Latin specific epithet suggests, because everyone's experience showed that it was defiant to being tamed for the garden and it was so beautiful. Collecting its seeds is a difficult matter: they are "buried" among the spines, which easily attach to fingers or gloves.

In 1987–1988, John collected the plant on a trip and David Sampson of East Sussex, United Kingdom, successfully germinated seed of and then propagated the scarlet gorse from cuttings, according to John, making it available through his nursery, Oak Dene Nursery (South Yorkshire). Flores and Watson Seeds continues to offer seed of it.

The specific epithet of *Fritillaria alburyana* commemorates Sydney Albury, a co-collector with John and Martyn Cheese on the seven-month-long Turkish expedition in 1966. Albury was present at the discovery of this species, but later died of altitude sickness on a remote mountain in Nepal, an admonition that plant exploration continues to pose life-threatening dangers. A member of the Liliaceae, *F. alburyana* grows in northeastern Turkey in stony, peaty soil at an elevation of 600 to 1000 feet (180–300 m). The determination of this fritillary as a new species was published by Martyn Rix barely a month before a Turkish botanist also published a different specific epithet (however, the first published had priority). It has bell-shaped, pale pink flowers with a faint checkered pattern; the plant stem grows to 4 inches (10 cm) high. John is not happy that the plant has proven difficult to maintain in cultivation. One of the first to prod it into bloom was the skilled plantsman Harold Esslemont of Aberdeen.

Oxalis squamata was an introduction from the first Andean trip in 1971–1972. Although John's initial collections were from a poorly growing population, Roy Elliott (United Kingdom), former AGS *Bulletin* editor and brother of Jack Elliott, succeeded in growing it and cited it as one of the best introductions from that Watson expedition. Because it cannot reliably be overwintered outside in the United Kingdom due to moisture (primarily USDA Zone 8), its stout rhizomes fare better if stored dry indoors. Otherwise, *O. squamata* (Oxalidaceae) is easy to grow and flowers readily, producing an umbel of five to twenty-five blossoms, which are deep rose to warm lilac-pink.

Fritillaria alburyana PHOTO BY JOHN WATSON

Alstroemeria werdermannii subsp. *werdermannii*
PHOTO BY JOHN WATSON

encountered on early collections by John in the 1970s and 1980s. In the 1990s they added *A. werdermannii* and *A. paupercula* (syn. *A. violacea*), both from coastal dunes or oases near the Atacama Desert, north of Santiago.

John and Anita find that the tropaeolums, a delightful group of plants, are among their favorites. Indeed they have provided seed of more than a dozen species in their annually issued seed list, and it is likely that one of the legacies of Flores and Watson will be their introductions and understanding of Andean tropaeolums. Initially few of their collections were grown in gardens (some are tender or half-hardy), but now as their culture has been better understood, most of the species have bloomed and a few have even won prizes at flower shows in the United Kingdom.

Alstroemeria werdermannii subsp. *flavicans* PHOTO BY JOHN WATSON

Tropaeolum hookerianum subsp. *austropurpureum* PHOTO BY JOHN WATSON

Tropaeolum rhomboideum is a spring bloomer, native to the cordilleras near Santiago up to 6600 feet (2000 m). Among introductions of horticultural merit are three subspecies of *T. hookerianum* from coastal Coquimbo Province: subsp. *hookerianum*, and two new to botany, subsp. *pilosum* and subsp. *austropurpureum*. The latter, according to John, is "totally unexpected rich purple tilting slightly toward a warmer reddish, or cooler bluish cast according to flower age."

Tropaeolum is a New World genus (Tropaeolaceae) of usually climbing plants, which range from Tierra del Fuego (Chile and Argentina) northward to Mexico. Its best-known species is *T. majus*, the common garden nasturtium.

Every plant hunting trip has its flat tires, dead batteries, severe weather, and washed-out roads—to mention but a few of the less-than-pleasant memories; however, the highlight of John and Anita's collecting trip in 1998—a year that enjoyed extra rains from El Niño—was at once a gratifying and delightful find: *Jaborosa volkmannii* (Solanaceae), a plant they had chased for years. John's exhilaration spills over in his seed catalog when he says, "What to say of a plant whose

Jaborosa volkmannii PHOTO BY JOHN WATSON

every part shouts class, and which can manufacture from volcano dust a perfume to upstage any female *habituée* of the Ritz?" This species was discovered growing in pumice on the lee side of a volcano at an elevation of about 5200 feet (1600 m). It is rosette-forming and grows no more than 3 inches (8 cm) in height with pure white, sweetly scented flowers that are long tubed, reminiscent of tobacco and jasmine flowers. The leaves are rusty bronze above and pale on the underside with contrasting bright blue veins. It is "a beautiful and distinctive plant, worth any amount of effort . . . to track down and establish in cultivation" (Beckett 1993). The genus name is derived from the Arabic *jaborose*, used for the name of the closely related *Mandragora*, the mandrake.

For nearly forty years, John Watson has been a fixture in the plant hunting scene. His early collections in the eastern Mediterranean and Middle East, and later collections with his wife, Anita, in western South America are well known to most serious plantspeople. Both phases of his career have resulted in important new introductions.

John Watson and Anita Flores de Watson PHOTO BY BOBBY J. WARD

Flores and Watson Seeds
c/o Martyn J. Cheese
Silvercove
Lee Downs
Ilfracombe
North Devon EX34 8LR
England

10

King of Epimediums
Garden Vision—Darrell Probst

I began to grow epimediums shortly after I visited the garden of Harold and Esta Epstein in Larchmont, New York, in the spring of 1991. Harold led a group of us through his vast collection of Japanese woodland plants, including *Hydrangea petiolaris* and *Schizophragma hydrangeoides*, both of which were climbing the trunks of oaks in the front yard. Spilling from borders onto paths were numerous epimediums, which Harold doted on as he lingered over them, responding to questions from his inquisitive guests. It was the largest collection of epimediums I had seen, and Harold clearly delighted in the group's interest as we listened to him under the high shade of his garden, La Rocaille.

Later I discovered Darrell Probst and learned of his interest in epimediums, for which he was developing a small nursery specializing in their identification and cultivation. When I wrote him for a catalog, I learned that his interest in epimediums was not a casual fascination; rather, it was profound and permanent. He, too, had visited Harold's garden in the early 1990s and become enchanted. At the time there were only a few taxa available in nurseries, and these were generally unappreciated by the gardening public. Finding the field wide open, Darrell embarked on a dual plan to acquire as many species and cultivars as possible, and to develop hybrids and to make horticultural selections at his garden, Cobblewood, in Massachusetts. He had several hundred different clones by the mid-1990s.

Darrell then learned from William T. Stearn, an *Epimedium* taxonomist in the United Kingdom, that three of his acquisitions were new species. Darrell immediately suggested that one of them ought to honor Harold Epstein (1903–1997), a past president of the North American Rock Garden Society. Thus, *E. epsteinii*, collected in 1994 in Hunan Province (China) for the Beijing Botanic Garden and sent to Darrell, venerates this passionate plant collector and renowned early grower of *Epimedium* in the United States.

In 1996 Darrell made his first trip to China to observe epimediums in their native habitat and to better understand their growth requirements. He returned with several species and a naturally occurring hybrid, *Epimedium ×omeiense*. Since then he has made or sponsored twenty-four expeditions to fifteen Chinese provinces, Japan, and Korea. The number of species under cultivation at his garden now exceeds eighty, up from the seven that were grown in 1994 when Darrell first dreamed of growing and hybridizing epimediums. At least fifteen hundred forms or clones are known. At least twenty-five species await full botanical description. Fully three-fourths of the currently known species have been described since 1975.

Epimediums are increasing in popularity among North American and British gardeners. The credit for such increased interest in the genus has been largely the efforts of a handful of people: William T. Stearn, who completed the revised monograph on *Epimedium* shortly before his death in 2001 (Stearn 2002); Robin and Sue White, who grew many plants for Stearn's botanical work at their Blackthorn Nursery in Hampshire (United Kingdom); Mikinori Ogisu, who collected epimediums extensively in China; and Darrell Probst, the leading proponent for new *Epimedium* introductions to North American gardens (Mathew 2002). Darrell is currently writing a gardener's guide to *Epimedium* culture, and he operates Garden Vision, a mail-order nursery.

Darrell is a native of Kennett Square, Pennsylvania, and became interested in plants at an early age, even tending neighbors' gardens. He studied horticulture at nearby Longwood Gardens, specializing in professional gardening, an intensive horticulture program. Darrell and his wife, Karen, moved to Hubbardston, Massachusetts, in 1987. He worked for a while at Tower Hill Botanic Garden (Boylston, Massachusetts), a public garden, and did landscaping for specialty gardens. He has an on-going interest in plant breeding and has worked on various genera, including *Tricyrtis* (toad lily), some of this breeding conducted for companies interested in developing new, garden-worthy selections. His interest in epimediums developed from his plant breeding studies and crystallized after his visit with Harold Epstein.

I asked Darrell what drives his passion for epimediums. He responded:

Epimediums are such tough and long-lived perennials requiring minimal care, yet they have delicate flowers, incredible foliage, and year-round interest. This is what captured and encouraged my interest in them as well as a desire to hybridize them. It is the thrill of the unknown, an insatiable desire to learn more and the incredible diversity we are still uncovering in the wild that has kept me on the edge of my seat wondering what we'll find next. And this is before the intensive hybridizing program gets going full scale.

His enthusiasm for epimediums was instantly heightened when, for example, he received an e-mail "out of the blue" from an Austrian telling him of a pink-sepaled form of *Epimedium macrosepalum* from eastern Russia. Darrell thought the flowers had only yellow sepals. A piece of the new form found its way into his garden.

John Lonsdale gardens in Exton, Pennsylvania, and has grown epimediums he acquired from Darrell, among others. John told me:

Darryl Probst epitomizes the modern day plant hunter. Specializing in the genus *Epimedium*, he has introduced numerous Chinese species into cultivation that were unknown to science. As a first-rate plantsman with an eye for the unusual, he has also collected other very special plants on his travels, particularly dwarf irises. . . . In addition to his frequent visits to China, he works with, and educates, local workers who continue surveying and collecting on his behalf while he is tending his plants in the United States. He also works closely with respected Chinese scientists in the evaluation and description of his collections. Not content with merely discovering new species, Darryl works ceaselessly and generously to introduce them to cultivation by efficient propagation, selection, and distribution via his nursery and extensive network of like-minded friends.

Descriptions of some species he has promoted follow.

Epimediums are members of the barberry family (Berberidaceae) and are kin to *Vancouveria*, native to western North America, and to *Podophyllum* (Mayapple). Species may be either deciduous or fully evergreen; some deciduous forms will hold their leaves depending on the mildness of winter (Schmid 2002). Darrell has observed that, unless desiccated by dry winter winds, the leaves of evergreen species usually last well beyond the emergence of new leaves, usually through the summer; they do not actually fall off, but slowly disintegrate.

Darrell has remarked that, of the thirty or so species he has observed in native habitats, epimediums grow best in "rich, organic loam on gentle-to-steep northeast- or northwest-facing slopes, in dappled shade" (Brown 2001). He has also seen them growing under deep shade thrown by *Cryptomeria japonica*, in nearly full sun, in wet and dry sites, and on moist limestone hillsides; thus, in general, they are adaptable. The leaflets of the compound leaves can be heart shaped, arrow shaped, or round, and the flowers, appearing in spring, are relatively small, nodding above the leaves, ranging in color from white to yellow and rose to violet. Epimediums usually spread from shallow growing underground rhizomes and are typically clump forming; a few such as *Epimedium leptorrhizum* are vigorous spreaders.

Epimediums are native to the eastern Mediterranean area and to eastern Asia (from central China to Japan and Korea). Between these locales, *Epimedium elatum* grows in Kashmir, *E. pubigerum* in Turkey, and *E. pinnatum* in northwestern Iran with subsp. *colchicum* in adjacent Georgia.

Linnaeus applied the generic name, *Epimedium*, from Greek, a reference to a now-unknown, different plant. Common names for epimediums include bishop's caps and fairywings because of the fanciful design of their inflorescence. John Gerard referred to the only known species at the time, *E. alpinum* from southern Europe, as barrenwort in his *General History of Plants* (1633 rev. ed.): "I have thought good to call it Barrenwoort in English . . . because (as some authors affirme) being drunke it is an enemie to conception." Gerard got his barrenwort from Jean Robin, herbalist to French kings Henri IV and Louis XIII; however, there is no evidence that this or any other *Epimedium* has contraceptive properties (Stearn 2002). Some people believe that the dried leaves of *E. sagittatum* are an aphrodisiac (*ying yang huo*, in Chinese) because, according to legend, goats become sexually active after eating the plant. The "sexual plants for goats" (as roughly translated from Chinese) became much in demand by humans in the 1990s, resulting in the uprooting of native *Epimedium* populations by the Chinese (Taylor 2002).

Epimedium flowers have two sets of four petals and four sepals. Depending on the species, one or the other may be expanded, large and colorful, with an arching "spur" for attracting pollinators, or reduced and altogether indistinct. The white sepals of *E. epsteinii* are the widest of any of the species, nearly 0.5 inch (1.25 cm), and they contrast with the plum-purple long-spurred petals, giving an overall bicolor effect. Flower stems may hold ten to thirty flowers. The plant,

with glossy evergreen leaflets, spreads 6–8 inches (15–20 cm) per year, forming a low ground cover, up to 10 inches (25 cm) high. *Epimedium epsteinii* was unknown in the West till 1994 and was published as a new species in 1997. It bloomed for the first time in the United States in Darrell's garden. Harold Epstein lived to see the plant named for him when Darrell sat down with Harold to tell him of three new *Epimedium* species that had been named. Darrell told Harold that the last of the three, *E. epsteinii*, was the most difficult to pronounce, causing Harold to flash one of his rare smiles.

Epimedium xomeiense is a naturally occurring hybrid from China. (Other natural hybrids are known but have not yet been described.) It grows on Sichuan's Mount Emei where populations of *E. acuminatum* and *E. fangii* commingle. Japanese plant explorer Mikinori Ogisu discovered this hybrid swarm. Several clones of it are now available from Darrell and other sources. In 1997 Robin White at Blackthorn Nursery named one clone collected by Ogisu 'Stormcloud'. The flowers of *E. xomeiense* have bronze-purple spurs with white inner sepals, "sometimes flushed

Epimedium epsteinii PHOTO BY DARRELL PROBST

with light purple or rose," Darrell says. Another clone, named 'Akane' in Japan, was introduced later in the United Kingdom, where it was inappropriately renamed 'Emei Shan'. It has pale yellow petals. ('Akane' is incorrectly spelled 'Akame' in Stearn 2002.) In 1993 Darrell acquired yet another selection (Co93002) from Harold, who grew it as a form of *E. acuminatum*. It is a shorter plant and its flower spurs are a darker plum color than 'Stormcloud' or 'Akane'.

Although known since the mid-1970s, *Epimedium wushanense* is relatively new to cultivation in the West. The flowers wowed Dan Hinkley when he saw it

in full bloom at Blackthorn Nursery, "feeling awestruck that such a plant was only just beginning to become known to Western horticulture" (Hinkley 1999a). The flowers, carried on open, airy panicles above the leaves, are white to yellow with tangerine-yellow to rusty orange spurs. The flowers may number up to one hundred per stem, with stems rising up to 4 feet (1.2 m) high, though 3 feet (0.9 m) is more typical. The plant has long, narrow leaflets, producing a beautiful mound of foliage. A selection named 'Caramel' has "true copper color" flowers (Branney and Draper 2000). Darrell has produced hybrids of *E. epsteinii* and *E. wushanense* and

Epimedium ×omeiense 'Akane' PHOTO BY DARRELL PROBST

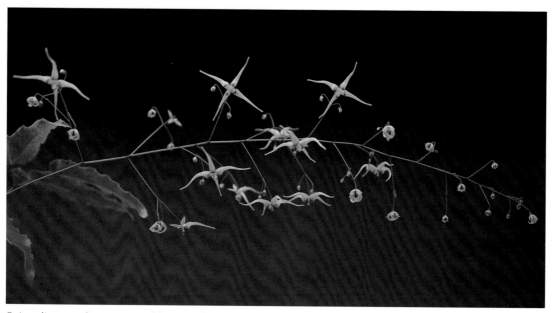

Epimedium wushanense, everblooming form PHOTO BY DARRELL PROBST

is making selections for garden-worthiness. The species's name derives from Wushan County (Sichuan, China).

Epimedium ogisui is named for Mikinori Ogisu, who discovered at least eleven new species and has reintroduced eight species known primarily from herbarium specimens. Epimedium ogisui was one of his 1991 collections in Sichuan. The flowers are among the most beautiful of the epimediums because they are pure white (occasionally there may be a hint of pink). The sepals and petal spurs are long and narrow and about the same length. Another species, named by William Stearn in 1998, also honors Ogisu's important work. Epimedium mikinorii, from China's Hubei Province, has medium-sized flowers with horizontal white inner sepals; light red spurs are held parallel to and are a little longer than the inner sepals.

Darrell's favorite epimedium, at least so far, is Epimedium fargesii ("I just can't get enough of [it]"). He saw it blooming at Blackthorn Nursery, from which he acquired a division, but later found it himself in November 2000 on a trip to Sichuan, where he collected clones from seven sites. The pendulous flowers, held about 18 inches (45 cm) high, have reflexed

Epimedium fargesii PHOTO BY DARRELL PROBST

Epimedium ogisui PHOTO BY DARRELL PROBST

inner sepals and petals; the inner sepals are pink or white while the petals are dark purple to lavender. The stamens protrude conspicuously. A casual look at the plant in bloom suggests it is a white *Dodecatheon* or a miniature badminton shuttlecock. The trifoliate, evergreen leaves are narrowly ovate, up to 4 inches (10 cm) long. 'Pink Constellation', a selection named by Robin White, has pink inner sepals and purple petals. The species was named in 1894 by Adrien Franchet to honor French missionary to China, Père Paul Guillaume Farges (1844–1912).

Epimedium grandiflorum occurs in northern Korea, southern Manchuria, and northern Japan. Because of its large geographical range, it is highly variable, and numerous named selections exist. Darrell has listed as many as fifty forms in his Garden Vision nursery catalog. The species has been known since the early 1830s when specimens collected in Japan were taken to the Netherlands, arriving in the United Kingdom by the late 1830s. The flower color varies from red-purple and light purple to yellow and white. Flower spurs are medium long and tapering. 'Princess Susan' has cherry-rose sepals and honors Harold Epstein's daughter. 'Pierre's Purple', with wine-purple flowers, was named for Pierre Bennerup of Sunny Border Nurseries in Connecticut. 'Purple Prince' produces dark red-purple flowers and has rose-colored new leaves.

Epimedium grandiflorum subsp. *koreanum* (syn. *E. koreanum*) has yellow flowers and appears to be more cold hardy than the typical species. Darrell has obtained several forms of this subspecies from various nursery owners. Dan Hinkley (1999a) reports that the largest epimedium he has seen was in northern Honshu, Japan, where he observed *E. grandiflorum* subsp. *koreana* reaching 3

Epimedium grandiflorum 'Princess Susan' PHOTO BY DARRELL PROBST

Epimedium grandiflorum 'Purple Prince' PHOTO BY DARRELL PROBST

feet (0.9 m) in height. In European nurseries, *E. grandiflorum* has been one parent of *E.* ×*rubrum* (the other parent was probably *E. alpinum*), *E.* ×*versicolor*, and *E.* ×*youngianum*. In Japanese nurseries it is possible to find hybrids of *E. grandiflorum* with other species.

In Japanese *Epimedium grandiflorum* is called *ikariso* (the grapnel plant), because the curved spurs on the flower look like a four-pronged grapnel, *ikari*, used by Japanese fishermen (Stearn 2002).

A new species has been discovered and described as a result of Darrell's research and collaboration in China. Darrell sent his collecting assistant, Joanna Zhang, on a trip to northern Guizhou Province, where she discovered *Epimedium dewuense*. Zhang found it on rocky, moist soils growing beneath scrub among grasses and other herbaceous plants. It occurs in a very limited area but is common within its range. The evergreen leaves have many erect, soft hairs on both sides—a feature rare among Chinese epimediums. Darrell reports that the species is fast growing and very floriferous, producing many flower sprays on stems 15–18 inches (37.5–45 cm) tall. The plant is tight, clump-forming, and probably cold hardy to USDA Zone 5.

After Darrell grew the plant, he realized it was a new species and forwarded the information back to his Chinese colleagues. *Epimedium dewuense* was published as a new species in 2003 in *Acta Botanica Yunnanica* by He Shunzhi, a professor and director of the Institute of Chinese Materia Medica at Guizhou's Academy of Traditional Medicine. Professor He went to the site reported by Zhang, collected herbarium specimens, and described it formally.

Epimedium grandiflorum subsp. *koreanum* PHOTO BY JAN SACKS

Epimedium dewuense PHOTO BY DARRELL PROBST

Darrell Probst standing next to the site where *E. ×wushanense* was found PHOTO BY JOANNA ZHANG

Darrell's goal has been to take epimediums out of the quiet shade of the garden and to dispel the misconception that they can only be used as groundcover. In doing this, he has thrust them into mainstream horticulture and to a more celebrated status through his nursery Garden Vision. No one today is doing more to promote and understand the genus *Epimedium*. Through his many collecting trips to China, Darrell is making this fascinating group of woodland plants more available to avid gardeners.

Darrell Probst
Garden Vision
63 Williamsville Road
Hubbardston, MA 01452
United States
www.home.earthlink.net/~darrellpro

11

Among the All-Stars

Josef J. Halda

Being a plant hunter is not safe, as Josef Halda will tell you. On his travels around the world, he has been questioned by local officials and detained by immigration officers leery of his baggage. He has ducked through areas of warfare and has picked up Lyme disease. None of these obstacles and personal risks has deterred him as he continues to travel, often with his wife, Jarmila Haldová, in search of seeds (O'Brien 1999). His travels constitute a geography lesson, requiring frequent atlas consultation to find the mountain ranges he has visited in diverse and remote locales: central and southwest Asia, Patagonia, Bolivia, Ecuador, Peru, Mexico, South Africa, Greece, New Guinea, and the U.S. West. He has also collected in the mountains of my home state of North Carolina. He continues to have a deep interest in the flora of the former Soviet republics. Overall his most frequent collections have been made in central Asia and China.

Josef also is a builder of rock gardens, using a method frequently called the Czech-style crevice garden, in which closely set rocks are turned on edge and upright, giving the roots of alpine plants plenty of downward running space. Phyllis Gustafson, a gardener in Central Point, Oregon, for whom he has constructed two crevice gardens, says of Josef:

> Because of Josef's interest in mountainous areas from an early age, he developed an understanding of how mountain masses are built in Nature and what elements constitute the placement of plants. Pulling this together with the sensibilities of an artist he has developed a unique style, which he freely passes on to interested gardeners, here in North America as well as those in the Czech Republic.

Josef estimates he has designed and constructed fifty rock gardens in the United States and Canada, including mini mountain-tops, such as Mount Halda at Siskiyou Rare Plant Nursery (Medford, Oregon).

Josef says he built his first rock garden when he was five years old and began traveling with his grandfather to the Czech mountains before he was a teenager. At the age of twelve, Josef became interested in plants and rock climbing, growing cactus and alpine plants in his mother's greenhouse (Gustafson 1995; Wrightman and Gustafson 2003). As a teenager, he began corresponding with

143

Lawrence Crocker, one of the founders of Siskiyou Rare Plant Nursery. Josef studied agriculture at Charles University (Prague) but left the university after the
Soviet invasion of 1968 (Kettler 1999). Subsequently he worked on restoring old
buildings in Prague and during this era had the opportunity to travel to Soviet-bloc
countries, all the while maintaining his interest in mountain climbing and plant
collecting. He published articles in the bulletins of the North American Rock Garden Society and the Alpine Garden Society, covering plant hunting in Bulgarian
mountains, the Julian Alps, the Karawanken mountains (on the border between
Austria and Slovenia), the Caucasus, the vegetation of the Fatra in the high Carpathians, and the flora of King's Rock in Romania—introducing readers to areas
little known from a horticultural and botanical standpoint.

I have heard Josef deliver many talks about his travels at gardening meetings over the years. He always captivates his audiences, coupling grand geographical tours with breathtaking images of plants (and therefore usually exceeding his
time allotment)! After one such lecture at the Denver Botanic Gardens, I asked
Josef how he decides what to collect. His quick response was, "I collect only
what is useful for people to grow [as] it makes no sense to collect seeds of plants
that people will kill because they don't know how to grow them." Then he added
that he collects for the beginner and for the advanced gardener, as well as plants
that simply suit him.

I also learned that, like most plant hunters, Josef has developed a variety of
ways to seek out new plants or to rediscover those that have been long lost to cultivation. He has spent considerable time looking at specimens in various herbaria, such as the one at Charles University (Prague), and those in Paris, Vienna,
Edinburgh, and London. Less accessible herbaria have been researched as well:
Beijing, Kunming, Moscow, Tashkent, Saint Petersburg, and Dehra Dun (India).
Herbarium sheets tell a lot about a botanist's work. Plants may be misidentified
or have incorrect location information (such as elevation, distance from a certain
town). Josef has discovered purposeful mislabeling in herbarium specimens,
probably to discourage subsequent collection by others.

Josef's collections tend to be at moderate to high elevations, the highest being
23,700 feet (7200 m) in the Pamir. When planning a seed collection trip, Josef may
choose to concentrate on a particular location, a certain elevation, a genus, or
some other method. At times, however, serendipity plays a hand, as when Jarmila
found a carpet of *Glaucidium pinnatum* in western Yunnan off the edge of a path.
If Josef runs out of collecting supplies, he uses what is available locally, once
using the pages of a telephone directory to press and dry plant specimens. If he
runs out of food in a remote location where he and Jarmila are camping to collect
seed, he hunts wild game.

In the 1990s Josef produced monographs on primulas, daphnes, and gentians, all three with extensive color illustrations and line drawings by Jarmila.
With James Waddick he published a book about peonies in 2004, and he is com-
pleting a monograph on violets. Josef figures he has named about 150 species of

plants and a number of forms and cultivars, but "no gentians or violets—yet," he says with a smile. He has named some species for his wife, with *jarmilae* the specific epithet.

Nurseryman Harvey Wrightman (Kerrwood, Ontario) has grown many of the plants that Josef has collected. Wrightman says:

> For me, Josef's greatest contributions are twofold. The monographs on daphnes, gentians, and primulas are priceless and will remain as important benchmarks for many years. He also helped to democratize the business of seed distribution by making available a lot of material we would not otherwise have seen.

Baldassare Mineo, proprietor of Siskiyou Rare Plant Nursery, says of him:

> Josef is a remarkable man with a diverse range of interests, capabilities, and talents. He has a strong personal motivation to accomplish one project after another as he confidently journeys through his life. He does not let obstacles that would deter many of us stop his progress. Thank God we have people like Josef who have the interest and determination to venture into unknown territories and find the new plants to make our gardening experience expand to the greatest extent possible.

A few of Josef's introductions follow.

Among the plants that Josef has collected from several expeditions to China is the tree peony, *Paeonia rockii* (syn. *P. suffruticosa* subsp. *rockii*), a member of the Paeoniaceae. It has large white flowers, up to about 8 inches (20 cm) across, with maroon blotches on the inside of the flower at the base of the petals, and golden anthers. *Paeonia rockii* grows to at least 6 feet (1.8 m) tall and about the same width. It is the wild relative of *P. suffruticosa*, a double form cultivated for centuries in China before reaching the West in the 1920s. It has been slow to gain prominence because of soil requirements and damage by late frost (Lancaster 1987). It has also been difficult to obtain because of infrequent seed set and problems in propagation by grafting (Grimshaw 1998). Some stocks sold have become virused, further hindering availability.

The specific epithet *rockii* honors a U.S. plant hunter of an earlier generation, Joseph Rock, who first collected the species in Gansu (China) around 1925. Josef obtained seeds of *Paeonia rockii* from mountains in Gansu, Hubei, and Shanxi Provinces.

Another peony that Josef collected is *Paeonia lactiflora* from the Altai (Mongolia), growing at about 6100 feet (1850 m) elevation. This species is the wild form from which most garden forms have been derived, according to the 2003 Wrightman Alpines catalog (Kerrwood, Ontario). Josef considers it to be among the best of the species.

Paeonia lutea is a collection from Mount Haba (Yunnan Province), but it also grows in Sichuan and southeastern Tibet on brushy slopes, among rocks, and in open spruce forests up to about 14,000 feet (4300 m) elevation (Halda and Wad-dick 2004). This shrub reaches up to 10 feet (3 m) high and its flowers, with yellow petals, are nearly 3 inches (7.5 cm) across. The specific epithet *lutea* means "yellow."

The Fatra is located in the western part of the Carpathian foothills in south-western Slovakia near Hungary. It has a modest elevation of 5825 feet (1770 m),

causing Josef to jokingly refer to the mountains as molehills (Halda 1984). Limestone and dolomite from the Triassic Period comprise these mountains. Indigenous plants found here include orchids, gentians, saxifrages, androsaces, and one cyclamen. Josef named the latter *Cyclamen fatrense* when he discovered it in 1971, but now it is considered *C. purpurascens* subsp. *purpurascens* (also sometimes listed as *C. purpurascens* var. *fatrense*).

Josef found the cyclamen in July and August growing in shady beech forests in the Low Tatras "on wooded slopes ablaze with the glowing pink flames . . . and the

Paeonia lutea in Yunnan PHOTO BY JOSEF HALDA

Cyclamen purpurascens subsp. *purpurascens* PHOTO BY BALDASSARE MINEO

woods was redolent with their fragrance." It has plain green leaves and large flowers and is considered in the normal variation range of *Cyclamen purpurascens* (Beckett 1993).

I grow the Fatra cyclamen in the light shade of a native *Magnolia tripetala*, far different from the landscape of its Slovakian home. Still it rewards me each summer with flowers, the same that had smitten Josef.

The high mountains of Pamir, a part of the eastern Himalaya, lie in the Tajikistan and Kyrgyzstan Republics, and western China. The eastern area is dry and consists of steppe or high alpine desert, while the western area is glaciated. In Persian *pamir* means "roof of the world" and in the language of Kyrgyzstan it means "desert" (Halda 1992b). In the Pamir, Josef has collected seeds of several dionysias (Primulaceae), including *Dionysia involucrata*, which grows on limestone cliffs at an elevation of up to 9500 feet (2900 m) and produces pink to rose flowers or occasionally plants with white ones. He found a population at higher elevation with smaller flowers and darker color. Josef says they germinate freely and they "love full sunshine and quite a dry summer" for best results in the garden. The species was introduced in the mid-1970s and is among the easiest dionysias to grow (Beckett 1993).

Another form Josef has collected is *Dionysia* aff. *gandzhinae*, from Gandzhino (southern Tajikistan). An inhabitant of dolomitic cliffs, it forms dense cushions about 4 inches (10 cm) across and 0.75 inch (1.9 cm) tall. The petals are bright pink to purplish and fragrant. Overall, it has the look of a diminutive *D. involucrata* (Halda 2001b).

Other *Dionysia* species that Josef has collected in the Pamir include *D. tapetodes*, which is fairly widespread and floriferous (often sweetly scented), and *D. hissarica* with yellow flowers, of which he has seen "thousands in full bloom on cliffs and walls, mostly under overhanging rocks," he says.

Androsace akbaitalensis (Primulaceae) is from the Pamir, Tien Shan, and other locations at alpine and subalpine elevations. In the Pamir, it grows at elevations between 12,500 and 18,400 feet (3800–5600 m). It forms a low cushion, 0.75–1.25 inches (2–3 cm) high, 20 inches (50 cm) across, with pale yellow to creamy white flowers, each about 0.4 inch (1 cm) in diameter (Halda 1992). The flowers are in umbels on very short stems. Josef has

Androsace akbaitalensis PHOTO BY VOJTĚCH HOLUBEC

Gentiana szechenyii PHOTO BY VOJTĚCH HOLUBEC

stone and dolomite in rocky slopes, pastures, and snowfields. The corolla is elongate-campanulate and pale blue to azure to mauve-blue. The cauline leaves are frequently tinged purple (Halda 1996; Beckett 1993).

Paraquilegia (Ranunculaceae) is a genus of plants that grow typically at high elevations from Pakistan to southwest China, to Afghanistan, and central and northern Asia. It is closely related to *Aquilegia* (columbine) but the flowers are solitary and spurless. *Paraquilegia microphylla* resides among rocky crevices, usually between 11,200 and 16,100 feet (3400–4900 m), often forming large clumps with flowers that are somewhat pendulous. The flowers vary in size and in color, being white, blue, or lilac depending on the location in the Himalaya (Polunin and Stainton 1997). Leaves are small (hence the specific epithet *microphylla*) with deeply cut lobes (Nold 2003).

Josef has found the species in the central Tien Shan (Kazakhstan) on cliffs, boulders, screes, and high alpine grasslands, growing in narrow, nearly microscopic crevices, always on thin soils (Halda 1991). He found that it is difficult in the garden and best grown in pots. *Paraquilegia microphylla* has a small root system, requiring good aeration and drainage, and a light soil mix. A photograph of the species by Yoshida (2002) taken in western Nepal suggests a superficial resemblance to *Anemone*. For this reason an ally of *P. microphylla* is *P. anemonoides*.

One of Josef's passions is *Daphne* (Thymelaeaceae), a genus of evergreen and deciduous shrubs of Europe and Asia. Some forms are small, suited to the rock garden or raised bed, while others are large and adaptable to the woodland and light shade garden. Josef's interest led him to write a monograph on the genus published in 2001, with illustrations by Jarmila. It is the culmination of forty years of growing, studying, collecting, and observing daphnes, both in their native habitat and in gardens.

Josef has introduced several forms of *Daphne arbuscula*, a plant of the Muran (Muranskya) region of the Carpathians in Slovakia, in crevices on limestone and conglomerate (Beckett 1993) in mid-elevations between 2300 and 4300 feet (700–1300 m). It is an evergreen cushionlike shrublet that grows to about 1.5 feet (0.5 m) tall. The flowers are rose to pink, and occasionally white. Among the forms that Josef has described are *D. arbuscula* subsp. *arbuscula* f. *albiflora* (white flowering) and *D. arbuscula* subsp. *arbuscula* f. *platyclada* (malformed, flattened stems). Among the cultivars are 'Jurajda' (snow-white blossoms; named for his friend and fellow seed collector Josef Jurášek, who collected it); 'Muran' (double rose-pink and "loosely compact habit"); and 'Tisovec' (a vigorous form with large pink flowers). 'Muran Castle' has short, dark, needlelike leaves, making a compact mound with medium pink flowers, according to the 2003 Wrightman Alpines catalog (Kerrwood, Ontario).

Another species that Josef has promoted is *Daphne aurantiaca* from northwest Yunnan and southwest Sichuan. It is a small evergreen shrub with bright yellow-orange, fragrant flowers. It grows to about 5 feet (1.5 m) tall (Halda 2001b). *Daphne aurantiaca* 'Little Gem' is a Halda selection from Haba Shan (Yunnan). It is a compact shrub with slightly purplish leaves and rich yellow flowers. *Daphne calcicola* is another form Halda has collected, with short decumbent branches, tiny leaves, and smaller lemon-colored flowers. The overall effect is a cushion-shaped, convex plant.

Daphne aurantiaca PHOTO BY JOSEF HALDA

Daphne arbuscula 'Muran Castle' PHOTO BY HARVEY WRIGHTMAN

Saxifraga jarmilae from Yunnan grows at an elevation of about 13,000 feet (4000 m). It is a stemless plant with white flowers about 0.5 inch (1.25 cm) across. Josef says it appears to be related to *S. oppositifolia*, but smaller.

Josef's collection of seed of *Meconopsis horridula* (Papaveraceae) is from Yulan Shan (China), though it also grows in Nepal. The flowers, which are about 2 inches (5 cm) across, may be blue or purple, and sometimes white and yellow. The plant grows to about 40 inches (100 cm) tall.

Saussurea tridactyla (Asteraceae) grows from western Nepal to southeast Tibet at relatively high elevations of near 18,000 feet (5500 m). The entire plant is densely woolly, columnar-shaped and cactuslike, and its flowers

Meconopsis horridula PHOTO BY JOSEF HALDA

Jarmila Haldová with *Saussurea tridactyla* PHOTO BY JOSEF HALDA

are deep purple, arising in a domed, terminal cluster atop the plant. It has basal leaves that are broadly lanceolate and woolly.

For years, Josef Halda has made seed from the most inaccessible of places available to rock gardeners the world over. His seed lists, together with his botanical monographs, have given armchair plant explorers hours of enjoyment. In doing so, he has joined the constellation of all-star plant hunters.

Josef Halda PHOTO BY BOBBY J. WARD

(seed list)
Josef J. Halda
Box 110
501 01 Hradec Králové 2
Czech Republic

12

Noah's Ark of the Plant Kingdom

Heronswood Nursery—Dan Hinkley

In September 1999, Hurricane Floyd churned menacingly off the North Carolina coast and meteorologists suggested it would take a rare path into central North Carolina. Anticipating water seeping into the basement, I began moving boxes, files, and books. Fortunately we were spared major damage, and as things settled back to normalcy I sorted through old boxes, intending to toss out items no longer important to me. I discovered an assortment of dusty plant catalogs including two early thin ones from Heronswood Nursery (spring and fall 1991), anorexic compared to the ones now issued which are ten times as large, averaging nearly three hundred pages and encompassing perhaps twenty-five hundred plants.

Originally Heronswood listed four employees, including owners and partners Dan Hinkley and Robert Jones. The nursery grew tremendously in the first decade and added considerable staff and plants. Todd Lasseigne, assistant director of the JC Raulston Arboretum (Raleigh, North Carolina), says that you need a sabbatical to spend enough time to fully cover the Heronswood gardens and nursery, so vast is its inventory. Scanning the catalog, you find a veritable Noah's Ark and registry of the world's temperate-zone plants. Dan neatly summarizes the catalog when he says, "Heronswood Nursery is a mail-order business that has deliberately remained a specialist without a specialty: we carry unusual, little-known plants that run the gamut from herbaceous perennials to woody trees, shrubs, and vines" (Hinkley 1997).

Dan grew up in northern Michigan and remembers gardening when he was three years old, tending a plate of moss on his bedroom window sill, waiting for avocado and orange seeds to germinate indoors, and sowing seeds in his parents' garden. He earned double undergraduate degrees in ornamental horticulture and horticulture education from Michigan State University, and a master's degree in urban horticulture ten years later from the University of Washington (Levine 1997; Cowie 2000). In 1987 Dan and his partner, Robert Jones, purchased about 7 acres (2.8 ha) on the Kitsap Peninsula, across the Puget Sound from Seattle, Washington. This would become their home, garden, and eventually Heronswood Nursery. While developing the nursery, Dan continued to teach horticulture at Edmonds Community College in Edmonds, Washington, and Robert worked as an architect, designing many of the features at Heronswood, including the 150-foot (45-m) long curving arbor. As the nursery grew and sales rocketed, eventually both gave up their jobs to run the nursery full-time, Dan dealing with the plants and Robert managing the day-to-day operations, including the all-important order fulfillments and on-site sales. Although in 2000, Dan and Robert sold Heronswood Nursery to W. Atlee Burpee and Company, they continue to operate under the Heronswood name.

I have visited Heronswood three times at different seasons. The plantings rival collections at botanical gardens and arboreta. Heronswood is a series of gardens for testing the seeds and cuttings that Dan has brought back to observe their habit, shape, and form, their garden worthiness or invasiveness potential. Near the house, there is a private garden, including some of Dan and Robert's favorites. Even here, the opportunity for horticultural education continues. On an August day, I saw for the first time the blossoms of *Eucryphia lucida*, a Southern Hemisphere shrub that I had admired at Bodnant Garden (Wales) without the flowers. Dan describes it agreeably in his catalog as having "exquisite, rather demure four-petaled white flowers."

I have heard Dan speak about his global travels and plant collecting at least a half dozen times. His presentations are unpretentious. It is easy to sense that his travels are not just about "the going there" to collect seeds. Rather it is the total experience that he absorbs, "the being there"—the people, culture, cuisine, and the fellowship of other plant hunters with whom he travels, such as Sue and Bleddyn Wynn-Jones of Crûg Farm Nursery (Wales). Dan says that the "traveling and seeing of plants in the wild helps me to see how to grow them in my garden and how to tell others to grow them." He has made nearly twelve thousand seed and cutting collections in fifteen years of travel. During his presentations he reminds the audience of his fear of introducing a new plant that is invasive. To that end he has partnered with Sarah Reichard of the University of Washington to help him objectively evaluate a plant for invasive characteristics. "If there is one thing constant among gardeners worldwide, it is their refusal to take another gardener's word when it come to invasive plants—especially when smitten by that momentary excitement of a new introduction," Dan says (Easton 1999).

Paul Jones, horticulturist at Sarah P. Duke Gardens (Durham, North Carolina), has traveled with Dan on three collecting trips to China. He told me:

> Dan has such an encyclopedic knowledge of plants that it is always a pleasure to travel with him. Botanically, and horticulturally, he is a tremendous asset to any expedition. Of course, he's also a wonderful person regardless of his plant skills. He's unfazed by bad weather, poor accommodations, or poor traveling conditions (excepting a little acrophobia). He's always jovial and humorous and, when collecting, unhurried and methodical. You won't find him at the head of a pack of collectors, but, time after time, at the end of the day, he'll have discovered more than anyone else.

A few of Dan's introductions follow.

I was surprised when I learned that *Paris* (Trilliaceae) does not get its name from that incomparable City of Love on the Seine. Rather it is from Medieval Latin *par* in its genitive case, meaning roughly "equal parts," or "like a pair," named by botanist Carl Linnaeus for the regularity or evenness of the parts in herb Paris (*P. quadrifolia*), the only European species. Paris the city, incidentally, derived its name from a tribe of Celtic Gauls, known as the Parisii, in the third century BCE.

That *Paris* (the plant) is one of the loves of Dan Hinkley is confirmed by his assigning an entire chapter to the genus and its allies in his book *The Explorer's Garden* (1999). Since his introduction to *P. verticillata* in South Korea, he has been smitten with this temperate woodland genus, just as he says he was with the bistros in Paris during his vagabond days along the Champs-Élysées. Depending on whom you ask and how you count, there are about twenty species of *Paris* and botanical allies scattered among three genera: *Paris*, *Daiswa*, and *Kinugasa*. Some authorities lump them all together as *Paris*, while others maintain separate generic distinction. They are grown for their umbrella-like whorls of foliage and their colored berries. Their flowers, except for the showy *P. japonica*, are often unappreciated. This assemblage of plants is closely related to *Trillium*, preferring moist, shady niches in the garden; however, they are generally more difficult to propagate, and colonies expand more slowly.

Roy Lancaster described the orange-red clusters of fruit on *Paris polyphylla* (syn. *Daiswa polyphylla*) he saw on the Milke Danda (ridge) and in other locations in Nepal in his five-man expedition in 1971 (Lancaster 1995). The plant also grows in China and India, and it was Dan's Holy Grail of plant finds, "the ultimate prize for searching hard enough and long enough," he says, when he finally encountered heads of its ripening, brilliant red fruit in eastern Nepal in 1995—and on the last day of a month-long collecting trip at that. It was "a treasure chest of ruby brooches," he writes euphorically, and later Sir Dan would sleep soundly under a starry Milky Way dreaming of how he found his knightly quest.

Other favorites of Dan include *Paris quadrifolia*, a woodland species that grows in colonies producing solitary flowers about 6 inches (15 cm) above the leaves and later, blue fruit. Also a favorite is *P. yunnanensis* from the dry, open woods above Lichang (or Lijiang) on the northwest Yunnan plateau (China).

Paris quadrifolia fruit PHOTO BY DAN HINKLEY

My introduction to fairy bells was *Disporum sessile* 'Variegatum' (considered by some to be a form of *D. pullum*). A few plants had been passed on to me mistakenly labeled as *Uvularia* or bellwort, a genus I knew from North Carolina. The following spring when new leaves emerged and I admired the splashes of creamy streaks and small, pendulous ivory-colored flowers or "bells," I began to wonder about the plant's identification. Not until I attended a lecture for a fund raiser for the JC Raulston Arboretum's education center, and Dan showed slides of *Disporum* that he had collected in eastern Asia, did I realize the true name of the plant. The plants I had were from Japan, not the U.S. Southeast, and my bellworts "morphed" into fairy bells! I have found that it is easy to confuse them as *Disporum* is kin to its look-alikes *Uvularia* and *Polygonatum*.

Disporum (Convallariaceae) consists of forty to fifty species, and, while five occur in North America, most are native to Asia. *Disporum cantoniense* is an evergreen species, growing as tall as 3–6 feet (1–1.8 m). Dan collected it in 1998 on Mount Emei, one of the four holy mountains of Buddhism in China. Because of the sacredness of the site, the forests are protected and thus Mount Emei is an excellent place to observe remnants of the lush subtropical forests of the Sichuan

Paris polyphylla PHOTO BY DAN HINKLEY

Basin; its hillsides are the source of many plants introduced into the West since 1970 (and previously by Ernest Wilson in the early twentieth century). When *D. cantoniense* emerges in the spring, the shoots look bamboo-like. Its flowers are white to purple. One selection, 'Green Giant', grows up to 10 feet (3 m), while another, 'Night Heron', "emerges with deep black-burgundy lustrous tones," writes Dan in his 2002 catalog. It's one that I want to add to my woodland garden.

Dan has collected *Disporum smilacinum* in South Korea and Japan. It has broad, *Smilax*-like leaves and is stoloniferous, forming a ground cover in light shade. It has starlike, creamy white flowers that produce a blue-black fruit. A cultivar of garden origin is 'Aureovariegatum', the leaves of which bear broad margins of creamy white.

Approximately fifty-five species of Solomon's seal or *Polygonatum* (Convallariaceae) are distributed in the Northern Hemisphere's temperate climates. They are excellent woodland plants whose graceful arching stems are reminiscent of algebraic polynomial curves, which add a fine touch of geometry to a dull understory. *Polygonatum falcatum* is a dazzling plant that Dan found on Kii Peninsula (central Japan). He reports the plant from which he collected seed was an astonishing 7 feet (2.1 m) tall and had lanceolate leaves nearly a foot (30 cm) long. Until recently, *P. odoratum* had been distributed erroneously by many nurseries as *P. falcatum*. From eastern Nepal, Dan added *P. oppositifolium* to his catalog, which he describes as rare with "leathery, dark green leaves in pairs along stems to 4 feet (1.2 m)."

Disporum cantoniense 'Night Heron' PHOTO BY DAN HINKLEY

One of the oldest plants in my garden is a big leaf hydrangea (*Hydrangea macrophylla*) that I purchased with a gift certificate from friends when I finished my graduate studies at North Carolina State University. It's a plant of no special lineage or selection as far as I know. It simply stood out and begged to go home when I toured Buchanan's Nursery (Raleigh). The puppy of a plant has now become full grown, unruly and shaggy—a Saint Bernard and an obese beast of a plant. I have whacked it back many times, pruning it after blooming, and shaped it when there has been damage from falling tree limbs. Still it has rewarded me now for more than two decades with large mop heads of blue flowers, and I would miss it terribly if it were not there. I am amazed when I look at the Heronswood catalog and find sixty selections of hydrangeas being offered—each with a distinctive provenance, collection site, or cultivar designation. Reading the list gives me the effect of a strong cup of java with the realization that I do not have nearly enough room to grow them all.

The approximately twenty-five species of *Hydrangea* (Hydrangeaceae) comprise shrubs, vinelike climbers, and even small trees. Dan's enamorment is evident when he describes standing on the Kii Peninsula (central Japan), and counting five species of *Hydrangea* in plain view around him—without turning his head.

The mountain hydrangeas offered in the catalog are selections of *Hydrangea serrata* that Dan has made on Japanese and Korean collecting trips, many from cuttings in the wild, and others arriving at Heronswood of "garden origin" amassed from various sources. They bear Japanese names that translate evocatively, such as 'Shirofuji' meaning "white-capped Mount Fuji" and 'Miyama-yae-Murasaki' meaning "deep mountain with many layers of purple." A handsome one, and perhaps Dan's favorite is 'Kiyosumi', which has pink fertile flowers surrounded by a ring of pink sepals.

Hydrangea serratifolia, collected in Chile by Dan and also native to Argentine Patagonia, is an evergreen, self-clinging climber that produces summer panicles of flowers up to 6 inches (15 cm) wide. Dan and the Wynn-Joneses (see chapter 6) collected *H. sikokiana*, the Japanese oakleaf hydrangea, in the Kinki District (Japan), and some selections were found in Japanese nurseries. It develops into a large shrub up to 10 feet (3 m) wide and tall; its light green leaves are slightly lobed and tomentose to felted.

In 1971 when Roy Lancaster journeyed through southeast Nepal, he saw *Dichroa febrifuga* (Hydrangeaceae), a shrub that was common in the forest above the village of Sedua (Lancaster 1995). It grows up to 2 to 3 feet (0.6–0.9 m) tall. The glossy, evergreen leaves are paired, elliptic, and toothed. Clusters of blue flowers are followed by metallic-blue fruit. Except for the fruit, *D. febrifuga* is easily mistaken for a small-leafed hydrangea. Dan first saw the plant at the University of British Columbia Botanical Garden (Vancouver), and later in 1995 on the Jaljale Himal (Nepal), where he collected a form with lavender-pink flowers and lavender-mauve fruit. The plant blooms in the late summer and the clusters of fruit remain on the plant through the winter. Dan believes it is cold hardy to USDA Zone 7b

Hydrangea sikokiana PHOTO BY DAN HINKLEY

or warmer, as it grows at low elevations from eastern Nepal to southwestern China and into Southeast Asia. It grows best in light shade to part sun.

Dichroa febrifuga, Lancaster said, is important to the Nepalese as a medicinal plant for mitigating fevers, especially malaria. The specific epithet refers to the use of the plant as a febrifuge, or fever reducer.

A plant I did not know until it appeared in the Heronswood catalog is *Asteranthera ovata*, a woody vine and monotypic genus of the gesneriad family (Gesneriaceae). It grows in Chile's Lake District and in southern Argentina, most often in cool moist areas, generally at moderately high elevations associated with wet forests of *alerce* (*Fitzroya cupressoides*). *Asteranthera ovata* has raspberry red to cerise tubular flowers. It is a show stopper when in bloom, and for this reason is known locally in Chile as *la estrellita* or "little star." Its stems, which may trail to 5 feet (1.5 m), have small leaves with scalloped edges. It is usually evergreen and is hardy to USDA Zone 8, at least in the Pacific Northwest.

When I moved to my present house in March of 1975, the first plant that I identified on the property, when it popped up under the deciduous shade along the steps leading to the porch, was *Podophyllum peltatum*, the native may apple. I decided then to call the house "May Apple"; the name has stuck and the colony continues to survive. There are about seven species of *Podophyllum* (Berberidaceae), one in eastern North America and the others in eastern Asia and the Himalaya. They are rhizomatous herbaceous perennials whose leaves are bold and umbrella shaped.

Dan has collected the egg-sized red autumn fruit of *Podophyllum hexandrum* in Yunnan Province (China). The flowers are pink, unlike the white of the American species. In 1999 he found *P. pleianthum* (sometimes classified as *Dysosma pleiantha*) in mountainous areas on Taiwan. It is a spectacular plant (I have seen it myself at Heronswood) with glossy, leathery, hexagonal-shaped leaves; its flowers are maroon to blood red and its autumn fruit hangs in clusters of silvery white. It is a must for my own garden.

The genus *Podophyllum* has undergone recent taxonomic review by Julian Shaw (Royal Horticultural Society) as reported in Stearn (2002). It recognizes new species, varieties, forms, and hybrids of *Podophyllum*.

I had to rush to my reference books when I heard Dan Hinkley talk about *Triosteum pinnatifidum*, only to find the species absent or a scant line noting that there is an eastern American native, *T. perfoliatum*. Though it is herbaceous, *T. pinnatifidum* (Caprifoliaceae) is a honeysuckle relative from China and looks superficially like *Hydrangea quercifolia*. It has large jagged leaves, small flowers, and white fruits that are held up above the plant. It is "beyond remarkable and mind boggling," shouts Dan about the plant he grows in his moist, shady garden.

Dan collected ripe, scarlet fruit of *Triosteum himalayanum* in northwest Yunnan Province, in the area near Zhongdian at 10,000 feet (3000 m) elevation. The plant was collected by Ernest Wilson in China between 1907 and 1910 for the Arnold Arboretum, as *T. himalayanum* var. *chinense*. It grows to about 18 inches

Podophyllum hexandrum with *Tiarella* flowers PHOTO BY DAN HINKLEY

Podophyllum hexandrum in flower PHOTO BY DAN HINKLEY

Stachyurus salicifolius PHOTO BY DAN HINKLEY

(45 cm), has papery lime-green leaves with glandular hairs; it has a terminal spike of unremarkable light green to yellow flowers. Roy Lancaster (1993), who saw it in Liuba (China), says that when it produces its "knob of juicy red berries . . . the plant is then worth its place in the garden."

Of the approximately six species of *Stachyurus* (Stachyuraceae), the most commonly known is *S. praecox* from Japan. All are large shrubs and most species produce flowers before the leaves expand in the spring, "while still in the grasp of winter." They range from the Himalaya to Japan. *Stachyurus salicifolia*, the willow-leafed stachyurus, is an evergreen plant that Dan got initially from the late J. C. Raulston, who acquired it in 1992 from the Shanghai Botanic Garden. A native of China, *S. salicifolia* has long narrow,

Triosteum pinnatifidum PHOTO BY DAN HINKLEY

willow-like leaves about 10 inches (25 cm) long and drooping racemes of yellow flowers in late winter. A specimen of this plant grows in the lathe house at the JC Raulston Arboretum. Whenever I see it I am reminded of J. C.'s horticultural generosity. Dan, a grateful recipient, writes of *Stachyurus*: "In the ranks of this genus, I find the most agreeable shrubs that have come our way in many years."

Helwingia (Cornaceae, or dogwood family) has also attracted Dan's attention and he thinks it deserves broader evaluation by gardeners. There are both evergreen and deciduous species of this woody shrub, all of which are native to Asia. In Yunnan and Sichuan Provinces, he has collected two species. *Helwingia chinensis* has broad, evergreen foliage and is curious in that the flower and fruit appear to develop from the surface of the leaf, a characteristic of the genus. Actually the leaf petiole and the flower peduncle are fused, giving it this odd appearance. The shrub grows to 8 feet (2.4 m) tall and 4 feet (1.2 m) wide. Dan has also collected a narrow leaf form of *H. chinensis*, which is perhaps a different species. He has collected the deciduous species, *H. japonica*, which grows to about 5 feet (1.5 m) tall. It possesses broad ovate, deciduous foliage. Both species are cold hardy in USDA Zones 6 to 10 and grow well in light shade and moist, well-drained soils (Hinkley 1997).

Dan Hinkley is a category of one in that he is probably the most indefatigable plant hunter today as he makes numerous collecting trips each year. Barry Yinger, owner of Asiatica and himself a plant hunter, says, "Dan has the highest profile of all contemporary plant hunters." Like a modern-day Tantalus, Dan shares the gods' ambrosia with mortals through his many plant introductions and is driven to continue to search out new plants. His plant hunting expeditions have taken him to exotic places, the envy of many gardeners: China, Nepal, Japan, South Korea, Taiwan, Vietnam, Turkey, Chile, and Mexico. The list continues to grow.

Dan Hinkley with a fruiting stem of *Polygonatum falcatum* PHOTO BY DARRELL PROBST

(mail-order source of plant material)
Dan Hinkley
Heronswood Nursery
7530 NE 288th Street
Kingston, WA 98346
United States
www.heronswood.com

13

Bulbs for Warm Climates

Thad Howard

I first met Thad Howard at the annual meeting of the International Bulb Society (IBS) in May 2000 in Lake Charles, Louisiana. It was a small gathering of bulb aficionados for a weekend of talks, reminiscences, and plant swapping. There was a presentation on daffodil hunting in Spain, a weighty talk on molecular systematics and phylogeny in Amaryllidaceae, and a lecture on bulbs of Europe and the Middle East. The most anticipated talk of the weekend was by Thad, who surveyed his five decades of travels to Mexico studying rain lilies (*Zephyranthes*). It was a rare treat to see slides of so many species, some in the wild and others in gardens. At the end of the organized program, John Fellers, a rain lily enthusiast from Auburn, Alabama, gave an impromptu presentation consisting of about 150 rain lily slides that Thad had "left out" or forgotten that he had even grown. Between the two of them, there was an extraordinary opportunity to witness nearly fifty years of plant hunting history and study of the Mexican rain lilies.

For many decades Thad has been a stalwart member of the IBS, where he has offered technical articles in the society's journal, *Herbertia*, and other presentations on collecting, cultivating, hybridizing, and growing bulbous plants. His travels in Texas, Mexico, Guatemala, Brazil, and Argentina have resulted in the discovery of at least thirty-five new species. He has named many species and others have been named in his honor, such as *Allium howardii*, *Habranthus howardii*, *Hymenocallis howardii*, *Polianthes howardii*, and most recently, *Sprekelia howardii*. *Herbertia* continues to record the ongoing fruits of his botanical interests. Thad's collecting trips are well known in IBS circles and he has shared anecdotes and reminiscences at after-dinner gatherings for years. The society honored Thad in 1970 with the Herbert Medal, its highest award, for his contributions to advancing the knowledge of bulbous plants.

Thad began practicing veterinary medicine in 1956 in San Antonio. A year later he opened Zephyr Gardens, a mail-order and on-site nursery that specialized in bulbous plants, in particular *Crinum*, *Hymenocallis*, *Sprekelia*, and *Zephyranthes*. He issued an annual catalog, six to eight pages long, on legal sheets, often illustrated with his own line drawings. He ended the operation of Zephyr Gardens in 1972 but continued his veterinary practice until retiring in 1995. He then moved to a new location and garden in Saint Hedwig near San Antonio, Texas. In retirement he has taken the time to compile his extensive knowledge in a book, *Bulbs for Warm Climates* (Howard 2001), the documentation and culmination of a half-century interest in plants by this prolific bulb and seed hunter of the twentieth century.

For years, Thad has traded, given away, and sold Mexican bulbs to numerous individuals and nurseries. Benefiting from his largesse are nurseries such as Tejas Bulbs (Steve Lowe), Yucca Do Nursery (Carl Schoenfeld), Peckerwood Garden (John Fairey), and Plant Delights Nursery (Tony Avent). Thad continues to travel to Mexico and he has several articles and plant descriptions awaiting publication.

Dave Lehmiller, a *Crinum* expert who lives in Beaumont, Texas, has known Thad for nearly two decades, traveling with him to Mexico and Guatemala on collecting trips. Lehmiller says that "Thad is a keen observer and notices details in plant characters that others overlook. And his memory is remarkable; he can recall salient taxonomic features of plants that he observed in the field more than twenty years ago." Thad told Lehmiller, "As a veterinarian, I have to spot subtle differences in things I see, since my patients don't explain them."

Thad always wants to share observations of rain lilies blooming, as well as seeds and bulbs. In a letter to me (13 May 2001), he wrote:

> This morning I found *Zephyranthes dichromantha* in flower. It is several months ahead of schedule, but who cares? It will give you a head start and perhaps you might get it to bloom in a year or so. I'll send you seed as soon as it ripens, and can send more later too. If you don't have *Z. clintiae*, I can send this to you. Because of its wine-red color, it is one of my favorites. I grow my rain lilies in the ground. . . . I also have *Z. lindleyana* in bloom now from my Mexican trip. It is remarkable in its being a dark rose rather than pink and it is setting a husky seed pod. It rarely make offsets, so must be propagated from seed. But it is hardier than most, so can be grown outdoors year-round. Do you want seed? This species blooms very early, along with *Z. atamasco*, and so opens the rain lily season each year. Mature bulbs will throw off-season flowers until fall.

Below are some of the bulbs that Thad is particularly proud of and that he had a hand in introducing into our gardens and greenhouses.

Crinums live a long time, easily outlasting the buildings around which they are planted and the gardener who put them there. I have seen them at old home sites in the U.S. South where only brick foundations remain. Because of this longevity, Thad says, "A crinum bulb represents an investment like a shrub or tree, rather than a replaceable annual or perennial." Commonly called crinum lilies, these species are members of the Amaryllidaceae, not the Liliaceae even though *crinon* in Greek means "lily." More than 150 *Crinum* species are distributed around the world in the tropics and in some temperate regions, and there are numerous cultivars and hybrids. Many have sweetly scented flowers. They have been a feature of southern U.S. gardens and landscapes since colonial times.

Thad was the first person to experiment extensively with producing complex crinum hybrids, that is, hybrids involving more than two species, according to Lehmiller, who considers Thad's best hybrid to be *Crinum* 'William Herbert', a selection with a central cherry-red band running the length of the white petals. Another good complex hybrid is *C.* 'Mardi Gras', with dark wine-red flowers. Thad says it is a "really beautiful plant." *Crinum* 'Stars and Stripes' is a hybrid of *C. scabrum* × *C. americanum* f. *erubescens*.

The crinums of Mexico and Guatemala have fascinated Thad, particularly the naturally occurring hybrids or those of garden origin, many of which are without clear lineage. He found *Crinum* 'Maximilian' growing in gardens in northeastern Mexico, including around Ciudad Victoria, an old colonial town. Its flower stems are glossy burgundy and the tepals are red, edged in white (tepals are flower parts of a monocot that are similar to the sepals and petals of dicots). Thad thinks one of the parents is likely *C. zeylanicum*, a native of East Africa and tropical India, now naturalized in parts of Mexico. In the Mexican state of Veracruz, he discovered a hybrid growing among a colony of *C. zeylanicum* and *C. loddigesianum*. He called it *C.* 'Marisco', Spanish for "from the sea," an homage to the state's coastal seafood industry. 'Marisco' has

Crinum 'William Herbert' PHOTO BY DAVE LEHMILLER

Crinum 'Mardi Gras' PHOTO BY DAVE LEHMILLER

narrow tepals that are white with red stripes. 'Veracruz', another hybrid, has cherry-red stripes on white tepals. Thad believes 'Veracruz' resulted from hybridization of a naturalized stand of *C. zeylanicum* and random crossing and backcrossing with the native *C. loddigesianum*.

Although they are herbaceous, *Polianthes* species belong to a group of plants often called the woody lilies (Agavaceae), which includes *Agave* and *Manfreda*. Probably the most well known is the strongly scented tuberose, *P. tuberosa*, whose oil is extracted for pomade and perfume. The Aztecs cultivated it for hundreds of years and used its oil for flavoring chocolate. Unfortunately the tuberose does not exist in the wild any longer and survives entirely through cultivation. *Polianthes* 'Sunset' is a hybrid of recent origin. It has a flower tube that is yellow inside and pink to red outside. Thad calls it a "lovely peachy yellow." One of the parents is *P. tuberosa*, while the other is a probable new species, yet unclassified (#2, Thad calls it), from the low hills of Oaxaca.

In many of Thad's travelogs he makes observations on pressures that native plants in Mexico are facing, particularly from overgrazing by livestock and by "encroachment of the plow." In one report (Howard 1986), he describes a trip in 1985 in which he was confronted by a local woman as he collected a few bulbs of *Polianthes*. She wanted to know why all her *plantitas* were disappearing, noting that the goats did not dig bulbs, they "only" ate the *leaves*. Thad patiently explained (he is fluent in Spanish) that the bulbs required leaves to manufacture food for flower set and growth. The woman seemed to understand and said she would "run the animals away from the colony [of *Polianthes*] by heaving stones at them" in the future.

Thad has devoted a great deal of time to studying and growing the Mexican *Hymenocallis*, naming ten species alone and three more as co-author. I have admired them and grow a few myself. From a distance I have trouble distinguishing *Crinum* and *Hymenocallis* when they are not in flower, as generally both have wide, straplike leaves. Of the two, I favor *Hymenocallis* and I grow "Tropical Giant," a majestic midsummer bloomer that could never be mistaken for a crinum. "Tropical Giant" quickly produced many offshoots, and I have tucked them around the garden where they brighten up light-shade spots.

Hymenocallis (Amaryllidaceae), or spider lilies, are a group of New World plants. The elegant flowers, from entirely white to ivory, have long, conspicuous outer tepal segments that suggest the common name (a yellow-flowering *Hymenocallis* 'Sulphur Queen' is classified by some taxonomists as *Ismene* 'Sulphur Queen'). Many *Hymenocallis* first open in the evening and are most fragrant at that time, attracting hawk moths and other dusk-time pollinators. The flowers then remain open day and night till they wither.

"Big Fatty" is a nickname given *Hymenocallis imperialis* by Thad. This form is found primarily in the state of Hidalgo, in south-central Mexico. It grows on the hillsides where locals collect it for selling, and it is a feature of area gardens, especially around Jacala (Ogden 1994). *Hymenocallis imperialis* develops a large bulb that grows a robust plant with broad leaves up to 5 inches (12.5 cm) wide. "Big Fatty" flowers in late spring, earlier than most spider lilies, and produces a large umbel of flowers with wide, white tepals. I acquired "Big Fatty" from the JC Raulston Arboretum (Raleigh, North Carolina) members' plant giveaway and I have grown it in light shade, where it blooms sparsely. I think it would grow better if I could find a sunnier spot for it.

Hymenocallis proterantha is a discovery by Thad in 1969 in the states of Jalisco and Colima, on the west central Pacific coast of Mexico. Thad says it has wide gray-green leaves and white flowers.

I have a strong memory of seeing Aztec lilies (*Sprekelia formosissima*) growing on a rocky hillside near the village of Puerta La Zorra in Hidalgo. My companions and I had to shoo goats away to get a closer look at the spectacular red flowers that had surprised us as we rounded a curve in the road. Without a doubt, these are among the most beautiful "lilies."

Sprekelia formosissima (Amaryllidaceae) ranges over much of Mexico. Thad found one selection that he called 'Orient Red' in a garden in San Antonio, Texas, blooming, surprisingly, in the autumn. He purchased a dollar's worth of bulbs for a nickel apiece from the owner, grew them, and began distributing plants to friends. Thad found that 'Orient Red' blooms reliably each year, but many clones of *Sprekelia* do not flower each year in cultivation. 'Orient Red' has a deep, rich red flower that blooms in the spring. According to Scott Ogden, who has collected

Sprekalia formosissima 'Orient Red' PHOTO BY TONY AVENT

with Thad in Mexico, fall blossoms have white stripes on the keel of the petals, but spring blossoms do not (Ogden 1994). The specific epithet *formosissima* means "very beautiful" in Latin, which indeed the Aztec lily is. Another species that Thad admires is *S. glauca*, which has gray-green leaves and typically produces flowers in late summer.

A newly discovered species, *Sprekelia howardii*, occurs on the Pacific coast side of Mexico in the states of Colima and Oaxaca. It is much smaller than the other two species and blooms with the first rains in the spring. In addition, its leaves are *Zephyranthes*-like, slender and lanceolate (Lehmiller 1999). The specific epithet honors Thad, who initially collected the "mini" *Sprekelia* in 1962 and 1963 and again in 1994.

The key to successfully growing Aztec lilies is, according to Thad, withholding water from plants and allowing the bulbs to dry completely during the winter, without disturbing them. The genus name honors J. H. von Sprekelsen, a German botanist and the mayor of Hamburg, who sent Carl Linnaeus a bulb of the plant.

Milla is a group of plants found primarily in Mexico. *Milla biflora*, ranging northward into New Mexico and Arizona, is probably the most common. Millas are members of the Themidaceae (a family split off from the Alliaceae, itself a split from the Liliaceae) that grow from corms and are commonly known as Mexican stars. All produce white flowers with green central-raised keels running down the underside of the tepals. Some are solely nocturnal bloomers, usually fragrant, opening at dusk and closing at daylight.

Thad laments the decline and disappearance of some *Milla* species during his half century of traveling in Mexico. In one of his travelogs (1981) he described seeing children combing the hillsides at dusk, gathering armfuls of *M. oaxacana* to peddle on the streets of Oaxaca to passing traffic and tourists (Howard 1982). "The damage that has been done to *M. oaxacana* populations is appalling, for the pressure is great," he says.

The best of the millas is *Milla magnifica*, from the Mexican coastal state of Guerrero, where it grows on the limestone hillsides around the old colonial city of Taxco (Howard 2001). Thad says that it is large, showy, and easy to grow in sun or shade, and that he has found it to reseed itself in the San Antonio area. Plants may have flower scapes 2–3 feet (0.6–0.9 m) tall and can produce as many as forty flowers clustered in an umbel, with only a half dozen open for a few days at any one time. The leaves are gray-green, onionlike, and hollow and can grow, under ideal conditions, to 3 feet (0.9 m). The flowers are large, 2–3 inches (5–7.5 cm) across. When I grew *M. magnifica* in North Carolina, the leaves tended to flop over soon after emerging; however, Thad thinks this plant is worthy of commercial production because of ease of cultivation in the forty years he has grown it. It does not have to be lifted and stored in the winter as it will tolerate moisture even while winter-dormant at temperatures to 0°F (−18°C).

Thad's interest in *Milla* continues. In 1999, he described three millas from Mexico: *M. mexicana* from the state of Puebla; *M. potosina* from San Luis Potosí and Nuevo León; and *M. filifolia* from Morelos near Cuernavaca (Howard 1999). Several known forms of *Milla* are yet to

Sprekelia howardii PHOTO BY THAD HOWARD

be described, according to Thad. The genus is named for Juliani Milla, eigh-teenth-century gardener to the Spanish court in Madrid.

The word *dandya* has at least three definitions. One is a dance performed during the Festival of Nine Nights, a Hindu religious celebration; another is a Triassic Period fish whose fossils are known from near Bergamo, Italy; and third, a genus of cormous plants in the Themidaceae (formerly part of Liliaceae), native to Mexico, and named for British botanist James E. Dandy.

Thad's introduction to *Dandya*, the plant, was in the state of Michoacán where he saw *D. hannibalii*. In 1964 he found a then-unknown *Dandya* among thorny shrubs and trees in Guerrero. From a distance, it looks like a *Dodecatheon*, or shooting star, as it has white, reflexed tepals. It opens at night and closes in the morning (Howard 2001). This new discovery was later named *Dandya thad-howardii* by Lee Lenz in 1971. It is easy to grow in a container, if kept dry during the winter, and breaks dormancy with the arrival of the first rains of the season. Thad thinks it is a plant worth having even though it is not particularly showy, for "the flowers are individually very unusual" (Howard 1983).

High on Thad's "want" list is the elusive *Dandya purpusii*, a plant that has not been found since its initial collection in 1911. It was reported in the state of Coahuila, on the Mexican northern border, adjacent to Texas, in a rather remote area, and Thad hopes that it still exists there. It was reported to have blue flow-ers. In 1999 Thad and Chris Peres (University of Wisconsin, Madison) collected an apparent close relative of it in Nuevo León; this form has pink to lilac flowers. As he continues to grow and study it, Thad believes this plant is likely the long-lost *D. purpusii* (Howard 2001).

Milla potosina PHOTO BY J. CHRIS PERES

Dandya purpusii PHOTO BY THAD HOWARD

There may be as many as 750 species of the widespread genus *Allium* (Alliaceae) with at least 130 occurring in North America. Most have the characteristic onion smell when the leaves are crushed. Scores of species occur in the U.S. Southwest and in Mexico, and Thad Howard has contributed much to the understanding of *Allium* taxonomy in that region (McDonough et al. 2001).

Allium canadense var. *florosum* is a form Thad found within a large colony of typical plants of *A. canadense* in east-central Texas, east of Waco. It is a particularly floriferous allium, growing up to 24 inches (60 cm) tall and with heads of flowers 3 inches (7.5 cm) across. Normally, this species produces mostly bulbils on the flower heads. Thad dubbed it "White Flag," because it attracted attention as it stood out among the otherwise normal plants. He has maintained it for a decade without diminution of quality or invasive tendency.

Thad described *Allium texanum* in 1990, from central Texas and Oklahoma. It is a midsummer flowering allium with umbels of up to a hundred starry white flowers. The plant grows in wet areas and can tolerate winter moisture. Thad has distributed this form to several nurseries, and seeds have become available in plant society seed exchanges.

On Thad's first trip to Mexico in 1953, he found the rain lily, *Zephyranthes verecunda*, and the prairie lily, *Cooperia drummondii* (syn. *Zephyranthes chlorosolen*), the first of these plants he had seen in nature. Thad found two other rain lilies on the trip, both unidentified at the time. One he dubbed *Zephyranthes* "Crepe" because of the crepelike, crinkled petals. Unfortunately that selection has been lost over the years. The other rain lily with yellow-apricot petals he called "Valles Yellow," as it was collected just below the tropic of Cancer, near Valles in San Luis Potosí, and

Allium canadense var. *florosum* PHOTO BY THAD HOWARD

it was distributed under that name for many years (Howard 2001). In 1990, Thad and Scott Ogden published the name *Z. reginae*, the queen of rain lilies, for "Valles Yellow." The plant flowers prolifically all summer long and self-sows freely.

To me, one of the most beautiful rain lilies is *Zephyranthes primulina*, whose flowers are light primrose-yellow with a pink-red tinge on the back side of the petals. I have grown it several times but each time failed to give it the winter protection it needs, as it, too, occurs below the tropic of Cancer. It grows along the old Pan American Highway, Mexico 85, near the town of Tamazunchale (pronounced "Thomas and Charlie") in San Luis Potosí, through which the Moctezuma River flows (Ogden 1994). On a trip there with Betsy Clebsch, John Fairey, and Mike Chelednik, I failed to see it in bloom as the spring rains had not yet arrived in the area. I would like to return to see it there someday. Thad and Scott Ogden formally described *Z. primulina* in 1990.

On our trip after leaving Tamazunchale, we were rewarded with the discovery in Tamaulipas of a small white rain lily with a green center and blush of pink on the outside petals; the flowers are about 1 inch (2.5 cm) across. It was growing along the roadside on the edge of a burned sugar cane field. Thad has tentatively given it the name *Zephyranthes modesta*. It is a plant he had seen in the area years ago but "lost."

Zephyranthes reginae PHOTO BY TONY AVENT

Zephyranthes dichromantha from east of the Sierra Madre Oriental in San Luis Potosí is a rare endemic of warm tropical valleys. It grows on clay soils, which at low elevation are prime lands for sugar cane cultivation in the area and, Thad believes, probably account for the scarcity of *Z. dichromantha* (Howard 1996). This rain lily produces light yellow flowers with bright red tips from midsummer till fall (Howard 2001). Discovered in 1991, *Z. dichromantha* was described and published in 1996 (Howard 1996). The specific epithet *dichromantha* derives from Greek and means "two-colored flower."

In addition to Thad's collecting and naming of Mexican rain lily species, he has produced and introduced many named cultivars. Among those in the trade are *Zephyranthes* 'Capricorn' (bicolored orange-red flowers) and *Z.* ×*ruthiae* 'Ruth Page' (bicolored deep rose-pink). He also produced hybrids of *Zephyranthes* and *Cooperia* in the 1960s but few of those

Zephyranthes primulina PHOTO BY THAD HOWARD

Zephyranthes ×ruthiae 'Ruth Page' PHOTO BY THAD HOWARD

crosses are available today. He believes the rain lily introduced by Yucca Do Nursery (see chapter 16) as Z. "Labuffarosa" is a hybrid between *Cooperia pedunculata* and a pink *Zephyranthes*. He suggests the proper naming should be ×*Cooperanthes* 'Labufaroseus'.

Thad Howard has spent a lifetime exploring the bulbous flora of Texas and Mexico. From the robust crinums to the delicate millas and lovely rain lilies, his many introductions have proven invaluable additions to warm climate gardens.

Thad Howard PHOTO BY BOBBY J. WARD

Thad Howard
1580 North Graytown Road
Saint Hedwig, TX 78152
United States

No longer sells plants.

14

Land of the Snow-covered Mountain

Mount Tahoma Nursery—Rick Lupp

One of the more memorable annual meetings of the North American Rock Garden Society was held in Tacoma, Washington, and included excursions to Mount Rainier National Park. It was high summer and the subalpine meadows at Longmire, Paradise, and Sunrise points, strewn with colorful plants, beguiled me into shooting several rolls of film while 14,410-foot (4380-m) Mount Rainier rose grandly in the background. It is not difficult to imagine Native Americans such as the Puyallup, the Nisqually, or the Yakama hunting, fishing, and berrying among the foothills of the peak they called Takhoma or "snow-covered mountain," now anglicized variously as Tacoma and Tahoma. It was in these high-elevation areas, while he was hiking and mountain climbing, that Rick Lupp first became captivated by rock and alpine plants.

In 1986 Rick selected the name "Mount Tahoma" for his start-up plant nursery, located at Graham in the foothills of Mount Rainier, which dominates the skyline there. Only when you walk among the tall trees of Rick's property does the mountain disappear from view.

Mount Tahoma Nursery is a small mail-order nursery specializing in choice rock and alpine plants from the mountains of the U.S. Northwest. The nursery is considered among the leading U.S. alpine plant sources. Rock gardener Loren Russell (2000) of Corvallis, Oregon, says that "Rick's commitment to propagating and growing these outstanding alpines provides a Noah's Ark . . . [and] without his work many would go out of cultivation in North America." As Rick's knowledge and skills in growing alpines have increased, he has expanded his nursery to include some of the fine alpines from Europe. Many of his seeds have crossed the Atlantic Ocean, where plants garnered awards at shows of the Alpine Garden Society with its exacting and legendary standards (Grey-Wilson 2000). One example is *Erigeron* 'Goat Rocks'.

A native of Seattle, Rick studied psychology at the University of Washington and at Central Washington University. His first job was in the airline industry as a customer service representative and then in air cargo. Rather than transfer at the airline's request to the East Coast after a sixteen-year career, he pursued his budding interest in alpine plants and opened Mount Tahoma Nursery, first while working part-time for six years and then full-time in the nursery for ten years.

Rick has brought into cultivation through his nursery many outstanding selections.

Rick travels to collect seed fairly often. He gets out into the mountains about ten to twelve times a year on average. Most of his trips are in Washington. When he can find the time, he also travels to Oregon, California, Idaho, and Montana, and approximately every two years he travels to Alaska. He says, "Most of my best plant finds have been in Washington. I know the flora well in our area and so when I see something special I recognize it as such right away."

Conservation of natural resources is an aspect of seed and plant collecting that is important to Rick (and other contemporary plant hunters as well). He told me:

> Buying or selling wild-collected plants seems to me to be a bad idea. Some make the argument that certain wild plants are so prolific that there is no harm in collecting and selling them. This view overlooks the fact that some populations would not be able to sustain themselves in the face of collection for sale even if, overall, the species is very prolific. I do not sell wild-collected plants. [However] I think that collecting seed in moderation has very little effect on wild populations, as very little of their seed produces more plants in the wild. Just one seed capsule can be enough to establish a plant in cultivation. I am sure that this view could be seen as hypocritical by those who think that it is also okay to collect plants, but we all have to draw the line somewhere.

When Rick collects seed in the wild, he takes only an infinitesimal percentage of the seed in a population. He explains that he needs so little to produce enough plants for his needs. Once a population is established in the nursery, he is almost always able to produce his own seed or propagate additional plants from cuttings or division.

I asked Rick about his success with plant cuttings from the wild. He responded:

> Unusual forms of plants in the wild are brought back to the nursery for propagation via cuttings. I never take more than three cuttings from an individual plant and more often I only take a single cutting. I rarely fail to establish a plant from even just one cutting.

Graham Nicholls, a garden writer and alpine nurseryman in Timsbury, Somerset (United Kingdom), has known Rick for a number of years. In *Alpine Plants of North America* (2002), a book that Nicholls authored and on which Rick consulted with him, Nicholls described Rick as a "plantsman extraordinaire":

> I do not give this description lightly. In fact he [Rick] could be described as a throwback to the great plant collectors like Lewis and Clark or James. Whether on field trips or in the nursery he is always on the lookout for new and exceptional plants that would be of horticultural value. For anyone seri-

ously interested in good alpines, a visit to Mount Tahoma Nursery is a must. Surely it is without any argument the best alpine plant nursery in the United States. Finally, I must pay tribute to Rick's generosity. From the first time I contacted him to obtain a start of Erigeron 'Goat Rocks', he has been very generous, allowing me to introduce many of his new plants into the United Kingdom via my nursery.

A few of Rick's best introductions follow.

Among the species of fleabane that grow in western North America are *Erigeron aureus* and *E. compositus* (Asteraceae). Both are fine plants—the latter displaying white, daisylike flowers and the former with golden-yellow flowers. In 1990, Rick found a naturally occurring hybrid between these two species in the Goat Rocks of the Cascade Mountains at 7000 feet (2130 m), just north of Mount Saint Helens in southwestern Washington. He noticed that volcanic ash from the eruption of Mount Saint Helens years earlier on 18 May 1980 continued to cover much of the area in wind drifts. Rick says:

> In early September of 1990, after an extended lunch break at the summit of Hawkeye Point, I decided to drop down a couple of hundred feet [about 60 m] to a small, rocky bench just below the summit, to get a better view of a large flock of mountain goats grazing about 1000 feet [300 m] below. There, among a large colony of *Erigeron aureus*, was a most unusual little daisy, its bright lemon-yellow flowers standing out vividly from the rich golden blooms of *E. aureus* . . . the plant being every way intermediate between *E. aureus* and *E. compositus* [which grows nearby].

Rick took a few cuttings from the plant back to his nursery, propagated it, and introduced it as *Erigeron* 'Goat Rocks'. On another trip he found one other plant,

Erigeron 'Goat Rocks' PHOTO BY RICK LUPP

but subsequent trips to the site have revealed a "dust bath" area made by the goats and no living plants in the area. Rick's find suggests that it now exists only in cultivation.

Erigeron 'Goat Rocks' produces solitary flowers, 1.5 inches (3.75 cm) across on 3-inch (7.5-cm) long stems with silver-gray, spatulate foliage. It is a compact, small, low-growing plant that forms a loose cushion. The irony of the discovery of this plant is that the goats "helped" Rick find the plant and yet they are responsible for its loss in the wild as well.

The Goat Rocks area has produced another fine plant, *Phlox diffusa* 'Goat Rocks Pink' (Polemoniaceae). This western, spreading or creeping phlox is a compact, mat-forming plant with needlelike leaves. Normally the five petals vary in color from lilac to pink to white. 'Goat Rocks Pink' has rich pink, overlapping petals. *Phlox diffusa* grows in widely distributed montane areas of western United States and British Columbia.

Phlox adsurgens, the woodland phlox, is a creeping species of open humus-rich forests. It grows in a rather limited area from about the Klamath River Basin on the Oregon-California border to near Corvallis, Oregon, on the western slopes of the Cascade and Siskiyou mountains at subalpine elevations of about 6500 feet (1980 m). It is a fine phlox but a bit finicky, requiring propagation by cuttings every couple of years to keep it going in the garden. *Phlox adsurgens* is an ally of *P. stolonifera*, a denizen of eastern U.S. woodlands. The great phlox guru, Edgar Wherry (1955), wrote that *P. adsurgens* is the periwinkle phlox, a winsome name I think, and "its flower hues are brilliant and charming, so that it is generally recognized as one of the most beautiful members of the genus."

No less charming is Rick's selection, 'Mary Ellen', from southern Oregon. It has rich pink petals with white bases and yellow stamens and makes a dense

Phlox diffusa 'Goat Rocks Pink' PHOTO BY RICK LUPP

Phlox adsurgens 'Mary Ellen' PHOTO BY RICK LUPP

mound about 2 inches (5 cm) high. Rick has found that 'Mary Ellen' will take full sun—at least in western Washington.

The moss campion, *Silene acaulis* (Caryophyllaceae), is a cushion-forming species that is circumpolar in distribution. In North America it ranges from Alaska southward to Colorado and New Mexico. It grows to about one inch (2.5 cm) high and spreads to about 12 inches (30 cm), producing rose-colored (occasionally white), stemless flowers. *Silene acaulis* tends to be a shy bloomer in cultivation and somewhat difficult to please; however, according to Rick, his selection, *S. acaulis* 'Tatoosh', is "a large-flowered, vigorous form that blooms for months on end [and is] no shy bloomer here!" This floriferous form is from the Tatoosh Range, located on the southern boundary of Mount Rainier National Park.

Douglasia (Primulaceae), or dwarf-primrose, consists of a few species that occur in North America and Europe. Some botanical authorities lump the North American douglasias into *Androsace*. *Douglasia laevigata* var. *laevigata* 'Packwood' (syn. *Androsace laevigata* var. *laevigata* 'Packwood') is from the southern Cascades, near Packwood, Washington. It produces large rich clusters of rose-pink flowers on 2-inch (5-cm) stems. Rick observes that it is "different from the norm in that it forms dense globose domes much like the best androsace."

The U.S. Rocky Mountains are home to about fourteen species of anemone or windflowers. Morphologically, the solitary flowers do not have petals but are made up of sepals that come in a range of colors, suggesting petals (Nicholls 2002). Each flower has thirty-five to seventy-five stamens surrounding a cluster of short pistils. *Anemone oregana* (Ranunculaceae, or buttercup family), the Oregon or blue windflower, is a stoloniferous anemone found typically in the cool open woodland and scrubby hills on the west side of the Cascades and on the Blue Mountains in Washington and Oregon. It reaches up to 12 inches (30 cm) tall and has one basal leaf and three deeply segmented stem leaves. 'Ellensburg Blue' originates on the drier east side of the Cascades in eastern Washington at an elevation of 4000 feet (1220 m). It has dark blue blooms and is similar in appearance to some forms of *A. nemerosa*, a European species.

Massachusetts rock gardener Geoffrey Charlesworth, author of *The Opinionated Gardener* (1988), wrote: "In a competition among groups of plants, penstemons would be close to the top of the list." He continued, "Some of the best-loved alpines are penstemons." About 275 species of penstemons or beard tongues (Scrophulariaceae) are native to North America, ranging from Alaska to Guatemala.

Rick discovered a pink form of *Penstemon davidsonii* var. *menziesii* in the Cascades. This mat-forming shrub with tiny serrate, evergreen leaves produces huge, soft-pink flowers. It grows to about 3 inches (7.5 cm.) tall and spreads to 18 inches (45 cm) in five years. In 1995, Rick introduced into cultivation another penstemon, *P. procerus* var. *tolmiei* 'Hawkeye' (syn. 'Alpinglow'), which he collected on Hawkeye Point at 7300 feet (2220 m) in the Goat Rocks area (Washington). The pink to ivory blossoms produce "a very sweet fragrance," Rick says. 'Hawkeye' reaches only 4 inches (10 cm) tall.

The first bellflower I grew was *Campanula americana* (now *Campanulastrum americanum*) in the Campanulaceae, a tall, late-summer bloomer that grows along woodland verges and streams in parts of North Carolina where I live. I failed to recognize that it was a biennial and after a few years I lost it altogether.

Very different in type of growth is *Campanula piperi* 'Marmot Pass', a short, rhizomatous bellflower that rambles over scree and slopes at Marmot Pass in the Olympic Mountains, the highest mountains in the Coast Range of Washington. Stems grow to 3 inches (8 cm) tall. Rick's selection produces "ice blue flowers with just a blush of lavender to the edge," he says. The flowers open flat, are just over 1 inch (2.5 cm) in diameter, and bloom for Rick in mid to late summer. Another of his selections is *C. scabrella* 'Ironstone' from

Penstemon procerus var. *tolmiei* 'Hawkeye' PHOTO BY RICK LUPP

Penstemon davidsonii var. *menziesii* 'Pink' PHOTO BY RICK LUPP

near the summit of Ironstone Peak, which reaches an elevation of 6800 feet (2070 m) and is located about 24 miles (40 km) east of Mount Rainier in the Cascades. The typical form of *C. scabrella* has blue-gray flowers, 1 inch (2.5 cm) across, which are formed in clusters of one to six. It grows to about 2 inches (5 cm) tall. 'Ironstone' produces icy blue flowers that stand out against the blue-gray foliage. Both *C. piperi* and *C. scabrella* are somewhat temperamental and require coddling to get them to grow in cultivation, including pot culture. They are worth the effort, but you will need to watch for slugs and put a bit of grit as top dressing.

Campanula 'Bumblebee' is an introduction Rick made during the mid-1990s. It is a happenstance, natural cross that resulted because a batch of seedling *C. piperi* 'Mount Tahoma' was growing adjacent to a flat of *C. lasiocarpa* at Rick's nursery. The result is a plant perfectly intermediate between the two forms. 'Bumblebee' has large, upfacing blossoms that are deep blue and somewhat funnel shaped, held on stems about 6 inches (15 cm) high. Graham Nicholls (2002) has grown the plant in both scree and troughs and thinks that the hybrid is more agreeable to cultivation than either of the two parents. Rick named the plant to honor the bees that made the cross.

Artemisias or sagebrushes are familiar plants in the U.S. West, covering thousands of arid square miles in vast sagebrush ecosystems. After a rainstorm, it is easy to detect the aromatic volatile oils that emit a near-turpentine fragrance. The genus name *Artemisia* derives from Artemis, the Greek goddess of chastity. Artemisias (also called wormwood) are the source of many medical products, including vulneraries (wound-healing medicines) and vermifuges. One species, *A. absinthium*, is the source of the strong herbal liqueur absinthe.

Artemisia senjavinensis (Compositae, or Asteraceae), the Bering Sea wormwood, is endemic to the Seward Peninsula (Alaska) west and north to the eastern part of Chukotka (Russia). It grows on calcareous sites among dry gravel scree and outcrops. The densely pubescent leaves have shiny white hairs, and the inflorescence consists of bright yellow heads. The plant rises from a woody stem, growing to a maximum of 4 inches (10 cm) tall (Lipkin and Murray 1997). Some consider the Russian and the Alaskan forms to be different species and treat the Alaska group as *A. androsacea*. Rick collected seed from the plant about 20 miles (32 km) north of Nome, Alaska, and has found it difficult to propagate from cuttings. He hopes to eventually distribute plants. The Conservation of Arctic Flora and Fauna Program currently lists this plant as rare.

Alaska is home to about forty species of willow (*Salix*), many of which are dwarf and suitable for the rock garden. One of these, *S. reticulata* (Salicaceae), grows about 6 inches (15 cm) high and forms colonies by layering of the stems (Argus et al. 2003). Secondary veins on leaf blades are decidedly impressed into the surface, giving the upper surface of the dark green, glossy leaf a distinct reticulate or netted effect, and giving the plant its common name, the web-leafed or net-leafed willow. Catkins, held just above the leaves, are rosy pink. *Salix reticulata* is typically circumboreal in distribution, but grows as far south as New Mexico. Rick's selection came from near the Delta River, north of the Alaska Range in east-central Alaska. He describes it as "beautiful mats of rounded, hairy, reticulated foliage with showy upright gray catkins." In the Alaska tundra, it grows in moist gravel areas, on sandy beaches, and along streams. In cultivation, it is easy to grow, but Rick says, based on his U.S. Northwest experience, it "likes a cool position" in the garden and moist conditions. It is difficult for areas with considerable summer heat.

Rick's nursery occupies an important niche in U.S. horticulture: it is one of the few remaining nurseries devoted solely to alpine plants. Through this venture, Rick has introduced a number of plants from his native Northwest that have been well received both in this country and abroad.

Rick Lupp
Mount Tahoma Nursery
28111 – 112th Avenue, East
Graham, WA 98338
United States
www.backyardgardener.com/mttahoma

Rick Lupp PHOTO BY BOBBY J. WARD

15

Something for Everybody
Northwest Native Seed—Ron Ratko

Winter Study Weekends of the North America Rock Garden Society take place during the short days of January and February. Conversations anticipate spring and summer days as members gaze out at frozen ground and snow drifts. At one such snowy meeting in Rye Brook, New York, Ron Ratko rolled in a huge suitcase-on-wheels and lifted it with one hand. He unzipped it, spread it open, and revealed cellophane packets of wild-collected seed, arranged alphabetically by Latin name. As eager, stir-crazed rock gardeners rushed to inspect Ron's seed, I quickly moved back to avoid being trampled by the "bulls at Pamplona."

From May till October, Ron is a denizen of the mountains in the U.S. West. From his home in California, he follows the cycle of flowering and seed ripening across the states and upward on mountain slopes, "foraging" like a mountain sheep during seasonal migrations. On trips that may be from six to eight weeks in duration, he travels and camps alone, enduring critters that raid his campground and bears that sniff his tent at night. His Northwest Native Seed catalog lists collection sites with charming names: Gravelly and Lost River ranges, Silver Mountain, Hells Half Acre, Railroad Ridge, Bob's Point, and Plunge Creek. Ron does not currently garden; he gave it up when he left the Seattle-Tacoma, Washington, area, where he grew up on a farm and learned plant names from his grandfather. His educational background, typical of many plant hunters, is wide and diverse, with focus and interest in musicology, electrical engineering, and botany.

Ron began Northwest Native Seed in 1992. The first catalog dated November of that year featured a drawing on its cover of *Campanula scabrella* from Washington's Mount Adams. Because of the demand, the catalog went into a second press run, but the printer collated it backwards from *Zigadenus* to *Abies*, unwittingly attracting both attention and sales. The geographical coverage of the first seed list included Washington, Idaho, and Oregon, but a year later Ron had expanded southward to California ("to support my collecting habit," he says). As his customer base grew, he enlarged the collecting range, responding to specific desiderata from customers in North America and the United Kingdom. He tells me that there always are orders for the popular *Lewisia kelloggii*, which Ron first listed in the 1995 catalog.

The demand for native seed has continued, and Ron has found that *Erythronium* frequently sells out, as do *Lilium, Iris, Fritillaria, Penstemon,* and any fresh seed of *Lewisia*. His British customers repeatedly request seed of bulbs, such as *Calochortus*. Ron's own personal favorites are the eriogonums (for their leaf texture) and lomatiums (for the color range of flower and seed head); he also likes members of the Apiaceae.

Rick Lupp, proprietor of Mount Tahoma Nursery (Graham, Washington) and himself a seed collector, says of Ron:

> Ron is a real standout as seed collectors go. He is very professional in his approach and preparation in the field. I have gone out with Ron on several occasions and have seen him in action. On first trips into an area, he records the populations on a small recording machine, noting unusual traits, size, color, etc. He is then able to return when the seed is ripe and collect from just the populations that he wants to introduce.

> Ron gets out into many areas that no one else visits for collection purposes and is able to introduce many plants that we would never be able to otherwise grow. His list provides a huge amount of information about the plants and their habitat, making the list a valuable resource in itself. I commend Ron for the very high germination rates that I get from his seed. He takes the time and effort to see that the seed is handled and stored properly from the time that it is collected to the time it is shipped. Many other seed collectors could take a lesson from Ron in this regard. I know of no better source for seed than Ron Ratko.

Andrew Osyany (Shelburne, Ontario), who grows seed he obtains from Ron, admires Ron's detailed methods and focused drive. He told me:

> In the seed-collector caste, Ron Ratko is highly regarded; he not only has a lot of interesting "names" in his catalog, but he also distributes clean and viable seed. He is unique among present-day collectors in providing the specific locales of his collections, along with abbreviated environmental descriptions. I have been to some of his locales and I know that he deserves recognition for actually finding many of the thinly occurring items. We don't associate danger with North American collections, but Ron has had some anxious moments when his actions were misinterpreted or he was in an area where he was thought not to be welcome. He works solo and during the season he lives in his truck. In the off-season he lives in herbaria, studying and planning future trips. He has been in the field for a long time now and has a superb overall grasp of the quite immense ecological changes in some areas.

Some of the seeds of native plants that Ron carries in his catalogs follow.

Lewisia kelloggii (Portulacaceae), a white-flowering species, was discovered by a physician, Albert C. Kellogg, in 1870 in the central Sierra Nevada (Davidson

2000). It is closely related to the more widely grown *L. brachycalyx* and grows at an elevation of 4,500 to 10,000 feet (1370–3050 m) in its range from California to Idaho. It perches near snow line in gritty, granitic sand where it spends most of the spring growing period in running water from snowmelt. Ron's initial seed collections were from a site in northern California's Sierra County and later in Madera County in central California. A member of a genus known collectively as bitterroot, *L. kelloggii* has fleshy green, spatulate leaves and short-pediceled flowers 2 inches (5 cm) across that crowd together over the small plant. Its seed are difficult to collect as they lie in a pod often located just below the soil surface. I once admired a plant of *L. kelloggii* growing in a trough but have since become content to nurture its less miffy relative, *L. cotyledon*.

At an after-hours talk one evening at the Rye Brook meeting mentioned earlier, Ron showed slides of *Heuchera elegans* (Saxifragaceae) photographed at an elevation of 8200 feet (2500 m) in the San Gabriel Mountains near Los Angeles (California). Commonly called alum root or coral bells, it forms mats of deeply green, crenate leaves. The panicles of flowers, about a foot (30 cm) tall, create a haze of red and white above the flat mat of leaves. Ron says, "The white petals are insignificant, but the narrow urn-shaped, rose-red calyces continue to display long after the petals have withered." At higher elevations, *H. elegans* is more compact with denser panicles of flowers. It is a plant that some alpine plant nurseries list in catalogs, crediting Ron as the source of the seed.

A typical Northwest Native Seed catalog contains up to four pages of *Eriogonum*, the wild buckwheats (Polygonaceae), consisting of about 150 species, mostly in the U.S. West. Nicholls (2002) describes the variability among species, all of which frequent arid areas. The flower color may be white to red, orange, or yellow, and flowers are of different sizes throughout the genus. Leaves may be silver to gray-green, woolly and tomentose to smooth, small or large—all clustered and presenting an overall mat or a cushion. LeRoy Davidson (1996) wrote eloquently of eriogonums: "The more refined among them are elegant indeed, constituting such gorgeous foliage plants that their flowers can be a mere distraction. Accordingly, nature, with the subtlety of a great artist, has given the flowers a subordinate role."

Among the jewels are *Eriogonum kennedyi* var. *alpigenum*, a silver cushion of a plant whose seed was collected from the

Lewisia kelloggii PHOTO BY GRAHAM NICHOLLS

Traverse Range in Ventura County, and the densely tomentose, oval-leaved *E. lobbii*, which Ron found in Tehama County, both in California. One of the loveliest is *E. ovalifolium* var. *nivale*, which forms a dense cushion of small silvery white, feltlike leaves and small pom-pom flower heads that are maroon in bud and yellow in flower. It is at home upon volcanic outcrops and scree slopes on Mount Aix in Kittitas County, Washington.

Eriogonum kennedyi var. *alpigenum* PHOTO BY RON RATKO

Erythronium citrinum PHOTO BY RON RATKO

Often thought of as a shade perennial, *Erythronium* (Liliaceae), the fawn or trout lily, is a bulbous plant that grows in North America. It has "evolved diverse forms and [has] adapted to habitats other than woodlands [it frequents] elsewhere" (Grothaus 2001).

From the Siskiyou Mountains in Josephine County, Oregon, Ron has collected *Erythronium citrinum*, a mottled-leafed species that produces creamy white to yellow spring flowers. In these mountains *E. citrinum* grows on serpentine gravel slopes in the light shade provided by Jeffrey pine (*Pinus jeffreyi*).

One of the loveliest trout lilies is *Erythronium hendersonii*, also native to the Siskiyous. It produces darkly mottled leaves and pale purple, reflexed flowers containing dark purple anthers. In Jackson

Erythronium hendersonii PHOTO BY GRAHAM NICHOLLS

County, Oregon, a source of Ron's seeds, *E. hendersonii* grows in the partial shade of Garry oaks (*Quercus garryana*), flowering before the oaks leaf out.

The flowers of the lemon lily, *Lilium parryi* (Liliaceae), are rich lemon-yellow and about 3 inches (7.5 cm) long. The throat of the flower may be spotted in red to maroon. Typically growing to about 3 feet (0.9 m) tall (Ron has found individuals as high as 7 feet [2.1 m] with seventeen flowers), this plant is found at high elevations in moist meadows, shaded stream banks, and hillside springs. Its geographical range, however, is limited to the mountains of southern California and Arizona. Ron's collections are from Metcalf Creek in the San Bernardino Mountains, California, at an elevation of 7350 feet (2230 m) in a mixed conifer forest.

Lilium parryi PHOTO BY RON RATKO

Though I have never seen this species in the wild nor smelled its fragrance, those who know it describe it as "exquisite," "delightful," and "powerful" with a "shockingly intense lemon-vanilla fragrance [that] fills the air in drifts." Ron says with characteristic constraint, "It is the finest West Coast lily (my opinion)." The specific epithet honors Charles Christopher Parry (1823–1890), a botanist-physician who undertook much of his collecting during the Mexican Boundary Survey, primarily in southern California.

Penstemons are the quintessential North American plant as the genus ranges from Alaska to Guatemala (there is a single isolate in northern Japan and the Kamchatka peninsula of Russia) and consists of at least 275 species belonging to the Scrophulariaceae. The common name, beard tongue, refers to the bearded staminode (sterile, vestigial stamen) found in many species. The tubular- to funnel-shaped corolla varies in color from white to blue and red. Penstemaniacs such as Bob Nold of Denver, Colorado, would say that penstemons are the nirvana of gardening. So popular are they that the American Penstemon Society honors this single genus. As there are many forms and sizes, species can be used in a border, pot, trough, or rock garden.

Ron collected seed of *Penstemon barrettiae* (section *Erianthera*) along the Klickitat River in Klickitat County, Washington, at an elevation of 1150 feet (3500 m). It develops rose to rose-purple flowers on 6-inch (15-cm) racemes, which develop above sedum-like, blue-gray evergreen leaves.

Penstemon crandallii subsp. *glabrescens* (section *Caespitosi*) is a seed collection from Rio Arriba County, New Mexico, in the Rio Grande Valley at an elevation of 8225 feet (2500 m). It is a woody shrublet, 2 inches (5 cm) tall, spreading to 6 inches (15 cm) wide. Ron writes that "the jewel-like, lavender-blue flowers with yellow bearded staminodes stand smartly above the foliage."

I once admired the rare blooming of a large population of *Frasera speciosa*, commonly known as monument plant or green gentian, near Breckenridge, Colorado. It is a phenomenon that occurs on a large scale at that location about once every two decades. Scattered throughout the meadow among the monument plants was *Calochortus gunnisonii*, or mariposa lily. The clean white petals of the mariposa (Spanish for "butterfly"), nodding in the wind, looked to me like cabbage butterflies darting about the subalpine terrain.

Calochortus (Calochortaceae, formerly Liliaceae) is a genus of western North America ranging from southern British Columbia to Mexico and eastward to Arizona. Its center of distribution appears to be California, where about twenty-five taxa grow. The bulbs of calochortus are edible. The Navajo and Hopi ate them raw or baked.

Ron sells seed of *Calochortus albus* var. *rubellus*, which hails from the Santa Lucia Range in San Luis Obispo County, a coastal county in central California. It is the darkest of the mariposas with 2-inch (5-cm) flowers that are deep, ruby-violet with a "translucent glowing quality." Ron says he found plants with six to fifteen flowers on branched 2-foot (0.6-m) scapes. Other *Calochortus* listings in the Northwest Native Seed catalog are *C. howellii* from Josephine County, Oregon, and *C. superbus* from (appropriately) Mariposa County, California.

Each fall when a local nursery receives its shipments of bulbs and displays them in wooden bins reminiscent of a country grocery store, the unmistakable odor emanating from bulbs of *Fritillaria imperialis* never fails to attract attention. I have never been nose to nose with a fox, except a taxidermic mount, but nursery catalogs say the odor of this species is that of a fox (some say "skunky") and that it repels moles (and perhaps customers as well). If these fritillary bulbs would only thwart voles and chipmunks, I would purchase a hogshead quantity.

The genus *Fritillaria* (Liliaceae) consists of about 150 species, of which about 20 taxa grow in western North America, extending east as far as the Great Plains. Ron found *F. biflora*, the chocolate lily or mission bells lily, in the San Rafael Mountains in Santa Barbara County in southern California. The large, nodding, bell-shaped flowers vary from dark emerald green to deep chocolate brown. Ron believes it is the finest of the California fritillaries.

From the North Coast Ranges in Lake County, California, comes *Fritillaria pluriflora*, or adobe lily, with "stunning" pink-violet flowers held above fleshy pale green lanceolate leaves. "Few fritillaries can compete in brilliance of color with the adobe lily," Ron suggests.

Lupinus polyphyllus (Fabaceae) typically grows to about 3 feet (0.9 m) tall and has 6- to 12-inch (15- to 30-cm) tall flower spikes. The flowers range from light to black purple, "the darkest color I have seen in a lupine," Ron writes in his 1999

Penstemon crandallii PHOTO BY PANAYOTI KELAIDIS

Fritillaria biflora PHOTO BY LOREN RUSSELL

catalog regarding the population he collected seed from in California's North Coast Ranges in Glenn County. In moist open areas of montane coniferous forests, *L. polyphyllus* can reach 6 feet (1.8 m) tall. It produces as many as seventeen leaflets per leaf, presenting umbrella-like luxuriant foliage, palmately compound and glabrous above and more or less hairy below.

Nine species of *Douglasia* (also considered *Androsace* by some authorities) occur in the western United States, including Alaska. *Douglasia nivalis* (syn. *Androsace nivalis*) is a real gem for the rock garden, crevice, or trough as the compact rosettes of narrow leaves develop into silver-gray, loose domes about 6 inches (15 cm) wide. Nearly stemless umbels of red-violet to wine flowers rise above the cushion. The rocky slopes of the Entiat Mountains in Chelan County, Washington, provided seed for this choice alpine.

Douglasia laevigata var. *laevigata* (syn. *Androsace laevigata* var. *laevigata*) grows in the Cascade Range of Washington and Oregon, and the Columbia River Gorge between the two states. Rosettes of shiny dark, evergreen leaves form dense cushions that are topped by pale to pink umbels of flowers. The cushions may be up to 3 inches (7.5 cm) high and 12 inches (30 cm) across. Graham Nicholls (2002) says that it is an easy-going species and recommends it for newcomers wanting to grow douglasias. *Douglasia laevigata* var. *ciliolata* (syn. *Androsace laevigata* var. *ciliolata*) grows in Washington's Olympic Mountains. It is an overall larger plant and the leaves are ciliate and toothed.

Douglasia laevigata PHOTO BY GRAHAM NICHOLLS

Douglasia laevigata var. *ciliolata* PHOTO BY RICK LUPP

Shy, unassuming Ron covers what is probably the largest territory of any seed collector operating in the western United States. His popular lists cover nearly the entire spectrum of plant families and biomes of this region, from high elevation *Lewisia* through coastal *Calochortus*.

Ron Ratko PHOTO BY BOBBY J. WARD

Ron Ratko
Northwest Native Seed
17595 Vierra Canyon Road, # 172
Prunedale, CA 93907
United States

as biologically diverse as Mexico. When John and Carl set out to establish Peckerwood Garden and Yucca Do Nursery, the popular perception of Mexican plants, even among knowledgeable horticulturists, was of tropical agaves, cacti, orchids, and bromeliads. Oh, how times have changed! The horticultural palette of Mexican plants now available and the knowledge we've gained on their culture and adaptability is nothing short of a botanical revolution! To find any other information on many of these plants, one must go back to the 1920s to Paul Standley's *Trees and Shrubs of Mexico*. That new species continue to be named from John and Carl's passionate pursuits speaks to the huge importance, not only to horticulture, but also to botany, of their monumental work.

From their earliest trips where they discovered the fastigiate evergreen *Magnolia schiedeana* 'Bronze Sentinel' (now *M. tamaulipana*) to recent collections of low elevation *Tigridia pavonia* (Mexican shellflower), John and Carl have expanded our botanical and horticultural horizons south of the border, offering a plenitude of new flora. Some of the plants that they have promoted and introduced follow.

When *Clethra pringlei* is in bloom at Peckerwood, you cannot fail to notice the pleasing aroma of cinnamon emanating from the delicate flowers. Known commonly as summer-sweet, this evergreen shrub is promoted by John and Carl through Yucca Do Nursery. One selection from a collection in the Mexican state of Tamaulipas is 'White Water', which produces 10-inch (2.5-cm) long panicles of bell-shaped, white blossoms. The flowers resemble a cascade of water and contrast sharply against black-green serrated foliage with a silver underside. The plant can reach 25 feet (7.5 m) high. It was found in the mountains near Puerto Purificación at an elevation of 4600 feet (1400 m), in a region that experiences snowfall. John and Carl have found this plant to be easily propagable via softwood cuttings.

Clethra (Clethraceae) consists of at least sixty species in tropical America, Asia, and North America, two of which occur in the United States. The genus name derives from the Greek *klethra* for "alder." The specific epithet *pringlei* honors Cyrus Guernsey Pringle (1838–1911), one of the key figures in systematic plant exploration and collecting in the southwestern United States, Mexico, and Cuba between 1881 and 1909. The Pringle Herbarium, at the University of Vermont in Burlington, houses many of his herbarium specimens.

Many Mexican mock oranges (*Philadelphus*) remain evergreen, unlike European and Asian natives that are deciduous. The several Mexican species grow in a range of elevations and habitats, though they favor rocky slopes and perch in crevices among boulders. John and Carl discovered their first Mexican mock orange on a hot day while they were hiking in the shade in a cool arroyo (wide ditch); they became overwhelmed by a knockout aroma of citrus with hints of cinnamon and honey.

One introduction, *Philadelphus* aff. *calcicola* from Nuevo León, produces an intense fragrance from flowers borne on long, arching whiplike branches. Another,

Clethra pringlei PHOTO BY CARL SCHOENFELD

Philadelphus 'Heaven Scent' PHOTO BY CARL SCHOENFELD

P. coulteri 'Bull's Eye', has a pink "eye" in the center of fringed white petals. *Philadelphus* 'Iturbide' sports 3-inch (7.5-cm) diameter flowers with bright yellow stamens. Another mock orange Yucca Do has promoted is *Philadelphus* 'Heaven Scent'.

One of the characteristics of the Mexican mock oranges (Hydrangeaceae) is their fickle growth form—some are vinelike, others treelike, and at least one species squats at only 1 foot (0.3 m) tall. In general, horticulturists and nurseries have thus far overlooked the natural variability and garden potential of the Mexican *Philadelphus* species. These mock oranges are cold hardy to at least USDA Zone 7. The genus name honors Ptolemy Philadelphus, an Egyptian monarch of about 300 BCE.

Eryngium venustum (Apiaceae), the Mexican sea holly, has a deep-growing, fleshy taproot like its distant relative the carrot, and thus requires little rainfall. Introduced originally as *E. umbellifera*, it has spiny evergreen leaves and thistlelike flower heads up to 18 inches (45 cm) tall. It displays a delicate, albeit formidable architecture. The overall shape of the plant is a flat rosette of finely cut foliage, almost doily-like, which hugs the ground. Seeds from this sea holly were collected at an elevation of 4000 feet (1200 m) in Tamaulipas. The plant has done well in gardens with full sun to light shade and well-drained soils from the Carolinas to the Pacific Northwest of the United States, surviving temperatures as low as 2°F (−17°C) in North Carolina. Another as yet unidentified *Eryngium* from La Peña, collected at an elevation of 8000 feet (2400 m), has robust, dark green foliage with few spines. For best effect in the garden, Carl says you will want to group several plants; but when doing so, you will need to wear gloves.

The poppy mallow or Mexican wine cup, *Callirhoë involucrata* var. *tenuissima*, produces a profusion of flowers that fancifully resemble a wine cup. The petals are of a softer violet-mauve color than other callirhoës. Another distinguishing characteristic is the finely dissected, blue-green evergreen foliage. John and Carl found seeds from this variety in Coahuila at about 8000 feet (2400 m). Yucca Do Nursery considers this poppy mallow one of the finest Mexican plants as it is more ornamental than native callirhoës.

Eryngium venustum PHOTO BY CARL SCHOENFELD

Callirhoë involucrata var. *tenuissima* PHOTO BY CARL SCHOENFELD

The name *Callirhoë* derives from the daughter of the river god Achelous in Greek mythology. The genus is a member of the Malvaceae, the cotton and okra family.

Along Mexican roadsides it is common to see salvias waving their spikes of blue, purple, or red flowers. While we may be familiar with the culinary sage (*Salvia officinalis*) from the Mediterranean, the Mexican sages adapt better to the growing conditions in the southern United States and are considerably bolder in color, shape, size, and texture. *Salvia* (Lamiaceae) has been one of the hallmark genera offered by Yucca Do Nursery over the years. In 1994, for example, its catalog listed fifty-four species or forms. Betsy Clebsch, who lives in La Honda, California, and is a salvia authority and author of *The New Book of Salvias* (2003), has traveled with John to see the Mexican salvias in their native habitat, noting that "it is quite a thrill to be able to do this because it tells you so much about soil, exposure, as well as growing companions."

Salvia microphylla 'San Carlos Festival' is a selection from a large colony found near San Carlos, Tamaulipas, in October 1992 at about 3800 feet (1150 m). It has rich magenta flowers and gray-green leaves. *Salvia microphylla* 'Hoja Grande' (Spanish for "large leaf") has oversized leaves that make it look decidedly exotic and tropical. *Salvia microphylla* 'Dieciocho de Marzo' (Spanish for "18 March," the national holiday celebrating the nationalization in 1938 of the petroleum industry in Mexico) is an exceptionally hardy form collected at an elevation of 6000 feet (1800 m) near the town of Dieciocho de Marzo in Nuevo León.

Salvia blepharophylla 'Dulce Nombres', a red-flowered form of the eyelash-leaved sage from the town of Dulce Nombres at the border between the states of Nuevo León and Tamaulipas in Mexico, was introduced by Yucca Do Nursery in 1992. Edging each leaf are small, yet visible, hairs ("eyelashes") that provide both the common name and Latin specific epithet. This cultivar is among the few salvias that grow well in light shade.

Salvia darcyi 'Galeano Red' (referred to in early Yucca Do Nursery catalogs as *S. oresbia*) has red flowers with delta-shaped, soft green leaves. It is a relatively rare plant found in a limited area at an elevation of 9000 feet (2700 m), where it grows to a height of 3 feet (1 m). Carl and John discovered this species in 1988 in Nuevo León. James Compton named it to honor William D'Arcy. Compton and D'Arcy are British botanists who accompanied John and Carl to the salvia site location in 1991.

Salvia ×*jamensis* is a hybrid swarm of Mexican salvias produced where populations of *S. greggii* and *S. microphylla* overlap (Clebsch 2003). One such natural population was discovered by John and Carl in 1988 and from that they introduced in 1991 a selection called 'San Isidro Moon', which produces pale creamy pink flowers set against a dark purple calyx. The specific epithet honors the town Jame in the state of Coahuila.

Salvia mexicana grows widely over east-central Mexico in a range of elevations. In the wild it reaches up to 9 feet (3 m) tall, but in cultivation it is somewhat shorter. The flowers on the typical form are dark purple. One of Carl and John's older introductions is 'Lollie Jackson', a selection obtained from the garden of Lollie Jackson in Houston. Jackson had found it in the mountains of Vera Cruz. Carl describes it as "broad growing with soft velvety leaves and extra long flower spikes congested with royal purple flowers."

To ascertain the hardiness of the Mexican salvias, Peckerwood Garden and Yucca Do Nursery distributed seeds and plants to Tony Avent (Plant Delights Nursery, Raleigh, North Carolina; see chapter 19), who gardens in USDA Zone 7b. Tony recommends delaying the cutting back of dead stems of Mexican salvias from the fall to the spring, thereby reducing winter damage to the crown from alternate freeze and thaw because the stems can fill with rain water. Salvias prefer bright sun and good soil drainage. By picking the right selections, it is possible to have salvias in bloom throughout the growing season.

The woody lilies are a group of plants that include agaves, yuccas, and related plants, which are assigned to the Agavaceae and the Nolinaceae, formerly considered part of the Liliaceae. Taxonomically these monocots are members of Liliflorae, a superorder, and share many characteristics such as number and arrangement of flower parts and having flowers borne on an elongated inflorescence (Irish and Irish 2000). John and Carl's collections in Mexico have added considerably to the palette of woody lilies and have been an integral part of Yucca Do's catalog offerings.

Agave montana is a recently described species that was formerly lumped with the *A. macroculmis* complex. One huge form from northern Mexico at La Peña

Agave montana PHOTO BY BOBBY J. WARD

Nevada (Nuevo León) at an elevation of 9,000 to 11,000 feet (3000–3300 m) has large gray-green leaves with sharktooth-like margins. This high-elevation agave is hardy and has large, artichoke-like leaf rosettes 2–3 feet (0.6–0.9 m) wide and tall. It is a non-suckering plant. *Agave gentryi*, also a new species, is closely allied to *A. montana*, but it is found at lower elevations of about 6000 to 8000 feet (1800–2400 m). *Agave* 'Jaws', a wonderful Yucca Do introduction, is a hybrid, probably between the two species as intergrades occur at elevations between the normal ranges of *A. montana* and *A. gentryi*.

The false red agave, *Beschorneria*, has large, sword-shaped, fleshy and fibrous leaves and grows in light shade, often along roadsides and hanging over cliffs. *Beschorneria septentrionalis* has green leaves and fuchsia-red flowers on a 4-foot (1.2-m) stalk of branched panicles. Yucca Do's collection comes from Tamaulipas at an elevation of 4100 feet (1250 m), and therefore is a very cold hardy *Beschorneria*. In 1991, Carl and John sent seed of *B. septentrionalis* to Martin Grantham, then horticulturist in charge of the Meso-American collection at the University of California (Berkeley) Botanical Garden. Martin did extensive research in crossing hardy and nonhardy forms of *Beschorneria*, including crosses with *B. yuccoides*.

Dasylirions or sotols are stemless, yuccalike plants that have long, pliable

leaves with teeth. *Dasylirion berlandieri*, the blue sotol, grows to 3 feet (0.9 m) tall. "Blue Twister," the bluest of the sotols, was found growing on a high gypsum plateau in Nuevo León in 1990. It was named for its leaves—3 feet long (0.9 m) and 1 inch (2.5 cm) wide—which appear twisting and undulating as if whipped about in the wind, a striking contrast to the white landscape surrounding them. "Blue Twister" retained its color when grown and tested away from gypsum-rich soils.

Manfredas form rosettes of leaves on stemless or nearly stemless plants. Most manfredas are deciduous. Leaves are often marked, fleshy, and brittle. Some of the blue-green leaves of *Manfreda undulata* (San Carlos site, Tamaulipas) have chocolate-colored spots. Leaf margins are often undulate or wavy. The flowers are green to brown. Plant size is only about 4 inches (10 cm) high and 15 inches (37.5 cm) wide, but the flower stalk may be 5 feet (1.5 m) tall. This plant typically grows in bright shade to full sun.

Beschorneria septentrionalis PHOTO BY ROBERT LYONS

Nolina nelsoni is a treelike species with a fairly limited distribution around Tamaulipas, Mexico. It grows to 20 feet (6 m) tall with stiff blue-gray leaves 1.5 inches (3.75 cm) wide and 4 feet (1.2 m) long. The inflorescence of tiny, creamy white flowers may soar an additional 6 feet (1.8 m). *Nolina* La Siberica form has 2-inch (5-cm) wide leaves, a 20-foot (6-m) tall central stalk, and a flower stalk of up to 6 feet (1.8 m). John and Carl collected this nolina in an oak-madrone forest near the town of La Siberica in Nuevo León at an altitude of 8380 feet (2550 m). It is one of the hardiest nolinas. The leaves of nolina are used locally for roof thatching.

One of the prides of Yucca Do Nursery is the array of *Zephyranthes* offerings in its catalog. Though commonly known as rain lilies, they are members of the Amaryllidaceae, making the genus more closely allied to narcissus, crinum, and snowdrops than to the true lilies (Liliaceae). The generic name means "flower of the west wind" (a reference to the origin of the genus in the Western Hemisphere, or more likely to the rain-bearing west wind).

John and Carl found a form of *Zephyranthes* called "Labuffarosa" in 1990 growing in deep shade among *Ilex rubra* and large granite boulders in the San Carlos mountains of Tamaulipas at an elevation of 3800 feet (1160 m). It was not in bloom—only the wide glossy foliage was present. Later in the summer on a return trip, they were rewarded by finding large, pale-pink flowers on plants that

Zephyranthes "Labuffarosa" PHOTO BY CARL SCHOENFELD

proved quite floriferous. "Labuffarosa" propagates easily from seeds and it now appears widely in retail garden centers. In the garden the flower stalk produces slightly drooping petals, which vary from white to rose often with tips that are near cerise. John and Carl have found this rain lily in only one relatively remote location, although other rain lilies (including a large *Z. drummondii* offered by Yucca Do Nursery as San Carlos form) grow there as well. In 1999, I made a trip to the site with John and Wade Roitsch (Yucca Do's propagator and gardener) and saw that the landowner had been grazing horses for some time without apparent jeopardy to "Labuffarosa."

Zephyranthes 'El Cielo' is generally the earliest of the rain lilies to bloom, producing flowers when the April rains arrive. It grows on steep slopes among Mexican beech (*Fagus grandifolia* subsp. *mexicana*) at a 4000-foot (1220-m) elevation. This cultivar, named for its collection location, Rancho del Cielo, a tropical cloud forest in Tamaulipas, has clear pink flowers with a pale green central eye. Overall, it appears rather pinwheel shaped.

Trips to Mexico have produced other rain lilies. One dubbed "Querétaro Yellow" is small, bright yellow and blooms all summer long. It is now identified as *Zephyranthes katherinei* var. *lutea*. The taxonomy of additional forms collected by John and Carl remains uncertain. This taxonomically challenged group includes the "*lindleyana* complex," plants that superficially resemble *Z. lindleyana* but which vary considerably in size, shape, and color of the flower. Thad Howard of Saint Hedwig, Texas (see chapter 13), has spent forty-five years studying Mexican

Zephyranthes katherinei var. *lutea* introduced as "Querétaro Yellow" PHOTO BY CARL SCHOENFELD

flora, primarily bulbs. Some of the rain lilies found by Yucca Do have been passed along to Howard for assistance in sorting out the taxonomy.

Lynn Lowrey first promoted Mexican oaks for Texas landscapes. For many years he tirelessly collected acorns of such species as *Quercus polymorpha* and *Q. rhysophylla*. These are evergreen oaks, which lose their leaves in the spring when a new flush of leaves replaces the previous season's growth. Yucca Do Nursery has introduced numerous other forms since the late 1980s. *Quercus* La Encantada form was found on the trip J. C. Raulston made with John and Carl in 1991. Near the village of La Encantada (Nuevo León) they discovered a colony of stately evergreen oaks at an elevation of 7000 feet (2100 m). The leaves are glossy, dark green, 1.5 inches (3.75 cm) long and 0.5 inch (1.25 cm) wide.

On another trip, John and Carl found at a still higher elevation *Quercus* La Siberica form (from the town La Siberica, also in Nuevo León, at 8100 feet [2500 m]), the leaves of which are generally ovate and dark green. Other forms of uncertain taxonomy include the Pinal de Amoles form (a small tree with elliptical leaves), *Quercus* aff. *fusiformis* (with scalloped leaves on twisting branches), and a shrublike big cup oak from Coahuila with blue-green foliage. *Quercus canbyi* has long narrow, scalloped leaves with a glossy sheen.

Most of the Mexican oaks in the plant evaluation program at the JC Raulston Arboretum in Raleigh, North Carolina, have survived temperatures down to 2°F (−17°C) without damage and some have survived even colder temperatures in USDA Zone 5 in Kansas, according to Carl.

Quercus polymorpha PHOTO BY BOBBY J. WARD

Sabal is a genus of about fifteen species of fan palms or palmetto that are found in the U.S. Southeast to northeast Mexico, the Caribbean, Panama, and Colombia. The species grow in a variety of open habitats, including low hills, coastal dunes, and swamps. Trunks may be tall and lofty to subterranean (Jones 1995).

In 1988 John and Carl discovered in Tamaulipas at an elevation of about 1500 feet (450 m) a trunkless form of *Sabal* growing in the shade of Mexican evergreen oaks, such as *Quercus canbyi* and *Q. rhysophylla*. At first they thought it was a juvenile form of *Sabal mexicana*. When they found it producing seed, they gathered some, which quickly germinated. They introduced the plant as *Sabal* Tamaulipas form (coll. no. T17-55), but they affectionately dubbed it "the Mexican minor sabal" (Schoenfeld 2001). They have also collected it 50 miles (80 km) to the south, where they discovered that the trunks run horizontally along the ground, some up to 4 feet (1.2 m) long. The form and growth habit of this "minor" sabal are clearly distinguished from those of *S. mexicana*. Despite its southern origin in a subtropical Mexican valley, *S.* Tamaulipas form is hardy to USDA Zone 7b, at least in Raleigh.

Sabal is a member of the Arecaceae (formerly Palmae). Its name is probably Native American in origin.

Yucca Do Nursery has also offered *Brahea decumbens*, a small palm with a reclining trunk terminated by an erect crown of silvery blue-gray foliage. A colony may spread to 10 feet (3 m) across, but attain a height of no more than 3 feet (1 m). The leaves of seedlings and offsets are green, while older plants develop the mature showy color. *Brahea moorei* is a trunkless palm that Carl describes as "graceful and elegant." It grows in the cool shade of evergreen oaks in the eastern flank of the Sierras in northern Tamaulipas. The fan of leaves becomes waxy as the plant ages.

Cornus florida var. *urbiniana* 'Pringle's Blush' PHOTO BY CARL SCHOENFELD

Two dogwoods (*Cornus*) have been introduced from John and Carl's travels in Mexico. A relic population of *Cornus florida* was discovered in the Sierra Chiquitas (San Carlos) in the spring of 1990, more than 300 miles (480 km) from the nearest similar trees in Texas. It is a small, isolated population growing among *Ilex rubra*, and the Mexican form of redbud, *Cercis canadensis* var. *mexicana*.

John and Carl also found *Cornus florida* var. *urbiniana*, the Mexican dogwood, at several places, including a canyon near Monterrey. It was growing at an elevation of about 4000 feet (1200 m) in light shade in woodlands of oaks, pines, and *Taxus globosa*. The white showy petals (actually

Cornus florida var. *urbiniana* in La Trinidad, Mexico PHOTO BY CARL SCHOENFELD

involucral bracts) remain fused at the tips, giving the bloom a Japanese lantern effect. One particularly striking form, 'Pringle's White', honors Cyrus Pringle. Another form with a hint of pink on the bracts is labeled 'Pringle's Blush'.

Exploring a much-neglected region practically in their own backyard, John Fairey and Carl Schoenfeld have brought back plants every bit as exotic as those from half a world away—from armored agaves and dasylirions to delicate rain lilies. They continue to expand the plant palette for those in the southern tier of the United States and beyond.

Carl Schoenfeld PHOTO BY BOBBY J. WARD

Carl Schoenfeld
Yucca Do Nursery
P.O. Box 907
Hempstead, TX 77445
United States
www.yuccado.com

John Fairey PHOTO BY BOBBY J. WARD

John Fairey
Peckerwood Garden
Conservation Foundation
20571 F.M. 359
Hempstead, TX 77445
United States
www.peckerwoodgarden.com

17

With Hellebores "Provenance Is Everything"

Phedar Nursery—Will McLewin

My fascination with hellebores began in the 1980s with an introduction to the Corsican hellebore, *Helleborus argutifolius* (then named *H. lividus* subsp. *corsicus*). It was a lonely runt of a plant with gray-green foliage, which I had received as a giveaway plant from the Friends of the North Carolina State University Arboretum (now JC Raulston Arboretum). It eventually became a robust specimen. I first learned of Will McLewin and Phedar Nursery from a hellebore list given me by Mike Chelednik, a member of the North American Rock Garden Society living in Greenville, North Carolina. He had seen a mention for Will's hellebore seed in a gardening magazine and made an inquiry. We combined an order to save on postage, and seeds arrived with such striking names as *H. foetidus* 'Sopron' and 'Sienna' and *H. multifidus* subsp. *hercegovinus*.

Through a series of high-profile articles in *The New Plantsman*, Will (and co-author Brian Mathew) guided (and beguiled) me farther along the hellebore road, instructing me as to the problems of nomenclature and taxonomy in this member of the buttercup family (Ranunculaceae). They also corrected impressions many gardeners have about hellebore "petals," pointing out that they are actually sepals (a modified calyx), and that some of the structures we call "leaves" are really bracts. Will and Brian's observations regarding species, hybrids, and wild populations of hellebores steered me through the contradictions and ambiguities in the literature—all of which further fueled my own interest in hellebores. When you have finished reading these articles, you are convinced that Will's goal of clarification and verification is worthwhile.

Brian Mathew (pers. comm.), now retired from the Royal Botanic Gardens, Kew, says of Will:

> It is very refreshing to work with Will McLewin as he takes nothing for granted, has a lively, innovative mind, and questions everything—exhausting at times! But Will has probably done more than any other person to make available pure seed of species of *Helleborus*. Will has taken a more botanical view of the genus and is adamant that "provenance is everything" and that statements about taxonomy (and the identification of plants in gardens)

207

should never be based on plants of unrecorded origin. Through his nursery he has set out to supply plants of known provenance.

Mathew goes on to say:

> Although Will is relatively uninterested in hellebores as purely ornamental garden plants, he has assisted greatly in their development by supplying reliable and accurate material of the wild species to be used as "building blocks" for breeding programs, such as that of Ashwood Nurseries [Kingswinford, West Midlands]. His journeys in search of hellebores, especially in the Balkans, have been more extensive and detailed than probably any previous researcher of the genus.

Will's goal has been to "reduce misconceptions and widespread confusion over identity and classification of hellebores" (McLewin 1993). He sees his work with species and hybrids as two entirely distinct activities. For species, the goal is to provide true species of known provenance with accurate collection information. For hybrids (*Helleborus ×hybridus*), he focuses particularly on flower spotting, as well as overall bloom form, and in doing so eschews the "endless list of names, many representing barely distinguishable plants alongside increasingly bizarre novelties."

Will does not see himself as a hunter or collector of new plants, although he has found some "almost by accident" (for example, *Helleborus croaticus, H. niger* Sunrise Group, and *H. niger* Sunset Group). His interest is in obtaining *true* examples of species hellebores and peonies (another of his botanical passions) so that there will be less taxonomic inaccuracy. He recognizes that for some commercial growers, exactness is a nuisance and that only a few of them will appreciate precision of plant names. He travels primarily to the Balkans, the center of hellebore diversity, particularly in the former Yugoslavia and neighboring countries. His goal is to make available authentic material from wild colonies for study, propagation, and selection of specimens with improved or unusual characteristics. Will made his first field trip to Yugoslavia in 1988 and has returned to the area two or three times each year since, including the difficult period during conflicts following the breakup of Yugoslavia and subsequent rise of nationalism and ethnicity.

His seed list provides respite from the simple flower descriptions and dull site collection statistics typical of many plant catalogs, as when he inserts things like the following from his 1999 seed list:

> Again we can confirm a definitive feature of hellebore seed collection—it usually takes place in fiercely hot sunshine among brambles, nettles, and hordes of ravenous insects. This year we were hoping for a bit of pouring rain among brambles, nettles, etc. But to no avail, so there were more than the usual quota of vows never to do this again. Once again some excellent collections raised spirits and once again ticks were a greater hazard than warring Slavs. We returned with one disputable collector's item—a Bosnian speeding ticket.

Then there is this bit of ordering advice: "We are happy to comply with regulations that serve a useful purpose; however if you suffer from Kafkaesque behavior by officials who seem bent on turning horticultural ignorance into an art form . . . then let us know."

Will is working with scientists at the Royal Botanic Gardens, Kew, employing molecular genetic techniques to evaluate the phylogenetic relationships within *Helleborus*. Using nuclear ribosomal DNA, plastids, and other subcellular analyses, Will and the molecular geneticists are studying the structure of the genus. Initial results support the six recognized sections and species that are clearly distinct morphologically; however, species in section *Helleborastrum* that are morphologically less well defined are also less clearly distinct at the DNA level at the sites on the genome used in the study (Sun et al. 2001).

Michael Fay, Royal Botanic Gardens, Kew, and co-author of the molecular genetics article, says (Sun, McLewin, and Fay 2001):

> Our work on hellebores basically confirmed widely held views about the relationships of the different species—*Helleborastrum* [the acaulescent hellebore species section] is a group of very closely related species, and our current data do not convincingly resolve some of the relationships, for example between *torquatus* and *multifidus*. To sort that out will require a lot more data.

Fay goes on to say that some of the other species are more easily distinguished. *Helleborus thibetanus* is closely related to the other species in *Helleborastrum*, but distinct enough to be kept separate. Much further afield (genetically speaking) are the remaining species. *Helleborus lividus* and *H. argutifolius* are a closely related pair, whereas *H. vesicarius*, *H. niger*, and *H. foetidus* appear to be pretty much isolated (Fay, pers. comm.). In these studies, Will was surprised to find that *H. vesicarius* was not different and thus not deserving new generic status.

Will grew up in East London, obtained a degree in mathematics from Reading University, and taught mathematics at Manchester University for twenty-seven years. He has been a fell-runner (a long distance hill and mountain runner) and an alpine mountain climber, scaling all the peaks in the Alps that are over 13,400 feet (4000 m) high, many of them solo. He is the first British alpinist to do so without the help of professional guides. When Will is not sorting out taxonomy of hellebores and peonies, he plays the French horn with the Palatine Wind Quintet, a group he founded in Manchester. He has always been interested in plants—growing them from the age of seven and going through a "tree" period. While teaching at Manchester, he began to garden more and more, and then hellebores began to take over as his avocation.

To help fund field trips, Will has set up Phedar Nursery, an acronym derived from "peonies, hellebores, erythronium, dodecatheon at Romiley," an homage to the nursery's early focus and plants that Will "just likes." (Romiley is the town near Stockport where he lives.) The sale of colorful hybrids for financial gain comes quite low in his priorities.

Gardeners who grow hellebores and who also have some interest in more information about the individual species and the genus as a whole would do well to get a copy of Will's "Extended Hellebore Notes," which Phedar Nursery makes available to customers. Will says that *Helleborus* is a genus whose characteristics are "endearing, intriguing, and infuriating." He unabashedly comments that while his interest is subjective, his observations of *Helleborus* are objective. The clarity and lucidity of his writing are a standard other nursery catalogs should emulate. Some of the hellebores and peonies that Will has promoted follow.

Helleborus dumetorum grows well in part shade in the wild, but the most vigorous populations Will has seen grow at the edge of the woods. *Helleborus dumetorum* is typically (but not exclusively) associated with shady areas, and Will has observed the species growing on low limestone hills in mature or scrubby deciduous woods (McLewin and Mathew 1996a) in Croatia and Slovenia, nearby southwestern Austria, and Hungary. These areas eventually become shady when the tree leaf canopy develops. Importantly, however, Will has also seen *H. dumetorum* in Slovenia as dense, bushy clumps growing in heavy, wet clay in open meadows (McLewin 1999). Among the sites, he has noted some differences in the forms from each of the populations—for example, the color, sheen, texture, and leaflet size. He has observed large dense colonies, groundcover-like, in mature woods, where *H. dumetorum* emerges in the spring and flowers before the leaf canopy develops, acting much like a spring woodland ephemeral.

Helleborus dumetorum is often neglected in cultivation as it is a small, green-flowering plant that grows to only about 10 inches (25 cm) tall. The leaves comprise three basic leaflets, two of which are further subdivided into nine or so parts. The leaves are soft and strongly deciduous, withering after flowering and disappearing completely by autumn. Among the sites where Will has collected seeds are Hungary (WM 0023) and Croatia (WM 9832). Will says rather sadly, "It's rarely a striking, eye-catching plant, yet people who grow it are almost invariably enthusiastic . . . that it remains so unsung says more about the singers than about the plant" (McLewin and Mathew 1996a). It is the one hellebore that Will most associates with charm.

Helleborus niger normally has clean white flowers, though in the garden some flowers turn pale pink after fertilization (pollination). On a tip from a colleague, his search for a "red" hellebore took Will to the Triglav National Park (Bohinj, Slovenia), where he obtained permission from the park's director to collect seed (McLewin 1992). In the high mountain range Will found populations of *H. niger*, a percentage of whose buds and flowers were pink to pink-red. He surmised initially that what he was seeing was flowers at various stages of aging, becoming darker after fertilization (McLewin 1992). As he looked at other, higher locations on the mountain, he found young, newly opened flowers that were distinctly pink, and he found others that had shed their stamens and were "really deep pink." Will decided that he had found a population with an extraordinary high degree of post-fertilization reddening. He concluded that once any flower on the

Helleborus dumetorum PHOTO BY DICK TYLER

Helleborus niger Sunset Group PHOTO BY DICK TYLER

plant is fertilized, all the others (even young one) are affected by the plant's hormonal change and become distinctly pink.

From opposite sides of the mountain about 24 miles (38 km) apart, Will collected seed from two sites from strains he dubbed Sunrise Group and Sunset Group, each with color variability. The former was growing in a clearing with some shade near a motorway at a tunnel under the Julian Alps (not in Triglav), the other in a more open, sunny area with grazing cattle nearby at a higher elevation in Triglav. The first of these populations also included pale yellow and striped flowers (McLewin 1996). Will reports that performance in the garden has been erratic, the plants not consistently fading to pink-red, and he assumes that climate differences are at play. In Slovenia, *Helleborus niger* is an Easter flower emerging from snow, which may be followed by mild, warm days. In the United Kingdom, rarely does snow cover it and it blooms much earlier. Will has gone back several times to monitor the populations and has noted greatly reduced flowering at the motorway site as vegetation and brush encroach on the hellebores.

Will's seed lists have included several forms of *Helleborus foetidus*. 'Green Giant' is a large hellebore from a seedling that appeared at Phedar Nursery, the original plant growing to nearly 4 feet (1.2 m) tall. It requires sufficient space to grow, as seedlings from it may reach a height of 2.5 feet (0.8 m) tall and be nearly as wide. The dissected foliage is bright green and the bracts are brighter than the typical form. Will's name for this form is a bit of a joke, as he thought of the Jolly Green Giant when he saw the overly large plant.

Helleborus foetidus 'Sopron' is a selection from seed Will collected at the Sopron Botanical Garden in Sopron, Hungary. The foliage is dark with a metallic look and its flowers are paler and somewhat more open than the normal form. The flowers lack dark tips. In the original plant, Will tells me, the dark tip usually on *H. foetidus* flowers is fainter and slightly inside the flower.

Helleborus croaticus was found by Will in Croatia and introduced into cultivation in 1993. It is now an accepted species, having been mistakenly regarded earlier as a form of *H. torquatus*. It has characteristics common to both *H. torquatus* and *H. atrorubens*. Will has collected it at three locations in Slovenia and northeast and northern Croatia, and suspects that it exists at more locations than he has been able to visit. In my garden it grows to about 12 inches (30 cm) tall and blooms in February with dark, slatey-purple flowers. Will found it in woodlands and in meadows. He says it is vigorous and seems likely to be an excellent garden plant. While it is close to *H. atrorubens* in characteristics, *H. croaticus* is a larger plant usually with minute bristly hairs largely absent in *H. atrorubens* and usually with the internal spotting and veining in the flowers more commonly associated with *H. torquatus*.

Helleborus orientalis is an acaulescent species from northern Turkey, Georgia, and the Ukraine. It is a distinct species, rare in cultivation, and is *not* the common garden hybrid known as Lenten roses and cataloged as "orientalis hybrids." The latter have highly colored flowers, are widely sold, and have been around for a

Helleborus croaticus PHOTO BY DICK TYLER

Helleborus torquatus PHOTO BY DICK TYLER

Helleborus atrorubens PHOTO BY WILL MCLEWIN

long time, beginning with breeding in the latter half of the nineteenth century (McLewin 1999); however, considering morphological characteristics, Will says that *H. orientalis* (the true species) is very likely the source of much of the genetic background for the so-called orientalis hybrids. He and Brian Mathew campaigned for the latter to be distinguished in the literature and nursery catalogs as *H. ×hybridus*, the original and correct epithet. Some catalogs now correctly list the Lenten roses botanically as *H. ×hybridus*, while others make a small concession by labeling them *H. orientalis* hort.

Adding a bit to the confusion is that in Georgia and the Ukraine, *Helleborus orientalis* is referred to as *H. caucasicus* by local botanists, which Will says may have merit to separate it from the Turkish population of *H. orientalis*. There are two recognized forms of the species, subsp. *guttatus* and subsp. *abchasicus*, separated primarily based on flower spotting in the former and flower color (dark pink) in the latter.

Will is continuing to sort out polymorphism in the Italian hellebores, *Helleborus multifidus* subsp. *bocconei*. He believes that it would be helpful to taxonomically divide two particular forms, both of which occur in large relatively homogeneous colonies. One group has many small leaflets like *H. multifidus* subsp. *hercegovinus* and *H. multifidus* subsp. *multifidus* but with larger flowers. The other has *H. odorus*-like leaves and large, almost white flowers that appear in late autumn.

Helleborus orientalis PHOTO BY WILL MCLEWIN

In other work on Italian hellebores, McLewin and Mathew (2002)
gave species status to *Helleborus viridis* subsp. *viridis* and *H. viridis* subsp.
occidentalis, designating them respectively *H. viridis* and *H. occidentalis*, a
change supported by molecular analy-
sis and again essentially correcting an
earlier mistake.

On one occasion when I visited
Will, it was a few days before Guy
Fawkes Day, the anniversary of the
Gunpowder Plot, a conspiracy to blow
up the English Parliament, on 5 November 1605, the day that James I was
set to open Parliament. It is celebrated
annually in the United Kingdom with
bonfires and the burning of effigies of
the conspirators. Will's porch and
kitchen were filled with bundles of
tied sticks and fagots and I wrongly

Helleborus multifidus subsp. *hercegovinus* PHOTO BY
DICK TYLER

Helleborus multifidus subsp. *multifidus* PHOTO BY WILL MCLEWIN

Helleborus occidentalis PHOTO BY DICK TYLER

assumed he was preparing for bonfire night. Upon closer inspection I realized he had just unpacked bundles of dormant shrub peonies for transplanting and growing on in his nursery.

Paeonia (Paeoniaceae) is Will's other interest, an interest perhaps as keen as that he has for hellebores. One of his specialties is supplying wild-collected peony seeds and young plants of known provenance through his contacts in China, Ukraine, Siberia, Azerbaijan, and elsewhere, and from his own collections, including Georgia. His mantra is that "species names on the plant ought to be correct." Too often peonies are passed along with a label from a nursery dealer who has no idea of the provenance or accuracy of the plant name, only that it "looks" right, he tells me. Will wants to be sure a given plant is the species it purports to be, especially for the sake of botanists and horticulturists who count on accuracy in doing hybrid work. For example, he thinks it unlikely that the species names in the records of A. P. Saunders actually refer to true examples. Saunders, at Hamilton College in Clinton, New York, undertook an extensive peony breeding program beginning in the early twentieth century (Hirshfeld 2003).

Will's annual peony seed list carefully distinguishes between wild-collected (herbaceous) species and varieties, seed from botanical gardens (especially in Georgia), and seed from plants in cultivation. The wild seed comes from places as far afield as Siberia (*Paeonia lactiflora*), the Altai (*P. anomala*), Ukraine (*P. triternata*), Georgia (*P. steveniana*), Turkey, Europe, and so on. He also supplies seed and plants of tree (shrub) peonies including hybrids of *P. rockii*. The specific epithet honors Joseph Rock, a U.S. plant hunter of an earlier generation who sent seed from plants growing in cultivation which may or may not have been examples of the true species. This neatly mirrors the present situation where almost all plants labeled *P. rockii* are actually cultivated hybrids (but none the worse for that). *Paeonia rockii* hybrids are becoming better known and more widely available, having been much sought-after but unavailable for many years. They are distinguished from the many well-known hybrids of *P. suffruticosa* by, among other things, a prominent purple-black blotch at the base of the petals and are in several ways a superior garden plant.

Dick and Judith Tyler operate Pine Knot Farm, a nursery specializing in hellebores in Clarksville, Virginia. They frequently make trips to nurseries in the United Kingdom and Europe, looking for hellebore stock, often visiting Will McLewin, whom they describe as "intense" when it comes to his passion for hellebores. Judith says:

> It would be hard to find a person with a more passionate dedication to a plant . . . than Will McLewin has to the genus *Helleborus*. As nursery owners, our job might be simpler if the extremely variable hellebore species were simply "lumped" into known groupings, but the pool of knowledge of the plant would be much smaller. Will's research has helped to sort out the muddle surrounding the green flowering species, and that information should help us in our attempts to duplicate the plant's natural growing conditions.

It is clear that no one has done more in the present day to elucidate the complex nomenclature of the genus *Helleborus* than Will McLewin. His field collections, many of which took place in the war-torn Balkans during the 1990s, coupled with genetic analyses, have improved the understanding of this previously misunderstood group of plants. Both the scientific community and keen gardeners have benefited from the fruits of his labor.

Will McLewin PHOTO BY BOBBY J. WARD

Phedar Nursery
Will McLewin
42 Bunkers Hill
Romiley
Stockport
Cheshire SK6 3DS
England
www.phedar.com

18

The China Connection
Piroche Plants—Bruce Rutherford & Pierre Piroche

During many years of horticultural involvement, I have witnessed hundreds of formal and informal garden talks and slide presentations covering a wide range of topics. The locations have ranged from large packed auditoriums to tiny, almost-empty classrooms. One memorable occasion was in August 1999 at a festive party in Portland, Oregon, at the home of Sean Hogan and Parker Sanderson (chapter 5), during the week of the annual Farwest Nursery Trade Show of the Oregon Association of Nurserymen. It was a small but diverse group of plant geeks, friends, and neighbors. Over wine and tasty hors d'oeuvres in the candle-lit "jungle" of the back garden, Bruce Rutherford of Piroche Plants (Pitt Meadows, British Columbia) showed slides and talked about his recent China trip. Among the images Bruce showed were some of the broadleaf evergreen shrubs and trees he had encountered, including the collection of members of the magnolia family (Magnoliaceae) at Kunming Botanical Garden and the flora of Lijiang, Zhongdian, and Bithai Lake in northern Yunnan. His impressive presentation attracted attention and hushed the crowd. That was my first introduction to Bruce and Piroche Plants.

Bruce is a native of Winnipeg, Manitoba ("that's a horticultural zone 3," he told me), and moved to British Columbia to work at the ski resorts. During the off season, he did landscaping and gradually developed a keener interest in plants, which included taking horticultural courses at area colleges. He joined Piroche Plants in 1994 and is the U.S. sales representative. Bruce lives on an acre (0.4 ha) in Mission, British Columbia, with long-time partner Stephan St-Germain. In this wooded, lightly shaded area they call Hammond Gardens, he revels in his passions of gardening, growing plants, photography, and writing.

In July 2000, I attended an annual meeting of the American Association of Botanical Gardens and Arboreta in Vancouver, British Columbia. Bruce, Sean, Peter Wharton (curator of the Asian garden at University of British Columbia Botanical Garden), and Chen Yue Kun (Piroche Plants and the Nanjing Botanical Garden) gave a formal presentation on Magnoliaceae. They discussed the diversity of the family, primarily in China, including endangered species and efforts to preserve them, newly described species, and plant nomenclature. They also talked about the introduction of new species into Western horticulture and hybridization possibilities. From the talk, I learned more about Piroche Plants and its relationship with the Nanjing Botanical Garden.

Piroche Plants was founded in 1987 by Pierre Piroche, a nurseryman from France, who had lived in British Columbia for years. He and his wife, Setsuko, have lived in and traveled to many different countries, including Setsuko's home of Japan. This wholesale nursery primarily grows landscape shrubs and trees for the Canadian and U.S. horticultural market. Pierre has long imported plants from many countries, including Japan. He developed connections with China soon after it opened its doors, knowing the vastness of its geography and flora.

Joint ventures with Western companies were very popular in China in the 1980s and into the 1990s when Pierre was introduced to He Shanan, the entrepreneurial director of the Nanjing Botanical Garden, who was hoping to develop ties with the West. The two created a joint venture in 1989 named Jiangsu Pipa Horticultural Services. Pierre invested time, money, equipment, and infrastructure as well as horticultural direction to this new Chinese nursery tucked away on the grounds of the botanical garden. The new company and Piroche Plants developed a joint strategy to collect seed and cuttings from the wild and from the garden, raise the plants in liner pots in Nanjing, and then export them to Canada.

Pierre requested that seed be collected from the northernmost and highest elevations possible within the range of each species to maximize hardiness. The program's ecological commitment requires a certain percentage of the stock be given back to the forest, planted by students through various reclamation programs. Also, Pipa allocates profits to plant conservation in the areas that the nursery searches for seeds. This unique enterprise with Piroche Plants was singled out as an example of an excellent biodiversity partnership at the World Summit on Sustainable Development in Johannesburg and Roodespoort (Bishop 2002).

Many of the plants that Piroche Plants sells are not entirely new to horticulture or gardens. What is different is that many are cold-hardy selections. The facility in Pitt Meadows consists of more than 25 acres (10 ha) of field and container production, 200 acres (80 ha) of tree fields, and a tissue-culture laboratory.

In general, Piroche Plants and Pipa are looking for overall improved forms and characteristics from new genetic material. The result is a line of plants introduced by Piroche Plants as the Wild Dragon series, currently consisting of seventy-five listings. Bruce told me about these introductions, some of which are marketed under the Canadian Ornamental Plant Foundation (COPF), a non-profit royalties collection agent operating for the nursery and floriculture industry, including plant breeders and growers.

I asked Bruce about working with Piroche Plants and Pipa. "It's an opportunity for such a fantastic international exchange," he said. He told me that many of the plants imported from Pipa are borderline hardy in the warmest parts of Canada, so the bulk of his clientele are in the United States. As an "insatiable plant geek," he has played a key role in marketing the large Piroche inventory to other plant aficionados.

Pat McCracken, a nurseryman in Zebulon, North Carolina, interested in the Magnoliaceae, says:

> Piroche has made many of these basically unknown species household names (especially on the West Coast). Garden centers in Portland and Seattle offer a wide range of evergreen *Magnolia* species (as well as *Michelia* and *Manglietia*) that would be completely unknown to the average gardener if Piroche wasn't there producing all these cool things. Piroche has made unusual plants *available*. That is a significant contribution.

Some of the nursery's introductions follow.

One family of plants that Piroche Plants has focused on is the Magnoliaceae, which consists of about a dozen genera and more than two hundred species of deciduous and evergreen shrubs and trees. The family is undergoing revision with some genera reduced and being subsumed into existing genera. For example, some authorities have reduced *Manglietia* to *Magnolia*, based on several lines of data, including DNA studies (Figlar 2001). The Magnoliaceae is among the oldest and most primitive of the Angiosperm families.

Manglietia insignis PHOTO BY TONY AVENT

Manglietia insignis (syn. *Magnolia insignia*) from south and central China is called the red lotus tree. It has large, evergreen leaves up to 10 inches (25 cm) long. Flower buds are produced in the fall and winter. The lightly fragrant flowers, 4 inches (10 cm) across, opening in the spring on the tips of shoots, are cup shaped with creamy white inner petals and pale pink to red outer petals. The fruit is elongated and dark purple-red. The tree will reach up to 40 feet (12 m) tall (perhaps taller) and 15 feet (4.5 m) wide. It grows in full sun to part shade and is hardy in USDA Zones 7 to 9. Piroche introduced the species in 1993 through Pipa, which had collected it in Sichuan. Bruce says the *M. insignis* has a wide but scattered native range in China, covering at least four provinces. Also, it is found in a variety of elevations from 3000 to 8000 feet (900–2400 m).

Another Piroche plant, a 1995 introduction, is *Magnolia chingii* (syn. *Manglietia chingii*). The flowers are creamy white

Magnolia chingii PHOTO BY TODD LASSEIGNE

and fragrant. This evergreen tree has large olive green leaves and its mature height is 35 feet (10 m).

I was introduced to *Distylium* at the JC Raulston Arboretum where *D. myricoides*, the myrtle leaf distylium, is planted in one of the new borders. It is a member of the witch-hazel family (Hamamelidaceae), which consists of many familiar garden trees and shrubs, including *Corylopsis, Fothergilla, Hamamelis, Liquidambar*, and *Loropetalum*. Less well known is *Distylium*, a genus of about a dozen evergreen shrubs and trees.

Piroche Plants introduced *Distylium racemosum*, a native of southwest Japan. In cultivation, it is a medium-sized shrub with glossy, leathery leaves up to 5 inches (12.5 cm) long. The red flowers, which have no petals, are produced in axillary racemes during early spring, and the cinnamon-colored fruit develops during the summer. In the wild *D. racemosum* will grow into a tree up to 50 feet (15 m) tall with a trunk diameter of 48 inches (122 cm). Called the isu tree, it is used for furniture because it has dense, lustrous wood, making it excellent for woodworking.

Distylium myricoides 'Lucky Charm' is another of the Wild Dragon series. Bruce says he thinks it deserves wider use in the landscape.

A close relative of *Distylium* is *Loropetalum* (Hamamelidaceae), a genus that

Distylium myricoides 'Lucky Charm' PHOTO BY TODD LASSEIGNE

made a splash on the horticultural scene in the early 1990s. In the southern United States where I live, it has become very popular, among the "top ten" plant introductions during the 1990s (Dirr 2002). Native to China, this evergreen shrub has small attractive leaves that vary from green to burgundy to purple. The branches tend to layer, one over the over, giving a striking appearance. The flowers, spiderlike and similar to those of witch-hazel, are pink to white, produced in the spring, and often in the summer with a second flush of growth. It is a fairly fast growing plant in the U.S. Southeast, achieving 6 feet (1.8 m) in a couple of growing seasons. *Loropetalum chinense* 'Fire Dance' produces hot-pink flowers against burgundy-red leaves. *Loropetalum chinense* 'Pipa's Red' is a low, spreading form with longer, narrower, and more pointed leaves, according to Bruce. The leaf color is also a rich burgundy.

Many consider *Nandina* (Berberidaceae) a run-of-the mill plant, one to be stuck in an uninteresting part of the garden, only to be further neglected while it quietly provides serviceability for years. Called heavenly bamboo, it was a plant I overlooked for years till I happened upon the large collection at the JC Raulston Arboretum. The common form of *N. domestica*, the only species in the genus, produces white flowers in the spring and red fruit in the autumn. Its tripinnately compound leaves are another attractive feature.

Loropetalum chinense 'Fire Dance' PHOTO BY TODD LASSEIGNE

Nandina domestica var. *leucocarpa*, a 1995 introduction, has cream to yellow fruit. Bruce says that it produces a plant true from seed. It grows to a height of nearly 6 feet (1.8 m). and has bright, yellow-green foliage.

Ilex (Aquifoliaceae) is a large genus of trees and shrubs that consists of deciduous and evergreen species, whose male and female flowers are usually borne on separate plants (dioecious). *Ilex latifolia* is native to China and Japan. 'Purple Power', a female selection of the species, grows to a height of 30 feet (9 m). It has extremely large, dark leaves up to 8 inches (20 cm) long and 3 inches (7.5 cm) wide and the teeth along the margin of leaves are widely spaced. The leaf petioles are bright purple. This holly produces greenish-yellow flowers in late spring and orange-red berries.

The banana shrub, *Michelia figo*, used to be commonly grown in the U.S. Southeast, but its use in the garden is now rare. Many who grew it considered it a type of *Magnolia*, and indeed, it formerly was classified as *Magnolia fuscata*. Southern gardener Felder Rushing (Jackson, Mississippi) says that when the banana shrub blooms and you become bathed in its heady fragrance of overripe bananas, "it's time to strip off socks and shoes and go barefoot" because summer is on its way (Bender and Rushing 1993). Today, some authorities have reduced *Michelia* back to *Magnolia*.

Michelias are native to China and are evergreen members of the Magnoliaceae. Piroche Plants has promoted several of the approximately forty-five

Nandina domestica var. *leucocarpa* PHOTO BY BOBBY J. WARD

known species. *Michelia maudiae*, a 1993 introduction, is a small tree that reaches 30 feet (9 m). It has silvery green leaves up to 7 inches (17.5 cm) long. The cupped flowers, produced in late winter, are 6 inches (15 cm) across and are produced in leaf axils. Each flower has nine to thirteen pure white, fragrant petals. According to Bruce, flower size is somewhat variable.

I am partial to *Edgeworthia chrysantha*, the paper bush, a gift to me from Sean Hogan. It is a plant that I admire year-round in my garden. Even before frost and leaf drop, the silvery yellow buds of *E. chrysantha* form by midautumn, lasting throughout the winter and opening in February with yellow, *Daphne*-like, tubular blossoms. In the winter the leaf scars and the gray-cinnamon-colored bark on the bare plant provide additional ornamental features. This stocky plant grows to 6 feet (1.8 m) tall and about 4 feet (1.2 m) wide with flexible branches. The deciduous leaves are 6 inches (15 cm) long, deep green above, and gray-green beneath. The species is a member of the daphne family (Thymelaceae) and native to China, but was introduced to Japan.

Edgeworthia chrysantha 'Gold Rush' is a selection with fragrant flowers that hang in terminal clusters. The flowers are covered in silky hairs which are responsible for the silvery white color when in bud. *Edgeworthia chrysantha* 'Rubra', a 1996 introduction, is similar to 'Gold Rush', except that it has smaller leaves and flowers that are bright red. 'Rubra' is sometimes listed as a form of *E. papyrifera*, currently an invalid name.

Michelia maudiae PHOTO BY BRUCE RUTHERFORD

The genus is named for Michael Pakenham Edgeworth (1812–1881), an amateur botanist who collected plants in India.

Melliodendron is a member of the Styracaceae, a family of eleven genera, the most well known of which is *Styrax*. *Melliodendron xylocarpum*, a 1994 selection and introduction by Piroche Plants, is native to south and central China. This deciduous-leaved tree grows to 40 feet (12 m) or more tall. Its leaves are bright green and up to 6 inches (15 cm) long. It produces single pink flowers, 2–3 inches (5–7.5 cm) across, in axillary corymbs, and they hang facing downward. When the fruit are formed, they look like small acorns. Bruce says it is a vigorous grower

Edgeworthia chrysantha 'Rubra' PHOTO BY TODD LASSEIGNE

and hardy to USDA Zone 7; in warmer zones it tends to remain evergreen.

Most of the dozen or so recognized species of *Bergenia* (Saxifragaceae) originate in temperate areas of east and central Asia (Upson 2001). *Bergenia emeiensis* was collected on Emei Shan (Sichuan) by Japanese botanist Mikinori Ogisu. It had been collected fifty years earlier, but was not described as a new species till 1988 (van der Werff 1999). In its native habitat it grows in woodland, shaded slopes, and rocky crevices. It has glossy, evergreen, basal foliage and, according to Tony Avent (Raleigh, North Carolina), who grows the species, it is heat tolerant in his woodland garden in the U.S. Southeast (unlike most bergenias). It blooms in very early spring with a 1-foot (0.3-m) tall spike (cyme).

Bergenia emeiensis 'Snow Chimes' is a large clone up to 20 inches (50 cm) tall and up to 40 inches (100 cm) wide. It has

Melliodendron xylocarpum PHOTO BY BRUCE RUTHERFORD

Bergenia emeiensis 'Snow Chimes' PHOTO BY BRUCE RUTHERFORD

large white to apricot-pink flowers, which fade to pink. They are sweetly scented, bell shaped, and produced over a long period, according to Bruce. The leaves of this evergreen plant turn reddish in winter.

As bergenias hybridize readily in cultivation, deliberate breeding programs have been undertaken. Crosses involving *Bergenia emeiensis* produce spectacular cultivars.

Piroche Plants's unique relationship with the fledgling Chinese nursery industry puts it in a rather unique position in Western horticulture. This partnership has enabled it to introduce a number of exceptional plants, particularly members of the Magnoliaceae, to Canadian and American consumers.

Bruce Rutherford and Pierre Piroche
Piroche Plants
20542 McNeil Road
Pitt Meadows,
British Columbia V3Y 1Z1
Canada
www. pirocheplants.com

Bruce Rutherford PHOTO BY BOBBY J. WARD

19

Hosta La Vista, Baby

Plant Delights Nursery—Tony Avent

Tony Avent has more fun with plants than most people, and his exhilaration is infectious. For ten years he and his spouse, Michelle, have operated the aptly named Plant Delights Nursery, a mail-order nursery south of Raleigh, North Carolina. To a public ever-demanding of new material for diversity in the landscape, Tony has responded with intelligence, passion, and humor, and, as a result, his nursery has become a fount of new garden plants. His collecting trips to Mexico, China, Korea, and Texas, his backyard excursions for native plants in the U.S. Southeast, and his own breeding programs have provided new fodder for testing, selecting, and introducing desirable plants.

Tony earned a degree in horticultural science from North Carolina State University. There he met and studied under J. C. Raulston, teacher, mentor, and director of the university arboretum. Upon graduation, Tony took a job as landscape director and horticulturist at the North Carolina State Fairgrounds, a unique opportunity that gave him the freedom to dress up the staid old grounds with agaves, yuccas, cactus, bananas, palms, a rock garden, and more. The site was widely admired by annual fair goers and weekend flea market visitors. During this time Tony became a volunteer curator for the arboretum's shade house, and with J. C.'s encouragement, took cuttings from the arboretum to try at the fairgrounds. During the sixteen years he stayed at the fairgrounds, he also managed to start a small private nursery on the side, opening Plant Delights Nursery in 1991. He shared his horticultural and gardening skills during this period by writing a weekly gardening column for the *News & Observer* (Raleigh, North Carolina) from which he dispensed sage advice and accurate information peppered with humor.

Tony's horticultural interests extend widely, from perennials and ground covers to desert succulents, rock garden plants, and woody plants. He has a singular passion for hostas, which he has been growing since he was an adolescent in Raleigh. In a breeding program launched in the 1980s, he has enhanced the hosta cultivar palette with such whimsical entries as *Hosta* 'Bubba', 'Red Neck Heaven', 'Tattoo', and 'Out House Delight'. The latter, referred to in his 1998 catalog as the "ugliest hosta in the history of hostas," sold initially for two hundred dollars each with scores of takers. His much-anticipated annual catalog has delightful descriptions, frequently imbued with humor as well as unbridled exuberance.

Tony has turned a tobacco field in southern Wake County, North Carolina, into a double bounty: on the one hand, Plant Delights Nursery; on the other, the Juniper Level Botanic Garden, featuring more than twelve thousand plants. Juniper Level serves as a display area and laboratory for plants he loves which, if you listen carefully to Tony, are just about any plants that will tolerate hot, wet summers and cool, wet winters in USDA Zone 7. A major aspect of the garden is the evaluation of cold tolerance—extending the range of tropical exotics, such as palms and aroids.

I have visited Tony's nursery and garden many times, often on plant sales days when the crowds are double parked along the rural road because his parking lots are full. He rarely fails to stop to talk to visitors, asking where they are from, or answering for the tenth time that morning which colocosias are the hardiest. On many of those occasions he has taken me aside to see a "private" stash of new plants, or an "amazing" color on a rain lily in bloom. It is amusing to overhear Tony in the garden with visitors describing plants; "amazing," "fantastic," and "great" are his mantra.

Tony's contagious enthusiasm spreads outside the boundaries of the U.S. Southeast. His horticultural style embodies a rare zeal for enriching our gardens, which puts him in ever-increasing demand as a speaker around North America.

Ken Druse (1996) has written: "Tony Avent searches for native plants that have been overlooked as garden possibilities." Tony's version is more direct: "I feel we need to encourage people to have more fun in their gardens!"

The list of Tony's plant introductions and the plants named by his nursery is ever-growing, and Tony's keen eye is a testament to genius and talent. A few of the plants that he has promoted and/or introduced follow.

Given his passion for hostas, it is not surprising that Tony has introduced a selection called *Hosta* 'Obsession'. Formerly a member of the lily family (Liliaceae) but now Hostaceae, the plantain lily or hosta is native to China, Japan, and Korea. There are about sixty species of this shade-loving plant, but there are thousands of cultivars and selections, many with distinctive foliage markings, which are the primary horticultural attribute.

Plant Delights's hosta introductions are of three types: selections from wild-collected seed, mutations or sports, and hybrids. The hosta gene pool and thus genetic diversity is maintained by introducing selfed plants from seed collected in nongarden settings throughout the plant's natural geographical range. Two forms of *Hosta venusta* resulted from Tony's trip to Korea in 1997. Collected with Darrell Probst of Massachusetts on Cheju Island at an elevation of about 2500 feet (750 m), one of these selections produces a 10-inch (25-cm) wide clump while the other produces larger leaves—both differing from the "standard" *H. venusta* type.

Tony also introduced a selection of *Hosta capitata* that develops 2-foot (0.6-m) wide clumps of long green foliage. He found seeds on Mount Chiri, Korea, from plants growing in full sun among daylilies.

Hosta 'Obsession' PHOTO BY TONY AVENT

Hosta 'Tattoo' (PP 11,603) and *H.* 'Obsession' (both 1998 introductions) are sports, the term for a plant exhibiting abnormal variation or departure from the parent stock or type in some respect, particularly in form or color. *Hosta* 'Tattoo' is a sport of *H.* 'Little Aurora' and presents rounded, brightly gold leaves surrounded by a wide green border and centered with a green, maple leaf "tattoo." *Hosta* 'Obsession', a sport of *H.* 'Sparkling Burgundy', is distinctive for its dark green leaves "with a near-black jagged border pattern."

Tony's goal in hybridizng hostas is to produce truly distinctive forms that are worthy of naming, and perhaps registering, from cross-fertilization of two taxa. He looks for new color forms and for plants that emerge later in the spring, thus avoiding frost damage, for example. He has proposed, perhaps in jest, a 10-foot (3-m) rule to hosta hybridizers: if you cannot recognize a new hosta by name from 10 feet away, that hosta should not be saved.

Hosta 'Carolina Sunshine', a 2001 introduction, is vigorous growing with long dark green, glossy leaves that have a butterscotch-yellow border. The plant, which may grow into a 40-inch (100-cm) wide clump, is a hybrid of *H.* 'Swoosh' and *H. tibae*, the latter native to the mountain flanks of Nagasaki Prefecture, Japan.

As Nature has shortchanged the plant kingdom, Tony remarks, when it comes to the color blue, he has sought to remedy this by inducing "Prozac moments of peacefulness" with *Hosta* 'Elvis Lives' (1990), a breakthrough cross that combined the blue color of *H.* 'Peter Pan' and the long, narrow leaves of *H.*

Hosta 'Tattoo' PHOTO BY TONY AVENT

'Green Fountain' to produce a plant with "wavy, tapered leaves of blue suede"—the consummate landscape plant for Graceland Mansion.

Two other hybrid introductions, popular with hosta addicts or funkiaphiles (the root is an old name for hosta), are *Hosta* 'Dixie Chick' and *H.* 'Potomac Pride'. The former is a small plant with thick, glossy, cream-edged leaves, and the latter consists of large, shiny green-black leaves and smallish, spiderlike flowers.

Hosta 'Abba Dabba Do' is a 1993 Plant Delights introduction. It has large pointed leaves with a yellow edge that widens as the plant grows older. Tony crossed *H. yingeri*, collected in Korea by Barry Yinger of Pennsylvania, and *H.* 'Golden Scepter' to obtain a hosta with glossy chartreuse leaves topped in mid-summer by starlike purple flowers. Tony named the plant *H.* 'Sweet Tater Pie' and introduced it in 1993.

Nerium oleander (Apocynaceae) is an evergreen shrub native to the Middle East and Asia and it is generally not cold hardy. In 2001 Plant Delights Nursery introduced *N. oleander* "Hardy Double Yellow" form, a hardy oleander, although Tony had shared cuttings of it since he found the plant in 1985. After Raleigh's 1985 "freeze-from-hell" in which the thermometer dropped to −9°F (−23°C), Tony said:

> I began a search in our local area for oleanders that had survived our killer freeze . . . there weren't many. One of the plants that I found was this form which, although burned from the cold, re-sprouted with great vigor. Atop the 6-foot (1.8-m) tall bushes are dozens of double light yellow flowers in late summer.

This form grows in sun to part shade, blooms in early summer, and provides repeat blooms sporadically. Once established, it requires little watering and easily propagates by cuttings. (All parts of the plant are poisonous.)

One of the plants that all gardeners and home owners can grow even in the absence of a green thumb ("it's a brown-thumb plant," Tony says) is the cast iron plant, *Aspidistra elatior* (Convallariaceae), an evergreen from eastern Asia. The plant produces stout rhizomes and bright, lustrous, ovate to lanceolate leaves that are deep green. Cast iron plants were popular house plants in the late nineteenth century and were able to withstand long periods of neglect and low-light levels (the perfect bar plant for watering with beer dregs). The authority on the English lan-

Nerium oleander "Hardy Double Yellow" PHOTO BY TONY AVENT

guage, the *Oxford English Dictionary*, says of the aspidistra that it is "frequently grown as a pot-plant, and often regarded as a symbol of dull middle-class respectability." Undaunted by this bit of across-the-ocean condescension, Plant Delights Nursery has introduced several selections that Jim Waddick (Kansas City, Missouri) made from wild-collected plants and seed from China. The forms, probably of *A. typica*, were found in Qing Cheng San Mountains in 1985 by Waddick and include 'China Moon,' 'China Star', and 'China Sun'—all spattered with pale yellow speckling and "freckles."

Other introductions are *Aspidistra caespitosa* 'Jade Ribbons' and *A. linearifolia* 'Leopard', the latter a form that grows almost to 3 feet (0.9 m) tall with 0.5-inch (1.25-cm) wide foliage. They are generally hardy in USDA Zones 8 to 10, preferring hot summers to thrive well.

Canna or canna lilies (Cannaceae) are New World natives of warm climates primarily distributed in Central and South America, the West Indies, and the U.S. Southeast. In some areas, particularly in the subtropics, they have become naturalized. Though introduced to Europe in the early seventeenth century from the West Indies, cannas did not become popular till the mid-nineteenth century. By the end of that century they had became valuable for their bold, broad tropical-looking foliage in summer beds.

Canna 'Pink Sunburst', introduced in 1996, was acquired by Tony from Sunburst Bulbs in South Africa; it has salmon-pink flowers and variegated leaves (the variegation has a pinkish background hue). According to Tony, it "is the hottest thing since summertime in the South." *Canna* 'Kansas City' is a smallish plant with yellow-variegated leaves (actually subtle green on green), a sport discovered by Jim Waddick. It produces butter-colored flowers and reaches a height of 4 feet (1.2 m). *Canna* 'Australia' (syn. *Canna* 'Feuerzauber'), from canna aficionado and guru Johnnie Johnson (Kentucky) via New Zealand, presents burgundy-black foliage with a satiny sheen and bright red flowers. It may attain a height of 5 feet (1.5 m) and is "a true stunner."

Vinca minor 'Illumination' (PP 12,132) is a groundcover periwinkle with a bright stable variegation. It was found by Christy Hensler of the Rock Garden Nursery, near Spokane, Washington. Christy recalls finding it growing in a bed of common *V. minor* when she was taking divisions to pot for 1995 spring bedding plant sales. Christy says (Hensler 2003):

> When I first saw it, it was little more than an inch [2.5 cm] in height but beautifully brilliant and unlike anything I'd ever seen in a *V. minor*. Needless to say, all work stopped till it was safely removed from the mother and replanted to its own area

Christy passed it along to Tony for testing and it was introduced through Plant Delights Nursery in 2001. *Vinca minor* 'Illumination' (Apocynaceae, or dogbane family) boasts brilliant golden leaves with dark green borders. It blooms in late spring with typical pinwheel-shaped blue-lavender flowers. Maximum plant

Canna 'Pink Sunburst' PHOTO BY TONY AVENT

height is 6 inches (15 cm); a single plant will spread up to about 4 feet (1.2 m). It is not so vigorous as the normal green form.

The Mexican yellow-eyed grass, *Sisyrinchium tinctorium* 'Puerto Yellow', was collected in 1994 by Tony on a trip to Mexico with Carl Schoenfeld of Yucca Do Nursery and John Fairey of Peckerwood Garden. It was found at an elevation of 1800 feet (550 m) near Puerto Purificación, a region on the border of Tamaulipas and Nuevo León. 'Puerto Yellow' is a member of the Iridaceae and thus has iris-like foliage and produces large bright yellow flowers from early spring to early summer. In a greenhouse it may begin blooming as early as January. Tony has found that it multiplies rapidly, forming a nicely compact plant to 18 inches (45 cm) wide and about 12 inches (30 cm) tall. The flowers, about 0.75 inch (1.9 cm) across, are held above the foliage. Although the plant is from Mexico, Tony has found it hardy to 0°F (−18°C).

Grasses are now being used increasingly in the landscape, thanks to passionate promotion by nurseries such as Kurt Bluemel (Baldwin, Maryland) and Greenlee (John Greenlee of Pomona, California) and by writers and designers such as Rick Darke (Landenberg, Pennsylvania). Plants in our gardens often take roundabout, sometimes winding routes before their horticultural potential is fully recognized.

Typical, perhaps, is the journey of *Pennisetum orientale* 'Tall Tails' (Poaceae),

Vinca minor 'Illumination' PHOTO BY TONY AVENT

the giant fountain grass, which Tony acquired from John Hoffman of Hoffman Nursery in Rougemount, North Carolina. Hoffman obtained his seeds from Mark Woods (Woods Nursery in Pennsylvania), who had received the seed from a USDA seed bank. It was a Pakistani collection being evaluated for forage potential. It took Tony's keen eye, however, to recognize the garden possibilities for this plant. Tony named and introduced it in 1998. *Pennisetum* 'Tall Tails' is a dense clumpformer with tan to pink fluffy plumes that may be 9 feet (2.7 m) tall. Its leaves are green to gray-green.

The blue love grass, *Eragrostis elliottii*, is another Plant Delights's introduction. In typical exuberance Tony describes this plant as the "most exciting native plant" that he has found in the last few years.

Sisyrinchium tinctorium 'Puerto Yellow' PHOTO BY TONY AVENT

Pennisetum orientale 'Tall Tails' PHOTO BY TONY AVENT

While driving in southern Georgia in early summer, Tony spotted the plant on a dry hillside, collected a tiny division, and took it to his garden at Juniper Level. There it grew into a 3-foot (0.9-cm) wide clump of narrow powder blue foliage, producing sturdy plumes that are still superb in the autumn.

The rush family (Juncaceae) includes about 225 species of perennial rhizomatous, grasslike plants that frequent low wet places. While most *Juncus* species produce cylindrical leaves that are erect and upright, *J. inflexus* 'Lovesick Blues' is strongly weeping, with steely blue foliage. It forms a mound about 3 feet (0.9 m) wide and 12 inches (30 cm) tall. This rush was a chance discovery as a seedling in the bog garden at Plant Delights Nursery. Tony finds that it does well in a bog or moist area of the garden.

Tony has gone through a baptisia phase, calling this eastern U.S. native "redneck lupine." Giving up on attempts with "real" lupines because they can not tolerate the North Carolina summer heat and high nighttime temperatures, he found surprises in growing the false indigo or *Baptisia* (Fabaceae). It is winter hardy to USDA Zone 5, can take drought and heat, and comes in a range of colors from near purple to blue, creamy white to bright yellow. He has promoted *B. australis* var. *minor*, generally overlooked by other nurseries, and *B.* 'Carolina Moonlight', an introduction of Rob Gardner of the North Carolina Botanical Garden (Chapel Hill). A hybrid of *B. sphaerocarpa* and *B. alba*, *B.* 'Carolina Moonlight' produces a 3-foot (0.9-m) wide plant with blue-green foliage and spikes of butter yellow flowers that are 18 inches (45 cm) long.

Baptisia sphaerocarpa, the yellow false indigo, is also promoted by Tony. A collection from Texas, this species produces yellow flowers and blue-green leaves in clumps 18 inches (45 cm) wide. Tony says it is hard to find a plant with more flower power. He says that in the wild a stand of these flowers looks like a "glowing mass of lit candles." The seed pod is distinct in that it is round and marble sized, not elongated and finger shaped as with most other species of baptisias.

Tony calls the aroid family "plants that only a mother could love" as some of them are sinister looking and go by such unappealing names as voodoo lily, dead horse arum, and green dragon. There are about thirty-two hundred species of aroids, many having been discovered since the

Juncus inflexus 'Lovesick Blues' in foreground PHOTO
BY TONY AVENT

1980s in areas formerly closed to plant explorations, such as Vietnam and Laos. Tony became interested in this vast group of plants, which includes relatives of jack-in-the-pulpit, in the early 1990s.

Many of the various species of *Amorphophallus* that Tony has promoted form giant underground tubers and produce huge flowers with a strong odor, attracting insects for pollination. He lists in his catalog *A. bulbifer*, *A. kiusianus*, *A. konjac*, and *A. konjac* 'Pinto', the latter a dwarf, rock garden–sized plant that grows to a mere 3 inches (7.5 cm) tall. The typical form of *A. konjac* grows to 60 inches (150 cm) tall. Tony currently grows seventy species, making his collection one of the top three in the world.

Tony also promotes *Sauromatum venosum* (syn. *S. guttatum*) or voodoo lily, *Arisarum proboscideum* or mouse plant, and several *Arisaema* species. Of the arisaemas, he writes a characteristically witty description (Avent 1997):

> If you are the voyeuristic type, then you will love arisaemas. Arisaema plants are one of the more unique members of the plant kingdom. Some plants are male, some are female, some are both, and some change back and forth (paradioecious). As a general rule, arisaemas are male when young, then when they build up enough energy to have babies, they switch and become female. The year after giving birth (fruiting), they will often revert back to being male.

Members of the aroid family (Araceae) have gotten a boost with the publication of a second edition of *Aroids: Plants of the Arum Family* (Bown 2000) and the publication of *The Genus Arisaema* (Gusman and Gusman 2002), about one of the popular members of the family.

Tony introduced *Eucomis comosa* 'Sparkling Burgundy' to the gardening public in 1997. The pineapple lily, as it is known, has dramatic purple foliage and grows to at least 20 inches (50 cm) tall. *Eucomis* is native to South Africa and a member of the Liliaceae (syn. Hyacinthaceae). Its name is from Greek meaning "fair headed" or "fair haired," an allusion to the bracts or crown of leaves above the inflorescence. Tony selected 'Sparkling Burgundy' in 1983 from seedlings he grew from Thompson and Morgan seed, having evaluated

Eucomis comosa 'Sparkling Burgundy' PHOTO BY TONY AVENT

Punica granatum 'State Fair' PHOTO BY TONY AVENT

it for fourteen years before its introduction. Visitors to the JC Raulston Arboretum in Raleigh, North Carolina, have raved over this plant in the perennial border for years.

The pomegranate's common name literally means, an "apple with many grains or seeds." The delicious fleshy fruit of *Punica granatum* (Punicaceae) can be boiled to make grenadine, a syrup or cordial. Although pomegranates are native from Turkey to the western Himalaya, they have become widely naturalized in the Mediterranean region. *Punica granatum* 'State Fair' is a hardy selection festooned with scores of tubular orange flowers. It later becomes loaded with fruit. The plant grows to a height of 5 feet (1.5 m) and is completely hardy to at least USDA Zone 7. Tony discovered this pomegranate among plants he grew from seeds. The cultivar name derives from the North Carolina State Fair Grounds, where Tony formerly worked.

Relying on both Tony's own collections and his network of plant geeks, Plant Delights Nursery has become a major conduit for new plants in the American nursery industry.

Tony Avent PHOTO BY BOBBY J. WARD

Tony Avent
Plant Delights Nursery
9241 Sauls Road
Raleigh, NC 27603
United States
www.plantdelights.com

20

The Eden That Is Quarryhill

Quarryhill Botanical Garden &
Saratoga Horticultural Research Foundation—W. A. McNamara

I had never seen Buddhist prayer flags till I visited Quarryhill Botanical Garden at Glen Ellen in California's Sonoma Valley. On a golf cart tour of the gardens, W. A. "Bill" McNamara, the garden's horticulturist and director, drove me to an overlook and a remarkable view of the gardens below, while the prayer flags fluttered nearby from a gentle breeze. The flags, said to bring happiness, longevity, and prosperity, pay homage to the countries from which many of the garden's plants came.

Quarryhill Botanical Garden was founded in 1987 by Jane Davenport Jansen, on 20 acres (8 ha) of garden space on hillsides above vineyards and among old stone quarries. Her mission was to advance the conservation, study, and cultivation of temperate plants from Asia. Jansen, who died in 2000, had originally planned a nursery on the site, but learning of the need to conserve Asian plants, changed her plans (Sanchez 1998). Quarryhill today holds one of North America's largest collections of Asian woody plants, whose provenance (wild source) is scientifically documented. The plants here are not merely of garden, arboretum, or nursery stock, generations removed from their original source, but newly collected by Quarryhill staff and others, primarily from China, Japan, India, and Nepal. It is Quarryhill's way of conserving genetic pools from native populations being threatened and decimated by logging, farming, roads, and other human pressures.

Bill says (Cascorbi 1995):

> The best thing for the threatened species is to preserve them in their native habitat, but in many cases this is not going to work. . . . there's not much time left for these plants [as] these habitats don't recover, in these steep forests.

Bill's hope is that "educational programs can be the route to help North American, European, and other gardeners to learn how to treat habitats with greater respect." He is optimistic that attempts at reforestation will continue, if not hampered by uncontrolled grazing (Sanchez 1998). Bill's hope is that the plants can be saved and reintroduced into their native habitats, but fears that it may be too late in some areas.

A native of Indiana, Bill was raised in Palo Alto, California. He majored in English at the University of California at Berkeley, where he worked part-time at local plant nurseries and continued developing his horticultural knowledge. After graduation and some international travel, he settled in Sonoma Valley in 1976 to start a family and begin a landscaping business. In 1985, he was hired to do some plantings at Jansen's home and for Roger Warner, the designer of the Glen Ellen garden. This led to further work there and, when Warner left Jansen's employment in 1987, she hired Bill as Quarryhill's assistant director (he became director in 1994). The staff has grown to ten people and includes a head of horticulture and a nursery manager, who propagates seeds and the occasional cuttings obtained from expeditions.

The first collecting expedition took place in the fall 1987 with Warner, Charles Howick of Howick Arboretum (Howick Hall Gardens, Northumberland), and Bill (who had not yet become a staff member at Quarryhill) as he was knowledgeable about plant taxonomy (Baumann 1995). The team went to Japan to the northern island of Hokkaido and the large, central island of Honshu. They brought back 474 accessions of seeds and cuttings, including *Acer buergerianum*, *A. cissifolium*, *Actinidia kolomikta*, *Rhus chinensis*, and *Ilex macropoda* f. *pseudomacropoda*. The resulting first young plants were placed in the ground in 1990.

Fueled by the success of this first trip, Bill went the following year to Sichuan (China). The expedition included botanists and horticulturists from the Royal Botanic Gardens, Kew, who wanted to reestablish ties with Chinese scientists. Aided by these annual expeditions, Quarryhill's collection has grown to well over twenty thousand accessions representing 425 genera.

Most of Quarryhill's collecting trips have been to China because so many species there are under pressure (some estimates place the total number of plants at thirty-one thousand species compared to eighteen thousand in North America, excluding Mexico). The expeditions occur in the fall of the year, but a few spring trips are planned to scout out potential sites, with a return in the fall to collect seeds and, sometimes, cuttings. Quarryhill has a partnership with the Chinese Academy of Sciences in Chengdu (Sichuan), whose staff and scientists host the group, assist in local arrangements, collecting, and taxonomy of plants. Field notes and seeds are shared equally by all collecting parties. Dried plant (herbarium) specimens are deposited at the Chinese Academy of Sciences, the California Academy of Sciences, and the Royal Botanic Gardens, Kew.

Bill says he has experienced many horticultural thrills in his travels for Quarryhill. A memorable one was in Modaoqi to the site of the original specimen (type tree) of the famed dawn redwood, *Metasequoia glyptostroboides*, a "living fossil" thought to have been extinct for five million years, but re-discovered in 1941. Bill's visit to the site in 1996 completed a connection, since Quarryhill has a single *M. glyptostroboides* obtained as a seedling from the University of California at Berkeley from the type specimen. Another thrill came in 1988 when Bill saw in China the presumed parent of modern tea roses, *Rosa chinensis* f.

spontanea, which had been rediscovered in 1983 by Japanese botanist Mikinori Ogisu.

Arrangements with the Chinese and others preclude Bill from directly growing plants for commercial trade (Fernandez 1996); however, Quarryhill has an arrangement with Saratoga Horticultural Research Foundation (San Martin, California), a nonprofit whose mission is to research, propagate, and introduce "new" and improved plants suitable for landscaping in California's Mediterranean climate. Bill sends along plants for testing and those deemed potentially good are passed on to growers who further propagate quantities for nurseries and landscapers. Rob de Bree, manager at Saratoga, told me that the partnership with Bill is a compatible relationship. "In an era where funding is tight, it is good to have partners like Quarryhill," he said.

Bill is considering expanding beyond the Saratoga relationship to include nurseries in the propagation and distribution of some of its holdings for wholesale and retail, particularly those plants from the first five years of the expeditions. These plants have had sufficient time to be monitored for any problems including invasiveness, a troubling aspect of contemporary plant hunting that is Bill's greatest concern for any Quarryhill introduction.

Robert E. Lyons, director of the JC Raulston Arboretum (Raleigh, North Carolina), has visited Quarryhill. He says:

> One can only wonder about the horticultural potential yet to be tapped within its collections. Bill McNamara has the responsibility for maintaining and enriching the collections of this West Coast gem and his influence is clear and widespread. Those of us who embrace the development of new landscape plants are appreciative of Bill's knowledge, dedication, and commitment.

Some of the plants that Bill has passed on to Saratoga for evaluation and some that are "in the pipeline" for evaluation by other nurseries include the following.

Illicium (Illiciaceae), the only genus in the family, consists of about forty-five species of shrubs to small trees in central to eastern Asia and in the U.S. Southeast, and northern Mexico. The leaves are glabrous, evergreen, and usually fragrant.

Illicium anisatum, or Japanese anise, was used historically in China as an insecticidal fumigant as its seeds are toxic. Its fragrant branches have been long used to decorate Buddhist graves.

Illicium simonsii grows to 10 feet (3 m) tall and has clusters of pale yellow flowers. I saw it coming into bloom when I visited Quarryhill and I have not forgotten the image of it. Bill says he first saw the plant in 1990 in southern Sichuan and northern Yunnan, identifying it with help from colleagues as *I. yunnanense*. Later botanists confirmed the identify as *I. simonsii*. Subsequently, they found large stands from which they were able to collect seeds. At Quarryhill the plants begin blooming in February and continue through March, providing a heavy

Magnolia-like fragrance (McNamara 2001). Even at temperatures of 18°F (−8°C), they continue to grow and thrive, though Bill says he thinks they would do better in light shade. Those in the garden have grown 8 feet (2.4 m) in seven years (McNamara 2001).

Schima is a genus in the camellia family (Theaceae), native from India to Southeast Asia. Once considered to be composed of several species, it now is thought to be a single species with highly variable forms, according to Bill's review of several keys and manuals.

Schima wallichii is an evergreen tree attaining a maximum height of 130 feet (40 m) (McNamara 1999). The leaves are elliptical, 3–10 inches (7.5–25 cm) long, with shallow-toothed margins. Bill believes he has two forms at Quarryhill. One form has blue-green foliage with entire leaves. The other has dark green leaves and toothed margins. Bill says that the creamy white flowers, 2.5 inches (6 cm) across, are showy and fragrant, having developed from white buds, not pink as he has seen referenced. At Quarryhill the species produces flowers in late summer and into fall.

According to Mabberley (1987), *Schima wallichii* is used as construction timber and has become an important tree for reforestation in parts of Southeast Asia. The genus name is believed to be derived from Greek *skiasma*, "shelter" or "shadow," an allusion to the tree's leafy, thick crown. Bill has collected *Schima* on

Illicium simonsii PHOTO BY BOBBY J. WARD

three expeditions, twice in Sichuan and once in Nepal. He says that in Nepal the bark is used in fighting intestinal worms and its leaves and roots for fever relief.

Michelia, a genus closely related to *Magnolia* (Magnoliaceae), consists of about forty-five species of primarily evergreen shrubs and trees. Some authorities assign it to *Magnolia*. It is distributed in tropical and subtropical Asia, including Japan.

Seeds of *Michelia compressa* were collected by Bill and his team on Shikoku Island (Japan) in 1989. The plant grows to 50 feet (15 m) and has fragrant flowers that are 2 inches (5 cm) across, white and tinged purple. Bill recalls looking a long time for the plant on Shikoku and having trouble locating it till he looked down and realized he was walking on its seeds that had fallen to the ground. Because of their origin, most michelias are tender (USDA Zone 9 or 10). One of the hardiest is *M. doltsopa* (Zone 9), but Bill believes *M. compressa* will prove even hardier.

In India, michelia are cultivated for the fragrant oil derived from the blossom to use in perfumes and cosmetics. Bill says he has seen vendors selling flowers of *Michelia* on the streets in China as a fragrance for automobiles. He is not sure of the species. The genus is named for Pietro Antonio Michele, an eighteenth-century Italian botanist.

The genus *Ilex* (Aquifoliaceae), known as holly, has at least four hundred species of trees and shrubs that may be deciduous or evergreen. The male and female flowers usually occur on separate trees. *Ilex dimorphophylla*, the Okinawan

Schima wallichii PHOTO BY WILLIAM MCNAMARA

Michelia compressa PHOTO BY WILLIAM MCNAMARA

Ilex dimorphophylla PHOTO BY WILLIAM MCNAMARA

holly, typically grows to about 5 feet (1.5 m) tall and up to 3 feet (0.9 m) wide. In 1989 Bill obtained seeds from the University of Kagoshima Botanic Garden, Kyushu (Japan), from a plant originally wild collected on Amami Island (Kagoshima Prefecture). From these seeds a fastigiate selection developed at Quarryhill. The female plant has a heavy, bright red fruit set and has grown now to 8 feet (2.4 m) tall and 1.5 feet (0.5 m) wide. It is an evergreen with a few spines on the mature dark green leaves; juvenile leaves tend to be spinier.

Until I talked to Bill, I had never heard of *Osbeckia*, a member of the Melastomataceae that includes the familiar *Tibouchina*, which *Osbeckia* resembles. About sixty species are known, most found in Asia and a few each in Africa and Australia. Osbeckias, consisting of perennials, subshrubs, and shrubs, are "hairy" (ciliate) and have showy flowers with four, sometimes five, petals. They have opposite, simple leaves that are somewhat leathery.

Osbeckia crinita (currently considered *O. stellata* var. *crinita* by the Royal Horticultural Society) was collected by Bill in Yunnan (China) in 1990. Its flowers, produced in the spring and summer, are lilac to pink with long yellow stamens. The plant grows to about 3 feet (0.9 m) tall and requires light shade. It is probably cold hardy to USDA Zone 8. Bill says it is herbaceous in California and in winter dies to the ground with a tuft of foliage remaining at the base. The genus name honors Peter Osbeck (1723–1805), a Swedish naturalist.

Corydalis became extremely popular in European and North American gardens in the 1990s, primarily from the introduction of the blue-flowered *C. flexuosa*. A member of the poppy family (Papaveraceae), the genus consists of at least three hundred species distributed in Asia in the Sino-Himalaya region (there are also European, North American, and South African species).

Corydalis linstowiana, a 1991 Quarryhill collection from Sichuan, is a tuberous-rooted species that produces a low groundcover about 8 to 10 inches (20–25 cm) high with a spread of 16 inches (40 cm). The foliage is blue-green, finely dissected, and fernlike. The tubular, fragrant flowers are pale blue, lifted on a spike above the foliage by about 6 inches (15 cm). The plant grows in partial shade and is hardy to USDA Zone 6. This species has already found its way into the nursery trade, and its seed has appeared in society seed exchanges. The genus name derives from Greek *korudallis*, for "lark," because the spurred flower fancifully resembles a bird's foot.

One of the stalwarts of gardens as a foundation and specimen plant is *Osmanthus*, a genus of evergreen shrubs native primarily to the Himalaya, China, and Japan (there are U.S. species as well). They tend to be slow growers and are somewhat overlooked till they produce late fall to early spring flowers, many of which are very fragrant, hinting of jasmine or gardenia. For this reason the flowers have been used to enhance the flavor of tea (Mabberley 1997).

Osmanthus delavayi is a Quarryhill collection from Sichuan. It is not a new introduction, as it has been in cultivation since the late nineteenth century; however, the selection blooms more profusely, Bill says, than the typical form. Over

Osbeckia crinita PHOTO BY WILLIAM MCNAMARA

Corydalis linstowiana PHOTO BY WILLIAM MCNAMARA

time, it grows to 6 feet (1.8 m) tall and about as wide (taller and wider in the U.S. Southeast). The leaves are lustrous and dark green, up to 1 inch (2.5 cm) long, on arching branches. The fruit is purple-black.

Osmanthus is a member of the olive family (Oleaceae) and comprises about thirty species. The genus name is from the Greek for "fragrance" and "flowers," and the specific epithet honors Abbé Jean Marie Delavay (1838–1895), a French missionary to China, who introduced the plant to France in 1890 (Hyam and Pankhurst 1995).

The Japanese alder, *Alnus firma*, is a member of the beech family (Betulaceae). This tree grows up to 30 feet (9 m) tall and 25 feet (8 m) wide. Bill says that at Quarryhill, it is only dormant for a short period (about three weeks)—from the time the old leaves drop until the buds begin expanding. Its best feature is its unfurling spring foliage, which is deep green and pointed with strong venation. When it flowers, its catkins are gold-colored. The Quarryhill collections were made on Honshu and Hokkaido (Japan), the first in 1987. One form, *A. firma* var. *multinervis*, collected on Honshu, has eighteen to twenty-six pairs of veins on the leaves, compared to the normal form with twelve to fifteen. It is a large shrub to 12 feet (3.6 m) tall, with smaller leaves and arching branches.

Another shrub that Bill introduced me to is *Luculia intermedia*, a member of the Rubiaceae, or madder family. *Luculia* is composed of five evergreen species, all from eastern Asia. They grow as large shrubs to small trees. *Luculia interme-*

Osmanthus delavayi PHOTO BY WILLIAM MCNAMARA

Alnus firma PHOTO BY WILLIAM MCNAMARA

Luculia intermedia PHOTO BY WILLIAM MCNAMARA

dia grows in the mid-elevation forests (Bill's collection in 1990 was in Yunnan at 7800 feet [2365 m]). It produces fragrant white flowers, fading to light pink, in terminal, round clusters.

Sedum cauticola is a member of the Crassulaceae or stonecrop family. A low sprawling, shallow-rooted perennial suitable for the rock garden, it grows to about 3 inches (7.5 cm) high. In the summer and fall it produces dense heads of small pink flowers, and in the winter it tends to die back. The leaves are gray with a red tint. Bill's collection was from Hokkaido (Japan) in 1987.

Acer pentaphyllum (Aceraceae) is a deciduous tree that grows to a maximum of 30 feet (9 m) tall and nearly as wide, giving the plant a rounded appearance. It has red petioles and opposite, simple leaves (but they are heavily divided to the petioles, resulting in five "leaflets"). In the fall, the leaflets turn yellow to orange and red. This maple is cold hardy to USDA Zone 7.

In 1929, plant explorer Joseph Rock discovered the tree on a National Geographic expedition, west of China's Yalung River (Yalong Jiang) at an elevation of

Acer pentaphyllum PHOTO BY WILLIAM MCNAMARA

10,000 feet (3050 m). A few plants from that expedition were distributed in the United States. By the early 1990s, hardly any existed in the United States from that collection or from a subsequent Chinese collection in 1937. It was Bill's goal to re-locate the species in the wild, initially in 1988 with botanists from the Chinese Academy of Sciences (Chengdu); however, Bill was unsuccessful on that trip and later ones (McNamara 2002).

In 1992 botanists at the Chengdu Institute of Biology surprised Bill with a packet of seed of *Acer pentaphyllum*. The seed germinated and all the seedlings survived. It is believed that all the trees of *A. pentaphyllum* in cultivation, except the ones at Quarryhill, are derived from a single tree at the Strybing Arboretum and Botanical Garden (San Francisco, California). The original trees at Strybing have died. Those currently in the nursery trade in North America are being subjected to "genetic depression," Bill told me. Finally, in 2001, Bill was able to see *A. pentaphyllum* in the wild, including a 33-foot (10-m) tall tree with a trunk diameter of 3 feet (1 m). A Chinese companion told him that this was probably the last surviving stand of *A. pentaphyllum*. Bill recalls (McNamara 2002):

> As the significance of his remark sunk in, I looked around again at the few trees in the distance. . . Goats and sheep grazed freely nearby. It was hard to imagine these few rare trees surviving another twenty years.

Numerous other plants are potentially garden-worthy introductions through Quarryhill, including two forms of *Cryptomeria japonica*, a yellow-tipped form and a dense form. Quarryhill has an extensive *Lilium* collection (Bill calls it his "little piece of Eden"), all from Japan and China. Introduction of *Rosa chinensis* f. *spontanea* also might be a possibility, all from the rich "Eden" that is Quarryhill.

Rosa chinensis f. *spontanea* PHOTO BY WILLIAM MCNAMARA

Bill McNamara and Quarryhill's unique manner of collection combine the best of both the horticultural and botanical worlds. With each plant's specific collection data recorded, the garden serves as a living museum of the flora of the Far East.

W. A. "Bill" McNamara
Quarryhill Botanical Garden
P.O. Box 232
Glen Ellen, CA 95442
United States
www.quarryhillbg.org/
Aboutus/index.htm

Saratoga Horticultural Research
Foundation
5185 Murphy Avenue
San Martin, CA 95046
United States
www.saratogahortfoundation.org/
index.htm

Bill McNamara PHOTO BY BOBBY J. WARD

21

Plants from the Fairest Cape
Silverhill Seeds—Rod & Rachel Saunders

Like most tourists who visit Cape Town, I went to Table Mountain for the commanding view it provides of the natural harbor of Table Bay and the Atlantic beyond. Locals peer up daily at the sandstone mountain as it has a reputation for weather prognostication, a function of the amount of dense mist or "tablecloth" covering it each morning. The summit, 3570 feet (1085 m) tall, is flat (you reach it by cable car) and offers a quick introduction to the flora and fauna of the Cape. Here you are tantalized with examples of the area's botanical richness: *Protea*, *Restio*, heaths (*Erica*), *Leucadendron*, orchids, and succulent *Crassula*.

When Sir Francis Drake stopped at the Cape in 1580 during his round-the-world voyage on the *Golden Hind*, he wrote in his log, "It is the fairest cape and the most stately thing we saw in the whole circumference of the globe." And surely it is, as the great Cape Floral Kingdom is designated one of the earth's six plant kingdoms. It is large, roughly the area of Portugal, embracing nine thousand species in about 960 genera with shrubs making up more than sixty percent of the flora. The shrubs comprise the *fynbos*, from Dutch for "fine bush." The *fynbos* receives the bulk of its rain in the winter and in the summer it becomes hot and dry, a tinderbox for wildfires. Plants here have adapted to the fire regimes, some species actually requiring smoke and fire to stimulate seed germination.

East of the Cape is the Drakensberg, a mountain range that begins near the kingdom of Lesotho and runs northward for about 620 miles (990 km) to Kruger National Park. The serrated appearance of its peaks led to its name: "dragon mountain" in Afrikaans; also known as *quathlamba*, or "wall of the upward pointed spears" to the local Zulus. The Drakensberg provides an elevated, cooler climate, for plants of alpine and subalpine habitat.

Rod and Rachel Saunders travel the Cape area and the Drakensberg (as well as much of southern Africa, including Zimbabwe, Botswana, and Namibia) in quest of seeds. They are owners of Cape Town's Silverhill Seeds, a business they have operated for fifteen years, their catalog offering a broad selection of southern African seeds, consisting of annuals, perennials, trees, shrubs, grasses, bulbs, and succulents.

Rod has lived most of his life in South Africa. He worked initially at the Johannesburg parks department and later became nursery manager at the famed

Kirstenbosch Botanic Garden (Cape Town). In between, he spent time traveling around the world, hiking and mountain climbing in South America, and running a tropical crop nursery for a year in Papua (New Guinea). Rachel, a native of Johannesburg, has a doctorate in microbiology from the University of Witwatersrand (Johannesburg) and worked in a research post at the University of Cape Town. She is editor of the bulletin of the Indigenous Bulb Association of South Africa. Both Rachel and Rod love the mountains, hiking, and the wilderness.

John Grimshaw, garden writer and gardens manager at Colesbourne Gardens (Gloucestershire, United Kingdom) says of the Saunders:

> Silverhill Seeds has been one of the unseen motors behind the resurgence of interest in South African plants. Its seed list is one of very few sources for reliably named seed of South African species from all over the country; if you want an annual from the Cape or a choice alpine from the Drakensberg it is to Silverhill that you must turn. As with all seed collections, many fall by the wayside, some survive as treasured specialists' plants, but very few become established garden favorites; what can certainly be said about the Saunders is that they have given us the opportunity to try.

The Saunders live on a small property in Kenilworth, a suburb of Cape Town. When the seed business took up too much of the space in the house, they relocated Silverhill Seeds a few minutes away and "now they have their house back." They own a tissue-culture and micropropagation business on an 18-acre (7.5-ha) track outside Cape Town, which includes production of *Zantedeschia* (calla), *Cordyline*, virus-free strawberries, *Gerbera*, *Streptocarpus*, *Ornithogalum*, and several species of rare *Aloe*.

Like other plant collectors, Rod and Rachel depend to a great extent on the weather and other factors for their seed collection. For their trips, sometimes planned on short notice, they must determine whether one area has received rain yet, or if another has had fires. Rachel told me of a harrowing experience a few years ago when they were stranded in the Chimanimani Mountains in eastern Zimbabwe in midwinter for three days due to unseasonal rains. They spent the days and nights trapped in a cave, separated from their car by a flooded river. During the wait, they endured wet sleeping bags and clothes, little food and—the worst—wet packets of seeds, but such extreme conditions are balanced by the many clear blue skies, cool crisp nights, snow-covered mountain peaks, orchids on the banks of an icy stream, and—most dear to these collectors—sheets of bulbs flowering after fires. Some of the plants that Rod and Rachel have promoted follow.

Dimorphothecas or African daisies are members of the Asteraceae. The genus *Dimorphotheca* consists of nine South African species of annuals, perennials, and shrublets in the Western Cape province and the Karoo region to eastern Namibia.

The Saunders found a white annual dimorphotheca on the west coast north of Cape Town, growing in sand. They managed to collect enough seed to pass on to a Johannesburg grower who "bulked it up" for them over three years. The selection, dubbed "Silverhill White," has become widely popular in South Africa, now having been distributed by Ball Straathofs, a large seed house that also markets seed from the Kirstenbosch Botanic Garden. *Dimorphotheca* "Silverhill White" is probably the main white annual form now grown. This compact plant grows to about 12 inches (30 cm) tall and produces large white flowers with dark centers. The Saunders recommend fall planting as it grows in the winter and flowers in the spring.

The genus name means "two shapes of seeds." The African daisy produces two distinctly different seeds: the seeds of the disc florets are round and ridged, while those from ray florets have two broad papery wings (Goldblatt and Manning 2000). *Dimorphotheca* is closely related to *Osteospermum*, the Cape daisy. Blurring of the taxonomy of the two has occurred in some cultivars that are marketed as *Osteospermum* but may be *Dimorphotheca* (Armitage 2001).

While traveling in the Drakensberg, the Saunders found a superb selection of *Jamesbrittenia breviflora* (also *Sutera breviflora*), with large red flowers rather than the normal small pink to lavender form. *Jamesbrittenia* (Scrophulariaceae) is commonly called the skunkbush as the leaves are fetid when crushed. Rod and Rachel selected the biggest and reddest flower, took cuttings and seeds, and sent cuttings to an agent in the United Kingdom, who sent them to various nurseries in Europe, Japan, and the United States for trialing. In the United States this

Dimorphotheca "Silverhill White" PHOTO BY ROD AND RACHEL SAUNDERS

plant is available as African Sunset and goes also by the common name bacopa, one of its earlier taxonomic names (Armitage 2001). The selection is used in hanging baskets, window boxes, patio plantings, and as a ground cover. It is a perennial, though it is usually grown as an annual. The genus name honors James Britten, a British botanist (1846–1924). The cultivar is 'Rarosil'.

In 1998 Rod and Rachel discovered a new species of *Romulea* (Iridaceae), a small, crocuslike bulbous plant, near Nieuwoudtville, north of Cape Town (Saunders 2000). Rachel explains how such a well-collected area could produce a new species:

> The reasons are simple. The new species (*Romulea discifera*) is yellow-flowered, and it grows in exactly the same areas as *R. montana*, *R. monticola*, and *R. hirta*—also all yellow-flowered species. Thus to an observer the new species is almost indistinguishable.

Rachel recalls that as they pottered along the roadside looking at *Romulea* they checked the corms and found a population that was uniquely flat "like a pancake." They took a few corms back to the Compton Herbarium at Kirstenbosch, where their suspicions were confirmed: a new species. The genus name honors Romulus, one of the founders of Rome.

In the same area a year later, Rod and Rachel found a new species of *Babiana* (Iridaceae) flowering from October to November (spring in South Africa). Babianas typically flower in early spring (July and August), and Rachel surmises it was a new find because nobody was there to see it in flower. She says, "It's a distinctive species with large, mauve, unscented flowers and an extremely long tube," but it has not yet been officially described.

Among the most popular seed Rod and Rachel offer is *Melianthus major* (Melianthaceae), which "seems to have become a 'cult' plant" as the Saunders sell many seed of this plant. *Melianthus* is a genus of six species of shrubs that occur in southern Africa. The leaves of *M. major*, the turkey bush or honey bush, have a strong unpleasant smell when crushed. The plant grows to about 7 feet (2 m) tall with sprawling, suckering purple branches (Goldblatt and Manning 2000). The honey bush has large attractive leaves about 18 inches (45 cm) long; they are divided into seven to thirteen toothed leaflets and have an over-

Romulea discifera PHOTO BY ROD AND RACHEL SAUNDERS

Melianthus major PHOTO BY ROD AND RACHEL SAUNDERS

all gray "bloom." The plant is frequently grown for its bold foliage. The flowers, produced in terminal racemes in the spring, have brick-red to bronze-red petals, whose rich nectar is fed on, and thus pollinated, by long-beaked sunbirds (*Nectarinia*). The plant is toxic when taken internally, but is used by locals as a poultice on wounds or bruises. It is a winter grower and requires a warm, sunny location in rich, well-drained soil that has plenty of water; in the wild it often grows on creek banks. It will take some frost if winter mulched (USDA Zone 8) and will send new shoots from the base in the springtime.

About 350 species of aloes (Aloaceae, formerly Asphodelaceae) grow on the African continent and nearby on Madagascar, Socotra, the Arabian peninsula, and Cape Verde Islands. They are rhizomatous perennials, shrubs, or trees with succulent leaves arranged in rosettes. The inflorescence is upright, candlelike, on a stout spike.

The aloes are among the first plants that Rod admired, having been introduced to the group when he found an old copy of G. W. Reynold's book *The Aloes of South Africa* (1950). He became smitten by these plants and began collecting seeds in earnest. A typical Silverhill Seeds catalog lists seeds of at least seventy-five species of aloe. At times Rod and Rachel spend up to three weeks solely searching for aloes. Collecting aloe seeds is easy, Rachel says, if you are there when the capsules open. They use an inexpensive, if novel, way to collect seeds: they shake the inflorescence into an upturned umbrella and then transfer the seeds to paper packets and treat the seeds with an insecticide.

Aloe reitzii is from a cold area (cold by South African standards, Rachel reminds me) of limited distribution in northern KwaZulu-Natal and the Belfast district of Mpumalanga, growing on rocky slopes in grasslands (van Wyk and Smith 1996). This species grows in areas that frequently get snow and an average of 30 inches (75 cm) of rain per year. It develops a stemless rosette of dull green leaves and produces red tubular flowers that point downwards and are pressed against the stalk, which may be up to 4 feet (1.2 m) tall. The specific epithet honors the South African Reitz family.

By contrast, *Aloe claviflora* has a much wider distribution in the dry interior of South Africa, growing in rocky areas, frequently in dense groups or colonies from rosettes that point outward, not upward. The inflorescences are not erect as in *A. reitzii*, but are slanted, nearly horizontal. The flowers are bright red and fade yellow to white with age. The species is suitable for warm locations (USDA Zone 10) and it comes from an arid area receiving less than 5 inches (12.5 cm) of rainfall annually. The specific epithet *claviflora* refers to "club-shaped flowers." In Afrikaans the common name for the plant is *kanonaalwyn*, meaning "cannon aloe," a reference to the oblique angle of the inflorescence (van Wyk and Smith 1996).

The restiods comprise a group of Southern Hemisphere plants that are the ancient precursors of the true grasses; they superficially resemble large rushes. Belonging to the Restionaceae, they are an important component of the *fynbos* community and consist of more than three hundred species in several genera. All

Aloe reitzii PHOTO BY ROD AND RACHEL SAUNDERS

Aloe claviflora PHOTO BY ROD AND RACHEL SAUNDERS

members of the family have separate male and female plants, the two forms often looking quite different (Cowling and Richardson 1995). Most members of the family are difficult to germinate unless given a smoke treatment from a fire deliberately set for that purpose or occurring naturally. The Saunders learned about restiods from Peter Linder, former curator of the Bolus Herbarium (University of Cape Town). The three collected often together, most frequently in the southern part of the Western Cape.

Elegia capensis is an ornamental restiod that grows to about 7 feet (2.1 m) and is commonly called broom reed, looking a bit like a giant horsetail (*Equisetum*). It has a graceful arching habit and takes sun to light shade. *Thamnochortus insignis* is a popular and easy-to-grow restiod, reaching to 8 feet (2.4 m) tall and attaining a spread of 10 feet (3 m). It is one of the few restiods with a commercial use: its culms are used by locals for roof thatching, which may last up to seventy-five years in arid areas. *Rhodocoma capensis* produces attractive arching stems about 7 feet (2.1 m) tall with feather-like foliage, reminiscent of the plumes of pampas grass. All three restiods are winter-rainfall plants. Their hardiness varies as they range from sea level to an elevation of 6600 feet (2000 m). They are sometimes found where snow lasts a few days and are rated hardy to USDA Zone 8, or colder with protection.

Elegia capensis PHOTO BY ROD AND RACHEL SAUNDERS

Ornithogalums (Hyacinthaceae) are a group of about 120 bulbous species with two main centers of distribution, one in the Mediterranean region and the other in South Africa. The genus is one of several that give Rod and Rachel immense pleasure and they have amassed a large collection. They have observed that many of the species flower best after the surrounding vegetation has been burned, and as a result, their collecting efforts target recently burned areas.

The most common and best-known species is *Ornithogalum thyrsoides*, locally called the common chincherinchee. The flowers are in conical racemes, long lasting, on stalks that may be 8–20 inches (20–50 cm) high. The tepals are shiny white to ivory and often darker in the center. This species grows on sandy flats.

Thamnochortus insignis PHOTO BY ROD AND RACHEL SAUNDERS

Rhodocoma capensis PHOTO BY ROD AND RACHEL SAUNDERS

Another common species is *Ornithogalum dubium* with orange, red, yellow, and occasionally white tepals. It is found on clay and gravel flats and lower mountain slopes. The Saunders are now propagating by tissue culture a population (possibly a hybrid) they discovered that has a range of color forms from pure white to deep orange. All the ornithogalums described here are considered hardy to USDA Zone 8.

Silverhill offers seed of another bulbous genus, *Lachenalia* (Hyacinthaceae), consisting of about 110 species producing variously colored flowers. The Saunders's catalog lists three pages of species, including *L. aloides*, the Cape cowslip, which grows on granite and sandstone outcrops. Several varietal forms exist. The plants have pendulous, tubular flowers varying from lemon yellow to apricot and white.

Lachenalias are fleshy plants and are difficult to press for herbarium specimens. On a trip to Namibia in a remote area, Rod and Rachel found a lachenalia that they photographed but could not collect a specimen of. Since then they have been back four times to look for it again, but because of severe drought in the area, they have not found it. This illustrates one of the problems encountered when trying to find new plants. The genus name honors Werner von Lachenal, an eighteenth-century Swiss botanist.

In the southern part of the Western Cape, the amaryllids flower in autumn, a time when most other bulbs are dormant. They send up flower stalks when the weather is still hot and dry, before their leaves appear. They seem to respond to fire, hence a good time to see them is after a wildfire: spectacular blooms become more pronounced against the bare, burned soil. *Haemanthus* and *Brunsvigia* are two of the members of Amaryllidaceae that Silverhill Seeds sells.

Haemanthus coccineus, the Cape tulip or paint brush, grows in scrub on rocky slopes from Namibia to Port Elizabeth (South Africa) near sea level. The coral to scarlet-red flowers, produced on 15-inch (37.5-cm) scapes, are crowded in a dense cluster.

Brunsvigia marginata, or the candelabra plant, is a mountain dweller, which flowers annually for a few years after fire has burned an area. It bears clusters of vermilion-red flowers. The seeds are recalcitrant in that the germination process begins as soon as the seeds ripen, even if

Ornithogalum dubium cream selection PHOTO BY ROD AND RACHEL SAUNDERS

conditions are not favorable. Thus, if there have been no autumn rains, the seeds germinate and perish.

Brunsvigia natalensis, the Natal candelabra, has pink flowers and grows in

scattered grasslands on scattered rocky out-crops up to an elevation of about 7600 feet (2300 m). The inflorescence may consist of thirty or more flowers on stalks about 1 foot (0.3 m) tall (Pooley 1998).

Brunsvigia orientalis grows usually in sand and often close to the sea. The plants have an interesting life cycle. Like the seeds of many other amaryllids, those of *B. orientalis* are perishable, so seed production must coincide with rain. The bulbs send up their flower spikes in autumn, when rain begins to fall. The flowers are usually pollinated by sunbirds, but if the Table Mountain pride butterfly is around, it is attracted to red and will also pollinate the flowers. The seeds set rapidly and, while they are ripening, the

Brunsvigia marginata PHOTO BY ROD AND RACHEL SAUNDERS

Haemanthus coccineus PHOTO BY ROD AND RACHEL SAUNDERS

Brunsvigia natalensis PHOTO BY ROD AND RACHEL SAUNDERS

pedicels of the flowers elongate to form a large, round seed head. The whole inflorescence then breaks off and rolls in the wind, distributing seeds as it goes. The seeds begin to germinate immediately and, if no rain falls within a month or so, they die. Leaves follow the flowering spikes, growing through the winter and becoming dormant again in spring when the weather heats up.

The genus name honors the Duke of Brunswick-Lüneburg (1713–1780), a patron of the arts and sciences.

Rod and Rachel Saunders reside in one of the richest floral kingdoms in the world, that of South Africa. Their amazingly diverse seed lists, with everything from grasses, to succulents, to trees and shrubs, have enabled people the world over to share in this bounty.

Rachel and Rod Saunders PHOTO BY DAVE LEHMILLER

Rod and Rachel Saunders
Silverhill Seeds
P.O. Box 53108
Kenilworth, 7745 Cape Town
South Africa
www.silverhillseeds.co.za

22

I Brake for Wildflowers

Southwestern Native Seeds—Sally Walker

In drawing up a list of contemporary plant hunters who are making notable contributions at the beginning of the twenty-first century, one would be hard pressed to find someone more modest than Sally Walker of Tucson, Arizona. As she quietly goes about the task of preparing seed for botanic gardens and mail-order clients around the world, she seems to go out of her way to avoid publicity.

When I first met Sally at a crowded banquet of the North American Rock Garden Society in Banff, Alberta, she expressed outright surprise at my interest in her seed business, Southwestern Native Seeds, which she founded in 1975 as Sally's Seedery and now operates with her husband, Tim. I had learned about Sally from Panayoti Kelaidis (Denver Botanic Gardens), who had included her name on a short list of those who are making important contributions as plant hunters and amateur botanists. "Really, you cannot overlook Sally Walker because she was a pioneer in the business of seed collection in the United States long before the current horticultural craze came about," Panayoti confidently affirmed. In 1996 Sally received the Marcel Le Piniec Award from the North American Rock Garden Society, an honor given to an individual whose efforts extend and enrich the spectrum of plant material available to our gardens.

Although my limited knowledge of Arizona geography had been learned from western movies, Sally reminded me that Arizona is not just a hot flat desert with cactus backdrops. She pointed out that the southern terminus of the enormous Rocky Mountains extends as far south as the White Mountains, which are about midway through the state on the Colorado Plateau. Near Tucson in southeastern Arizona, the malpais of the Chiricahua, the Santa Rita, the Pinaleno, the Huachuca, and the Santa Catalina mountains rise to roughly 10,000 feet (3000 m) and then plummet to flat broad deserts that lie at 2500 to 4000 feet (760–1200 m). Huddled against the borders of Mexico to the south and New Mexico to the east, these mountain ranges comprise part of the Basin and Range Physiographic Province. This is Sally's "backyard" for seed collecting because she believes, quite frankly, that there are more interesting plant species here than in other regions of the state; however, her foraging area is much wider, bounded by a perimeter of about 400 miles (640 km), the expanse that she can reasonably manage to collect in during a season.

Managing Southwestern Native Seeds is a year-round business. It involves numerous collecting trips (Sally most frequently camps along the way) up to two months long and several week-long trips hoping to find ripe seeds in areas where the rainfall has been generous. The tedious, time-consuming tasks associated with cleaning, packaging, and mailing seeds usually occupy the fall of the year at a time when late, extended-season seed collections are also needing attention. And, yes, there is the catalog to prepare and mail.

I wondered what Sally's fascination is with Arizona's landscape and its native wildflowers. She carefully explained that topographic isolation combined with localized rainfall produces a distinguished floral diversity in the forested high Arizona mountains and low valleys, a region that is botanically and meteorologically related to Mexico to the south. This area delights in a shag rug of spring flowers that spatter-paint the area following the long-duration, light winter rains from the southwest and west from November to March (at elevations above 5000 feet [1500 m], there is snow fall during this period). It also luxuriates in a bonus of welcomed, late season flowering during the short-duration rainfall, often heavy, which occurs in July through September. At a time when the area most appreciates a break from the relentless parched dry heat, these pronounced July rains spill over into southern Arizona from the Mexican monsoons. Unlike southern Arizona with its distinct spring- and summer-flowering seasons, Mexico boasts a summer rainy season bloom but a diminished spring season of wildflowers.

Finding new plants is the result of skilled eyes, patience, and years of experience, including frequent revisits to catch the plants in seed. Sally has an automobile bumper sticker that reads "I Brake for Wildflowers," and as some discoveries are made at more than 50 mph (80 kph), you would probably not want to tailgate her on the highway. Except for her bold bumper sticker, Sally is without pretension and generally prefers the shutters of anonymity.

Sally and Tim mail a simply produced annual catalog (they have not missed a single year) to customers around the world. Sally adorns the catalogs with her own pen-and-ink drawings of flowers and plants. The catalogs are the sole connection most of her gardening customers have with the native flora of the U.S. Southwest. In this catalog, which also functions as a newsletter, Sally lists and codes plants by predominant flower color, outstanding features, plant size, elevation where collected (to assist in estimating hardiness for other regions), and the origin of the seeds by county. The list includes annuals and perennials as well as succulents, shrubs, and a few trees—many of which are available from no other source. The 2000 catalog—a bit atypical in being more extensive than most of her seed lists—identified fifty counties in Arizona, New Mexico, California, Colorado, Montana, Texas, Utah, and thirteen states in Mexico. It included old timers from catalogs of previous years but also featured new discoveries, which are the main quest of Tim and Sally's trips.

A native of Bournemouth, England, Sally studied at the Waterperry Horticultural School, famous for Valerie Finnis, a teacher there. From there she went to

Jack Drake's Alpine Nursery (Aviemore, Scotland) and then to the W. E. Th. Ing-wersen Nursery (East Grinstead, England). Sally emigrated to New Zealand and worked at the rock garden in the parks department in Invercargill. While in New Zealand, she wrote numerous articles for the New Zealand Alpine Garden Society on rock garden plants. After that she came to the United States in 1963 and worked four summers as a propagator at Western Hills Nursery (Occidental, California). She founded a seed business in 1975 called Sally's Seedery and changed the name a few years later to Southwestern Native Seeds. Her husband, Tim, was born in Dayton, Ohio, and received a degree in forestry at North Carolina State College. He has worked for the U.S. Forest Service when not assisting Sally in the seed business. The following are a few of the exceptional plants that Sally has introduced.

Southwestern Native Seeds has promoted two primroses, *Primula rusbyi* and *P. ellisiae*. Henry H. Rusby discovered *P. rusbyi* in the Mogollon Mountains of New Mexico in 1881. Rusby, a professor in the College of Pharmacy at Columbia University, New York, also collected in Arizona and along the Orinoco River of Venezuela. *Primula rusbyi* grows on cliff ledges and the forest floor, generally in the shade of conifers in the high mountains of southern Arizona and southern New Mexico up to 9000 feet (2700 m). The species ranges southward into Mexico in the state of Zacatecas and into Guatemala. It is a rainy season (summer) bloomer with basal, toothed leaves and a 10-inch (25-cm) tall flower scape that produces up to eight flowers having rose-magenta petals and a yellow eye. In the

garden, this primrose is hardy in the Portland, Oregon, area (USDA Zone 8), Sally has learned from customers. Sally's diligence in searching out the location of plants has its compensations. After looking repeatedly and unsuccessfully for thirty-five years for *P. rusbyi* at Rustler's Park in the Chiricahuas (Arizona), a site with old records of its known occurrence, she thrilled at finally finding a small patch of plants on a trip in 2000, following unusual early season rains. She also found it for the first time in the Pinaleno Mountains in the fall of 2000. For years now, this species has been found in new localities, one of which is below the tropic of Cancer in the Sierra de Chapultepec (Zacatecas, Mexico).

Primula ellisiae is closely kin to *P. rusbyi*, the two differing primarily in the shorter scape and larger calyx in *P. ellisiae* and the color of the flower, a deep purple

Primula rusbyi PHOTO BY TIM WALKER

Primula ellisiae PHOTO BY PANAYOTI KELAIDIS

with a yellow eye. This primula was first described in 1902 and commemorates Miss C. Ellis, who had earlier collected the plant in New Mexico. This species also grows on the summit of White Mountain (Sierra Blanca) in New Mexico. It, too, is a rainy season (summer) bloomer and is hardy to about 6°F (−14°C) or USDA Zone 7, at least in the U.S. Northwest.

In the early twentieth century, *Dodecatheon dentatum* subsp. *ellisiae* (Primulaceae) was known only from the Sandia Mountains, east of Albuquerque, New Mexico. Now it is known at elevations of 8000 to 9000 feet (2400–2700 m) in other locations in New Mexico as well as several sites in Arizona. Commonly called shooting star, it has fairly large, basally attached thin leaves up to 4 inches (10 cm) long and 1.5 inches (3.75 cm) wide. The scape bearing the white-petaled flowers (the only white species in its range) may approach 8 inches (20 cm). Shooting stars frequently grow on the banks of mountain streams, where the moist soil means they do not have to wait for rains to produce flowers. If they have seeded among the shady, drier edges of conifer forests, they must wait for the summer rainy season.

Sally's favorite plants are bulbs, including shellflowers. Known botanically as *Tigridia* (Iridaceae), the genus consists of approximately twenty-five species ranging throughout Mexico and into Guatemala, growing at mid-elevations from about 5,000 to 10,000 feet (1500–3000 m). The Aztecs grew the Mexican shellflower, *T. pavonia*, for its edible bulbs more than a thousand years ago. The genus name derives from Latin *tigris* for "tiger," alluding to the spotted markings on the flowers that are reminiscent of the ocelot, the "tiger" of Central America. The common name, shellflower, refers to the shell-like appearance of the petals of the red and yellow flowers.

Tigridia pavonia is the most commonly available species and produces the largest, showiest flower in the genus. It has pleated leaves and short-lived flowers that are red to orange and pink, commonly spotted or blotched black. The plants crave rich, well-watered soil and partial shade. I have seen them growing in Mexico in the light shade of pine and oak forests, although some grow in *llanos*, or rainy season boggy meadows.

Other species include *Tigridia dugesii* with bright yellow tepals (Durango, Mexico); and the crimson and cream *T. bicolor* from Oaxaca, which Sally reports growing among the spiny *Hechtia* (a bromeliad), and *T. matudae* under *Abies religiosa*. Other tigridias include *T. chrysantha* (yellow), *T.*

Tigridia pavonia PHOTO BY BOBBY J. WARD

durangense (lavender-mauve tepals), *T. multiflora, T. mexicana,* and *T. vanhouttei* from the mountains of San Luis Potosí.

The genus *Calochortus* (Calochortaceae) ranges from Guatemala northward to British Columbia and eastward to western Nebraska. We know it as mariposa lily from the Spanish for "butterfly," which the bloom fancifully resembles, although the genus name is from Greek *kalos* and *chortos* meaning "beautiful grass." More than half of the fifty-two taxa are native to California. Less well known are the Mexican species that start their flush of growth in their native habitat in May to June during the beginning of the rainy season.

Calochortus barbatus is the most widespread (in terms of geography and habitat) of the mariposas in Mexico. The yellow flowers, have a handsome reddish purple "beard." Two other Mexican species are *C. venustulus* and *C. ghiesbreghtianus*—the former is bearded with clear yellow flowers, while the latter sports small deep-wine petals. Confusingly, there is a similarly named species, *C. venustus,* from California; it has white flowers.

Agastache, a member of the Lamiaceae or mint family, is found in North America and eastern Asia, growing in canyons among rocky substrates at elevations up to 6000 feet (1800 m). *Agastache rupestris,* or Mexican hyssop, grows to about 2 feet (0.6 m) or less in height and up to 15 inches (37.5 cm) wide. It has a

Calochortus barbatus PHOTO BY PANAYOTI KELAIDIS

1-inch (2.5-cm) long orange-red corolla and extremely fragrant leaves. A form (#2) from the western limit of its range in Arizona was the 1997 choice of Plant Select®, a cooperative venture between the Denver Botanic Gardens and the Colorado plant nursery industry. Introduced as Sunset Hyssop, it has "bold brushes of sunset orange flowers from August to frost."

The Patagonia Mountains in southern New Mexico are habitat for *Agastache barberi,* which has tubular flowers about 1.5 inches (3.75 cm) long; its corolla is purplish pink and the calyx is rich dark purple. The beautiful and extremely fragrant *A. aurantiaca,* with golden-yellow flowers from far south in Mexico, is a newer addition to Southwestern Native Seeds's catalog.

The genus name is from Greek *agan* and *stachys* meaning "many spikes," alluding to the numerous flower stalks. Currently, agastaches are becoming popular among gardeners, including Ginny Hunt of Seedhunt in Freedom, California. She has made several selections from *A. rupestris*. Though from the U.S. Southwest, agastaches will grow in the eastern United States. Richard Dufresne, who formerly grew them in western Massachusetts and has grown them most recently in raised sand beds in Greensboro, North Carolina, in USDA Zone 7 says, "They are reliable bloomers and will start during midspring and get stronger through the summer to finish in autumn with loads of blooms" (Dufresne 1999).

Columbines or *Aquilegia* are members of the buttercup family (Ranunculaceae). *Aquilegia micrantha*, the alcove columbine, has both showy flowers (pink to cream) and attractive glossy, deep green leaves. The Arizona columbine, *A. desertorum*, has delicate glaucous leaves and attractive red and yellow flowers. It is a plant of the mountains above 7000 feet (2100 m), not the desert as its specific epithet would suggest. A long-spurred columbine from the Baboquivari Mountains (Arizona) has yet to be described botanically. It bears large flowers that are two tones of yellow, one pale and the other bright yellow. The spurs may stretch to more than 4 inches (10 cm). Sally and Tim added this columbine to their catalog in 1996. It appears be a relative of *A. chrysantha*, possibly ranging into Mexico. David Salman of High Country Gardens (Santa Fe, New Mexico) sells plants of this form of columbine, obtained from Southwestern Native Seeds. He calls it Swallowtail™ and tells Sally that "the intense blue coloration of the foliage has been an unexpected bonus."

Aquilegia micrantha PHOTO BY PANAYOTI KELAIDIS

Monardella arizonica (Lamiaceae) is a little-known mint that produces beautiful lavender flowers in August and September during the rainy season. Sally finally found this plant after taking fifteen trips into five mountain ranges because it had been misreported to be a spring bloomer and is very rare. Although most monardellas are much smaller, this species can develop into a woody subshrub, branching to 5 feet (1.5 m). The plant is highly fragrant and attracts butterflies—as well as seed collectors. It grows at mid-elevation ranges up to about 4000 feet (1200 m).

The genus name is a diminutive of *Monarda*, itself named after Nicholas Monardes, a Spanish botanist and physician of the sixteenth century. The nearly twenty species of *Monardella* are native to western North America.

Another member of the mint or sage family (Lamiaceae) is *Salvia*, the largest genus in the family. *Salvia arizonica*, or Arizona sage, is a creeping perennial with numerous trailing stems that produce luxuriant glabrous foliage and indigo-blue flowers. The plant is at home in light shade and woodland settings, where it grows up to an elevation of 9000 feet (2700 m) and thus is one of the hardiest of the Arizona salvias.

Salvia henryi, a bright red sage, grows at slightly lower elevations in similarly forested areas. If there is sufficient rainfall in the winter and summer it may produce flowers twice a year. *Salvia davidsonii* is a plant of the high desert, producing bright red flowers in the spring. Both *S. henryi* and *S. davidsonii* grow on limestone.

Salvia henryi PHOTO BY PANAYOTI KELAIDIS

Richard Dufresne, a salviaphile, has successfully grown *Salvia arizonica* in North Carolina, where "it forms dense clumps, sometimes becomes leggy, and produces lots of flowers . . . and it's hardy."

Penstemon stenophyllus (Scrophulariaceae) is primarily a Mexican species, although it ranges into Arizona. The genus name is from Greek for "five stamens." The species has smooth leaves and produces blue flowers late in the growing season. Unfortunately it is not widely known or grown. Both *P. pinifolius* (pine needle penstemon), which grows up to 10,000 feet (3040 m) elevation, and *P. barbatus* (golden-bearded penstemon) have red flowers and are well-established garden stalwarts. Other Mexican penstemons such as *P. kunthii* and *P. wislizeni* are worth growing.

Two members of the Alliaceae that make appearances in Sally Walker's seed list are *Bessera* and *Behria*. *Bessera elegans* or coral drops (Alliaceae) is a cormous perennial from Mexico. It has threadlike foliage and wiry stems from which red flowers droop. Less common and less widespread are the pink and purple forms. Besseras typically grow in semi-shade in pine habitat, but sometimes range to the coastal lowlands and palmetto savannas.

Behria tenuiflora (synonym *Bessera tenuiflora*), a plant known only from Baja California (Mexico), is a relative of *Bessera*. It grows on rocky hillsides and on sandy flats near sea level. The dark red corm produces a pendent umbel bearing flowers of bright red-orange with yellow venation in September through October. Leaves are narrowly linear to 12 inches (30 cm) long.

Milla biflora (Alliaceae), a mountain species known as Mexican star, is closely kin to *Brodiaea* and *Ipheion*. It ranges from Guatemala, through Mexico, western Texas, and New Mexico, reaching its northern limit in the southeastern counties of Arizona at elevations to 7000 feet (2130 m). At times, rainfall is insufficient to break dormancy, especially in Arizona. One of the bellwether indicators for Sally is the milla in Paradise Cemetery in the Chiricahuas, near her former home; when it is in bloom, Sally knows millas will be in bloom in prime collecting locations. The basal leaves are grasslike and up to 15 inches (37.5 cm) long. Waxy-looking, white, funnel-shaped (salverform) flowers grow on 2.5-inch (6.25-cm) pedicels that sit on a 10-inch (25-cm) stem. This species usually blooms in August to September.

Sally found one form (Walker #2) with large, showy white flowers up to 3 inches (7.5 cm) across in the Mexican state of Durango at an elevation of about 8500 feet (2580 m). She reports that it has a delicate fragrance and, in areas where it grows in Mexico, children sell bouquets of it to passing motorists.

Penstemon stenophyllus PHOTO BY TIM WALKER

Bessera elegans PHOTO BY TONY AVENT

Veteran seed-collector Sally Walker has done more for the flora of the south-western United States and adjacent Mexico than nearly any horticulturist working today. From this seemingly inhospitable climate, she has introduced a number of exceptional garden plants.

Sally Walker PHOTO BY BOBBY J. WARD

Southwestern Native Seeds
Sally and Tim Walker
Box 50503
Tucson, AZ 85703
United States

23

In the Land of the Golden Fleece
Wild Collected Seeds—Vojtěch Holubec

The Caucasus Mountains, forming a bridge between Europe and Asia, have constant snow on the tallest peaks. The isthmus carrying these mountains lies between the Caspian and Black Seas and is the land of the Golden Fleece and of Jason and the Argonauts. I think of this region and Vojtěch Holubec each time my local FM radio station plays Mikhail Ippolitov-Ivanov's *Caucasian Sketches*. This musical postcard draws heavily on folk music, particularly from Georgia, Armenia, and Azerbaijan, where Vojtěch (pronounced "voy-check") has hunted for rock and alpine plants among cliffs containing relic vegetation dating from the Tertiary Period. One section of the music, "In a Mountain Pass," evokes images of a caravan of plant hunters, struggling in the thin air on a misty morning with the sunlit plains of Colchis stretching below them.

Vojtěch, a Czech agronomist-geneticist by training, has probably made more collecting trips to the Caucasus than any contemporary plant hunter. His focus has been in the Russian Federation, Georgia, Armenia, and Azerbaijan. Within Russia, he has focused on the botanically rich western Caucasus (Kabardino-Balkaria and Ossetia), and the region on the border of Chechnya. Other locations in which he has collected include the Tien Shan in Kyrgyzstan, Kazakhstan, Kamchatka, Altai, Mongolia, Turkey, and most of the mountainous areas of Europe. He has also collected in the United States, primarily in the West.

Vojtěch's interest in plants and gardening began when he was a fourth grader. His father, seeing his enthusiasm, gave him a 7- by 10-foot (2- by 3-m) plot of land to tend, and on this parcel he built his first rock garden, using local stones, grit, and native plants. As a Boy Scout, he had gone to the mountains of Slovakia and recalled the plants he saw there, but his first alpine collecting trips were to Romania and Bulgaria in 1968. By the time he was sixteen years old, he joined the group of Czech rock gardeners who were just starting the Rock Garden Club of Prague in 1970. Soon he was corresponding with Norman Singer of the American Rock Garden Society (now North American Rock Garden Society or NARGS). Norman encouraged his fanaticism and initially sponsored his membership in NARGS. As he continued his education in agronomy and crop science in the Czech Republic and later in Texas, studying plant breeding and genetics of wheat and cotton, rock and alpine plants were never far from his mind. Soon other trips with fellow Prague rock gardeners began in earnest. He compiled seed lists from his trips, and he issued his first commercial seed list in 1993.

Today, Vojtěch's rock garden is considerably bigger than the one he tended at the age of nine. It is full of boulders—some so big that he had to hire cranes to lift them into place. When I visited him in his garden it was late afternoon. He explained the layout of his rock garden, which is organized by geographical regions: Europe with plants from the Balkans, Alps, and Pyrenees; Asia with collections from the Caucasus, Turkey, Central Asia, and China; and so on. By the time we had completed the tour and had reached the part of the rock garden covering the western United States, it was dark, and we saw the remainder of the garden by flashlight. Here on one side of the house I could just barely see a large collection of witches'-brooms (abnormal tufted growths of small branches on trees and shrubs), which belong to David, Vojtěch's eighteen-year-old son. The son's obsession with plants seems no less passionate than that of his father at the same age.

When we left his garden, I asked Vojtěch what his motivation is for collecting, growing, and selling seeds of rock garden plants. He said that when he joined the Rock Garden Club of Prague, he met many people who had his same interest and it was okay to be "crazy" for saxifrages (he had up to three hundred forms at one point):

> I gained a lot of friends and traded plants with them, as well as with neighbors. I prefer to grow plants which I collect myself, because I can get a feeling for the locality and the plant's needs. I can grow plants from seed I collect myself, rather than from an anonymous seed list.

He also said the reality is there is an economic side to his "craziness" for alpines. "I get some help with the family budget from seed sales and I can take larger plant hunting expeditions."

When I asked Vojtěch about overcollection of seeds from wild populations, he said:

> It is important to have a feel for plants—knowing when the population is weak or strong. I never collect from poor or endangered populations, but I am against the 'fanatic greens' who think all seed collecting should be forbidden. If humans had not collected and used seeds from the wild, we would never have had economic plants, plant breeding, or cultivars.

Andrew and Sue Osyany (Shelburne, Ontario), who grow seeds obtained from Vojtěch, readily sing his praises:

> Fortunately for us, Holubec wears many hats. He has a fabulous knowledge of rock garden construction techniques and an impeccable sense of design. Affecting a wider range of gardeners is his personal seed collection and his participation in many of the jointly organized Czech ventures. Holubec is a principal plant researcher for the groups, studying up on what might be found, and afterwards spending many hours identifying the collections.

Like a taxonomic god, he loves every plant, regardless of garden interest; he has included in his catalogs a fair number of items with "minor flowers." Being a relatively young man, he should have many years of collecting left in him, and no doubt he'll go to visit areas where he has not been before. We hope he keeps going back to Central Asia (from Turkey to the Altai mountains) and that he will produce some floras. As he is already a published author, and an excellent photographer, we may be in luck. Holubec is a very kind person, generous with plants and totally unwilling to say anything critical about competitors and other gardeners.

Some of the plants that Vojtěch has promoted follow.

If there are 375 species of saxifrages as some references suggest, then there are 373 species that I *cannot* grow in my garden in the U.S. Southeast, an area with high night temperatures during the wettest months of the year. Plants from dry lands struggle to survive here. Without perfect drainage and shade, alpine saxifrages will not last under these extreme conditions. I rely on *Saxifraga stolonifera* from China and Japan, and the U.S. Southeast native, *S. virginiensis*. Both accept dry shade and in my garden are the sole representatives of *Saxifraga*, a genus of plants much respected by rock gardeners.

A scan of Vojtěch's seed catalog reveals seeds of a dozen or so *Saxifraga* species. One introduction from Vojtěch (and the group of Czech rock gardeners he collects with) is *Saxifraga dinnikii*, an inhabitant of Balkaria, a semi-autonomous republic in the northern Caucasus bordering Georgia and Chechnya. *Saxifraga dinnikii*, from 1996 and 2003 collections, grows in dolomitic crevices and fine scree, often in deep shade on north-facing slopes between 7,000 and 12,000 feet (2100–3600 m) (Holubec 2001). It belongs to subsection *Kabschia* in section *Porphyrion* and forms flat green cushions 1.25–4 inches (3–10 cm) wide. It produces lovely rose-colored flowers on 0.75-inch (2-cm) long pedicels.

Also here, high up among crevices Vojtěch found *Saxifraga columnaris*, a superb purple-rose-flowering species, which was not in cultivation even though it has been known since 1892. *Saxifraga columnaris* grows on south-facing slopes "in fissures of dolomitic walls . . . predominantly inhabiting small or large overhangs attached to the underside fissures in the ceiling or [they are] hanging like wasp's nests," Vojtěch recalls in this rather evocative description. This plant grows on southern exposures and requires moisture, which is usually available from deep fissures or from passing rain clouds, according to Vojtěch.

Vojtěch points out that the Caucasus is a region with a diversity of species from *Saxifraga* section *Porphyrion* (the mat or cushion-form types)—perhaps as many as twenty-five species. Some of these grow in overlapping locations, and Vojtěch has collected several interesting hybrids. Two that he found in the wild and described are *S. ×dinninaris* (spec. hybr. nova), a hybrid of *S. dinnikii* and *S. columnaris*, and *S. ×columpoda*, a hybrid of *S. columnaris* and *S. scleropoda*. The group of collectors with Vojtěch on a 2003 expedition to the area found other hybrids and they are being evaluated for garden worthiness.

Vojtěch's passion for saxifrages has included introduction of a red-flowering form of the normally white-flowering *Saxifraga albertii*, from Kyrgyzstan. This form is a compact cushion plant and rather difficult to grow. *Saxifraga khiakensi* is a proposed name for a most likely new species of silver *Saxifraga* from the Caucasus. It is a dwarf plant closely related to *S. cartilaginea*, but with one to three flowers per pedicel and compact cushions. Vojtěch found it on Mount Khiakh on the border of North Ossetia and Chechnya.

When you read Vojtěch's end-of-year letters to gardening friends, you realize just how dicey contemporary plant hunting can still be, particularly in remote areas. There may be sticky political situations and tribal fighting, and suspicious border guards unaccustomed to dealing with foreigners who say they are entering the country solely to collect seeds for their flower gardens ("Oh, yeah?"). On one such trip in the Caucasus, some members of the Rock Garden Club of Prague (whom Vojtěch affectionately calls "people who are crazy for alpines and mountain plants") were taken by the army and jailed for two days for "violating border laws." They were attacked and robbed by thieves with guns, had to pay a bribe of seventy (U.S.) dollars, had flashlights stolen, and then, upon their release, were honored with "important guests" status at a celebration by the local villagers.

Fortunately the precious seeds were not confiscated and gardeners now have the opportunity to enjoy three potentillas (Rosaceae) from that scary trip: *Potentilla divina*, *P. oweriniana*, and *P. porphyrantha*—the best of the high Caucasian potentillas, Vojtěch believes. *Potentilla divina* and *P. oweriniana* are densely tufted cushion plants with "silvery downy," decorative leaves. They both have relatively large flowers. In the case of *P. divina*, the flowers are rose to bright pink, while *P. oweriniana* has yellow flowers. The Alpine Garden Society *Encyclopaedia of Alpines* says *P. oweriniana* is "[a] desirable species but not easy to please" (Beckett 1994). The third species, *P. porphyrantha*, has similar, but smaller downy foliage, and pink flowers. All three species grow in crevices, but in geographically different places: *P. divina* along the main ridge of the Caucasus, *P. oweriniana* on the northern Rocky Ridge (called Skalistyj Khrebet), and *P. porphyrantha* in Nagornyj Karabakh on the border of Armenia and Azerbaijan.

You can gauge the value of campanulas (Campanulaceae) in rock gardens by the number of entries in the seed exchange of the North American Rock Garden Society and other societies whose members trade garden seed with one another. In these annual listings you will find a hundred or more campanula choices in a typical year. Taxonomists recognize some three hundred species, most of which produce lovely bell-shaped flowers, most often in shades of blue, purple, or lavender. As many bloom in mid- to late summer, their "cool" colors tone down the yellows of members of the Asteraceae that parade across the garden at the time. Vojtěch has added to this palette, and says, "The Caucasus is a paradise for campanulas" as there are just under one hundred *Campanula* species there.

One of the best campanulas, endemic to the Caucasus (the Mount Fisht region) and new to cultivation, is *Campanula dzaaku*, which grows in limestone

Saxifraga dinnikii PHOTO BY VOJTĚCH HOLUBEC

Saxifraga columnaris PHOTO BY VOJTĚCH HOLUBEC

crevices at about 6900 feet (2100 m). It has large light blue flowers and glossy, leatherlike linear leaves.

Campanula autraniana has dark blue to deep purple, solitary bells that hang from thin pedicels. Its leaves are cordate-lanceolate and up to 2 inches (5 cm) long. This species is another one of the "endemic gems of Mount Fisht," Vojtěch reports.

One of the most striking species is *Campanula kryophila*, whose leaves are spatulate up to 0.4 inch (1 cm) long. The flowers, borne solitarily on 1.25- to 2-inch (3- to 5-cm) stems, are pale blue, widely cylindric, and about 0.6 inch (1.5 cm) long. Vojtěch has found this campanula twice, always in volcanic ash on Mount Elbrus and Mount Kazbek.

Another beautiful species is *Campanula ardonensis*. It is a bit similar to *C. dzaaku* with leaves that are linear, and shallowly dentate. Flowers are solitary, hanging bells that are 1 inch (2.5 cm) long on 4- to 5-inch (10- to 12-cm) long stems. The color is very dark blue.

Kyrgyzstan, a landlocked Central Asian republic, received independence from the former Soviet Union in 1991. Its dominant geographical feature is the great peaks of the Tien Shan range ("Heavenly Mountains" in Chinese) and associated valleys, lakes, and glaciers. High among glacial moraines and granite soil, Vojtěch found *Pyrethrum leontopodium*, a lovely member of the Asteraceae. Growing at 12,500 feet (3800 m), up to the edge of glaciers far above the treeline, this woolly little daisy has a yellow eye and white ray flowers. It seems that a plant from such an elevation would be impossible to grow at lower elevations; yet it does. Vojtěch considers this plant one of the best of all of his introductions.

Campanula dzaaku PHOTO BY VOJTĚCH HOLUBEC

Campanula autraniana PHOTO BY VOJTĚCH HOLUBEC

Pyrethrum leontopodium PHOTO BY VOJTĚCH HOLUBEC

In herbal lore, King Gentius, the second-century ruler of Illyria (the lands east of the Adriatic Sea, now the Balkan Peninsula), is credited with discovering the medicinal properties of *Gentiana lutea*, the yellow gentian, whose roots were the source of tonic bitters, used to cure Gentius's army of a mysterious fever.

Gentiana verna subsp. *oschtenica* (Gentianaceae), another of the yellow gentians, is a denizen of the western Caucasus; it is closely kin to *G. verna*, a blue-flowering species. *Gentiana verna* subsp. *oschtenica* has pale- to lemon-yellow petals, unique within section *Cyclostigma*. It grows among boulders in meadows at alpine and subalpine elevations of about 7240 feet (2200 m), always on limestone. Vojtěch found it in the Mount Fisht and Oshten regions.

The navelseed or *Omphalodes* (Boraginaceae) consists of about thirty species of plants, primarily from temperate areas in the Northern Hemisphere. I was fooled once when I saw a cluster in a rock garden and immediately concluded that *O. cappodocica* was really a mislabeled *Myosotis*, so similar in appearance are the flowers and growth habit. *Omphalodes lojkae*, from the Mount Fisht region of the Caucasus, has very large, sky blue flowers and gray, waxy leaves. It grows to about 4 to 6 inches (10–15 cm) tall among rocky places, including limestone crevices. It's an excellent alpine, closely related to *O. luciliae*, a more commonly grown rock garden plant.

Draba (Brassicaceae) comprises about three hundred species. *Draba ossetica* (and its subsp. *racemosa*) grows in the Rocky Ridge in the northern Caucasus, on

Gentiana verna subsp. *oschtenica* PHOTO BY VOJTĚCH HOLUBEC

Omphalodes lojkae PHOTO BY VOJTĚCH HOLUBEC

Draba ossetica PHOTO BY VOJTĚCH HOLUBEC

the same dolomitic limestones where *Saxifraga dinnikii* and *S. columnaris* occur. It has white hairy cushions like *D. polytricha* and grows on rocky walls, often in cold, wet places. Unlike other "hairy" drabas, it has white flowers. Usually white-flowering drabas (*Leucodraba*) are not so nice and compact, but this is an exceptional delight. The cushions are 1.3–6 inches (3–15 cm) wide. They bear large open flowers on thin 1.3- to 2.5-inch (3- to 10-cm) long stems. Though published in 1893, this is believed to be the first introduction of *D. ossetica*, according to Vojtěch.

Though relatively young, Vojtěch has made many trips to the Caucasus and elsewhere that have yielded some extraordinary finds. His collections have found a place in rock gardens worldwide.

Wild Collected Seeds
Vojtěch Holubec
Sídlištní 210
165 00 Prague 6
Czech Republic
www.delonix.cz/Gb/seminum.php

Vojtěch Holubec PHOTO BY BOBBY J. WARD

Saint Josef of the Rocks

Wild Seeds of Exquisite Alpines—Josef Jurášek

On an agreeable afternoon and a meal at the Three Fighters pub in Prague, Josef Jurášek and Vojtěch Holubec related stories to me about their numerous foreign plant hunting expeditions. There were frightening revelations of run-ins at remote areas where highway robbers demanded money and cameras, but fortunately not their concealed collection of seeds. We drank pilsner beer, whose name, they proudly boasted, derives from Pilsen (Plzen in Czech), the West Bohemian city where the drink was first brewed. During lunch, Vojtěch served as my English-to-Czech-and-back-again translator on questions I posed to Josef about his long-term love affair with rock and alpine plants.

At the end of the meal, both invited me to view plants in the old Charles University Botanic Garden, where we saw the famous parasol-shaped *Ginkgo biloba* 'Prague' (syn. 'Pragensis'). From there they took me to a rock garden at the nearby church of Saint John on the Rock. This place of worship has an appropriate name because the Rock Garden Club of Prague leases land from the church for an especially fine collection of rock and alpine garden plants. Here, in a walled area beside the church, club members have put in a host of plants among crevices, upon scree, and in troughs, covering the rocky landscape. Saint John on the Rock is also the site of the club's plant sales and large annual exhibitions, including the show of early spring bulbs and saxifrages, followed in May by a three-week display of at least one thousand spring-blooming alpines, both highly popular. Vojtěch and Josef have played a dominant role in the success of the club and its public outreach, turning the grounds of the Bohemian baroque church into a veritable garden of pleasant delights.

Josef Jurášek is one of three contemporary Czech plant hunters profiled in this book. Along with Josef Halda and Vojtěch Holubec, he has added much plant material to our gardens over the last few decades. The three men have traveled together to Albania. Vojtěch and Josef Jurášek have collected together in Tibet; while in the Caucasus and Turkey, they collected together and independently. Andrew Osyany (Shelburne, Ontario) has grown seeds collected by these three. He has also assisted in providing North American contacts for Czech seed collectors. Osyany says, "Jurášek 's gift is the ability to find the not-so-obvious treasures in any given terrain. His gift to us is his steadfast refusal to distribute tax-onomical-delights-only plants."

Alpine plants are a passion for Josef, but he expresses it with controlled enthusiasm, which complements his low-key, reserved demeanor. He patiently describes unusual plants—many unfamiliar to me—that he has collected, taking pains to carefully spell Latin epithets derived from geographical locations. What you sense from him is a sort of Ahab-in-search-of-the-great-white-whale excite-ment for alpines. During our conversation, I learned from Josef that his favorite collecting areas are the Balkans and Turkey because "the areas are rich, interest-ing, and the plants will grow in my garden." As evidence, he has made fifteen trips to Turkey. His focus on this area has not impinged on his travel time to Rus-sia, Kazakhstan, Tajikistan, Mongolia, China, and Tibet, as well as several coun-tries neighboring the Czech Republic. He has been producing a seed list since 1987, primarily of alpines, serving customers in northern and western Europe, North America, and Japan. His most popular plants are androsaces, primulas, saxifrages, corydalis, and gentians. His most neglected are the Leguminosae. "They are beautiful and worth growing, so it's difficult to understand why peo-ple do not order them," he observes with puzzlement. "For example, it is a shame *Oxytropis* are not grown more, as they are beautiful plants."

I asked Vojtěch what it is like traveling and collecting plant seeds with Josef. He responded:

> There are many prominent rock gardeners in the Czech Republic—some of them never leave their pet-plants, others go to the mountains to enjoy nature and to relax on holiday. Only a few rock gardeners go to really "wild" places to discover and bring back plant novelties. Those individuals must be able to withstand harsh climates and threats where there are political hot spots. Those people are very individualistic and very different. Josef Jurášek definitely belongs to such a group. He has good instinct to go to the right places to find the best plants. He has introduced a lot of excellent alpines that are valuable for horticulture. Josef is always full of jokes that make peo-ple laugh, especially when he is sipping beer. Beer is his second love. In the garden he has green fingers, able to keep plants for years, which other peo-ple would shortly kill. Sometimes we have tough discussions, but we enjoy joint collecting and we have a feeling we can always rely on each other in hard times.

Josef was born in Prague in 1948, the second child of Slovakian parents. Thanks to Josef's father he was introduced to natural areas of the country as a small boy and often made hiking trips to the woods with his father. Here he found plants and trees that attracted his attention and as he grew into a teenager, he began growing plants for himself. Now Josef has been collecting and germi-nating seeds and growing plants for more than three decades. His passion for plants has continued with the founding of his seed business, Wild Seeds of

Exquisite Alpines (Prague). From a strictly conservation standpoint, Josef says that he does not believe seed hunters are destroying nature, as some people may suggest. "Seed collectors are saving most of the endangered plants [and] putting them into [garden] culture." Some of the plants that Josef has introduced and/or promoted through his seed catalog follow.

Centaureas (Asteraceae) hail from the Mediterranean region to Turkey (Asia Minor). Josef found *Centaurea pestalozzae* in the Boz Dağ area of western Turkey, where it is endemic, growing at 7080 feet (2150 m) on scree. The bright yellow-ish flowers, about 1.25 inches (3 cm) across, appear in early summer on stemless to very short stems (pedicels). The leaves are pinnatisect and are in a rosette. Josef recommends this species for dry and sunny places in the garden.

Josef found *Gentiana boissieri* in the Bolkar Dağ and Taurus in Turkey, up to an elevation of 7,200 to 10,500 feet (2200–3200 m). It is endemic there in dry grassy places. In the summer it produces deep blue to purplish bell-shaped flowers in clusters of one to three. Compared with some gentians, the flowers on *G. boissieri* are smaller, 0.75–1.25 inches (2–3 cm) long. The shiny, ovate, green leaves grow on stems to about 3 inches (7.5 cm) tall. An excellent trough or scree plant for limy soils, this species resembles a smaller version of *G. septemfida*, a plant long grown by rock gardeners.

Gentiana terglouensis is a compact plant Josef collected in the Julian Alps, where it grows in alpine areas on bare wolds, among rocks, and limy screes. It forms small, flat cushions to 2.5 inches (6 cm) and produces dark blue flowers in midsummer (Halda 1996). Josef says it is an excellent plant for troughs or lime-

Gentiana boissieri PHOTO BY JOSEF JURÁŠEK

stone crevices in full sun. Overall, *G. terglouensis* looks like a congested *G. verna* (Beckett 1993), but, like a proud parent, Josef says it is a "better growing plant, much nicer than *G. verna*." Its range is the Maritime alps to western Switzerland, growing on limestone rocks and slopes between 6300 and 8900 feet (1900–2700 m). It grows among companion plants of *Campanula zoysii*, *Draba aizoides*, *Linum aretioides*, *Lloydia serotina*, *Petrocallis pyrenaica*, and *Saxifraga crustata*—quite a sight to behold (Halda 1996).

Campanulas (Campanulaceae) are one of Josef's great interests and he lists several in his catalogs each year. *Campanula choruhensis*, one of the choicest European campanulas, is a new introduction from the Choruh River Valley (Tortum) of eastern Turkey, where it grows at 5900 feet (1800 m). It is a stunning bell-flower—the unopened bud-bell is ribbed and pink to rose and then, as it fully opens, becomes ivory white with a hint of pink on its outer petals. The bells stand out against the gray-green leaves. Josef recommends this species for raised bed, trough, pot culture, or even a wall as it is a chasmophyte, or crevice dweller. One of its champions is Graham Nicholls (2003):

> *Campanula choruhensis* grows in a range of soils despite the rigors of its native habitat. After flowering in May or June, the stems die back in autumn to a central rootstock, and during winter, plants growing outside look quite bare. In the alpine house, however, plants usually have a little green showing.

Bob Stewart of Fowlerville, Michigan, praises it in his Arrowhead Alpines nursery plant catalog for 2003: "This is just about as good as it gets . . . a challenging plant worth any effort to please, definitely not for beginners." Josef says he has found it growing among igneous rocks in dry areas in Turkey.

Campanula seraglio is from the Sarigol area of eastern Turkey. It is a crevice dweller with large white to pink flowers, growing at about 3900 feet (1200 m) elevation. Josef collected seeds from it, thinking it was *C. troegerae*, a plant also from Turkey. When he got complaints from his customers that the identification was not correct, he checked into it more fully and found it described in Davis's *Supplement to the Flora of Turkey* (1965).

Campanula pulvinaris is a beautiful compact-forming cushion campanula growing to about 1.5 to 2 inches (4–5 cm) high. Its single flowers are erect, violet-blue, and 0.5 inch (1.25 cm) long. The leaves are ash-gray to silvery and clustered in a rosette. The plant grows in rocky areas at an elevation of 7200 to 8900 feet (2200–2700 m). Josef collected it in eastern Turkey (Kop Gecidi) and at Palandoken. He says it needs dry conditions in winter and is excellent for the alpine house. Josef likes it so much that he uses it as the logo for his seed business.

Androsace villosa subsp. *palandokenensis* (Primulaceae) was the preliminary name given in Josef's seed catalog for this plant collected in the Palandoken Mountains of eastern Turkey at elevation 10,200 feet (3100 m). It was such a good plant that he investigated it further and found it had been earlier named as *A.*

Campanula choruhensis PHOTO BY JOSEF JURÁŠEK

Campanula pulvinaris PHOTO BY JOSEF JURÁŠEK

glabrata. Josef says that it grows on dry screes and rocky areas and produces rosettes of green leaves and cushions of white flowers.

Androsace delavayi is a cushion-former, growing to about 6 inches (15 cm) wide. Its flowers are almost stemless, one per stem, and small (up to 8 mm in diameter) (Beckett 1993). The population of plants that Josef found in Yunnan and in Nepal has rose to nearly purple flowers, but others in the Himalaya are creamy white. It is a high elevation plant growing up to 16,500 feet (5000 m). Josef says it is a superb plant. He found it in foggy, but not wet, areas.

Grassy bells or *Edraianthus* species (Campanulaceae) are early summer bloomers. About two dozen species are centered around the Balkan peninsula to the Caucasus at elevations of 6600 to 8900 feet (2000–2700 m). The plants typically have upward-facing, bell-shaped flowers, either solitary or as a terminal group.

Edraianthus montenegrinus produces one to three mauve to blue-violet large flowers on small stems. The leaves are narrow and densely hairy. The species was introduced into cultivation by Josef from seed collections he made in Albania and Montenegro. As a cushion-type plant, it appears to be closely kin to *E. pumilio*, a species favored by rock gardeners. Because it blooms in summer, Jurášek finds that it grows best in sunny spots among dry crevices or scree.

Josef has also offered seeds of *Daphne velenovskyi* (Thymelaeaceae), an evergreen species originally collected and named by fellow Czech plant collector

Edrainanthus montenegrinus PHOTO BY VOJTĚCH HOLUBEC

Edrainanthus montenegrinus detail PHOTO BY VOJTĚCH HOLUBEC

Daphne velenovskyi PHOTO BY JOSEF JURÁŠEK

Josef Halda in 1981. A relative of the well-known *D. cneorum*, it grows in southwest Bulgaria on Mount Pirin. It is found on open grassy slopes and alpine meadows among limestone and dolomitic rocks (Halda 2001a). The flowers are rose to bright red. Josef says it is excellent for the rock garden because it is a dwarf, compact shrublet growing to 4 inches (10 cm) tall and 12 inches (30 cm) wide. *Daphne velenovskyi* is densely branched and has glaucous leaves.

More of Josef's favorite plants are the primulas (Primulaceae), and he frequently lists several in each catalog. Josef reminded me that the specific epithet of *Primula deorum* means "of the gods." This species is endemic in the Rila Mountains of Bulgaria in wet, marshy areas at about 6600 feet (2000 m) elevation. Its leaves are oblong, somewhat leathery, smooth, and shiny, 6 inches (15 cm) long and 0.75 inch (2 cm) wide (Beckett 1993). The flowers are bright purple-pink and 0.6 inch (1.5 cm) across. Baldassare Mineo (Medford, Oregon) grows *P. deorum* successfully in humus-rich soil that is well drained and in part shade.

Primula dryadifolia produces rose-purple flowers that are 0.75 inch (2 cm) across, supported on 2- to 4-inch (5- to 10-cm) stems. The leaves are evergreen, small, and farinose beneath. Because it is a denizen of high, cold areas, this plant is difficult to grow in lower elevations. Josef collected it in Yunnan and Tibet, where it grows usually at the highest elevations (16,500 feet [5000 m]), on mineral scree, and on the shady side of rocks.

Primula graminifolia is a tiny plant with linear, almost grasslike leaves and purple flowers. It comes from Tibet, where it grows at an elevation of up to 16,500 feet (5000 m). *Primula subularia*, also from Tibet, is a mat-forming small plant found in wet areas, sometimes in standing water. It produces rose-purple flowers.

Josef's discerning eye, coupled with a willingness to travel to dangerous, barely accessible regions, makes him one of today's most important alpine plant collectors. The importance of many of his introductions is only beginning to be realized.

Joseph Jurášek PHOTO BY BOBBY J. WARD

Josef Jurášek
Wild Seeds of Exquisite Alpines
P.O. Box 251
152 00 Prague 5
Czech Republic
www.jurasekalpines.com

Natives Preferred

Woodlanders—Robert McCartney

I had never seen an American dingo, or Carolina dog as it is also known, till I saw one at Woodlanders Nursery in Aiken, South Carolina. The breed is a descendent of the canines that accompanied the Paleolithic ancestors of Native Americans across the Bering Strait from Asia to North America. The dog is found in the southeastern United States and is about as native to the South as a dog can get. It is appropriate that a nursery owner who specializes in American native plants also has a native breed of dog.

The opening page of one Woodlanders catalog quotes Thomas Jefferson: "The greatest service that can be rendered any country is to add a useful plant to its culture." Jefferson wrote that in 1800 when he was summarizing his life's contributions. Such a credo appears to be the guiding principle that Robert "Bob" McCartney and the co-owners of Woodlanders have set in the twenty-five years of the nursery's operation.

A native of James City County, Virginia, Bob obtained an undergraduate degree in wildlife management from Utah State University and a master's degree in game management from Louisiana State University. He worked several years for the Virginia Department of Wildlife and then took a job in 1966 as a biologist at Colonial Williamsburg, working in landscaping and plant propagation, increasing his knowledge of Southeast native plants, and introducing many plants there from various sources, including native plants collected throughout the South. At that time few nurseries specialized in native plants. One exception was Tom Dodd, Jr., a nursery owner in Semmes, Alabama, near Mobile, whom Bob visited to learn more about native plants.

Landscaping in the South had long consisted almost entirely of plants from two sources. The first was the old Fruitland Nurseries in Augusta, Georgia, a nursery run by the Berckmans family from before the U.S. Civil War till the early twentieth century. It offered azaleas, camellias, photinias, gardenias, hollies, and osmanthus, all stalwarts of Southern gardens. The other similar supplier was Pomaria Nursery in Pomaria, South Carolina, also established in the nineteenth century and operating into the twentieth century.

In 1980 Bob met Robert and Julia Mackintosh, who had recently founded Woodlanders. He joined the Woodlanders partnership and with them set the initial goal for the nursery: "To seek out and propagate the beautiful but neglected plants of the [U.S. Southeast] region . . . and to offer them for sale." As the nursery grew, the Mackintoshes, McCartney, and George Mitchell, Woodlanders's propagator, expanded their vision in the early 1990s to include plants from around the world that are suited in USDA Zones 7 to 9. Woodlanders has reached out since to areas such as the Middle East, South America, the Far East, and the Mediterranean for sources of plant material. Bob has been to Argentina and Bermuda and to nurseries in the United Kingdom. The nursery is unusual in that it is mail-order only, no walk-in or on-site sales, except at an open house held for eight days each April (orders can be placed in advance and picked up at the nursery during the shipping season).

On my last visit at Woodlanders, Bob stopped me at the door to the office and proudly showed off a blooming *Begonia boliviensis*, a plant that I had also grown. He and fellow plant hunters had found it in Argentina on a collecting trip in 2002. When asked about what motivates him in his horticultural passion, he spoke of his long-term interest in plant communities, even when he worked in wildlife biology:

> Woodlanders has given me the opportunity to explore the possibilities for using little-known native plants as horticultural subjects and to introduce these to the gardening public. These, along with new introductions from around the world and a chance to focus on the enormous but long-neglected opportunities for horticultural innovation and diversity in the Deep South (Zones 8 and 9), have been my motivation.

Bob said he does not take regularly scheduled trips (they are too expensive). He said that he gets a steady infusion of plants from his own collections, from friends, and from collectors overseas, who send him seed. He also gets plants from the people who found them, and these "foundlings" have become introduced through Woodlanders.

Todd Lasseigne, assistant director of the JC Raulston Arboretum (Raleigh, North Carolina) and a Southerner himself, appreciates the plants that Woodlanders has promoted over the years. He says of the co-owners:

> Robert and Julia Mackintosh and Bob McCartney have made Woodlanders a household name in the world of mail-order nurseries. Their offerings of southeastern U.S. natives at reasonable prices continue to distinguish Woodlanders as an icon among all nurseries. Their impact on American horticulture, of greater importance than is generally known, has brought us many southeastern U.S. plant treasures. In the early 1980s, Woodlanders grew plants now considered common, but at the time, were nearly impossible to find. That is Woodlanders's ultimate contribution to horticulture: one of the progenitors of the modern, diverse American garden!

Ken Druse, in his book *The Collector's Garden*, points out that when he travels around the United States, one of the nurseries that plant collectors consistently mention as a source for new plants is Woodlanders. Woodlanders's mission to provide hardy Southeast native and exotic plants in its catalog has been successful. It has also brought horticultural attention to an area generally largely overlooked except in the writings of Elizabeth Lawrence and Caroline Dormon. Some of Woodlanders's introductions follow.

The Arkansas amsonia or Arkansas blue star, *Amsonia hubrichtii* (Apocynaceae), is native to Arkansas and Oklahoma. Like other species in the genus, it produces small, steel-blue star-shaped flowers in late spring. In the fall, the thin, almost needlelike leaves turn a glowing banana yellow and then a golden brown, a highlight in the garden in the late season, particularly in mass plantings. The plant is suitable for large borders as it reaches a height and spread of about 3 feet (0.9 m). It grows best in sunny locations in well-drained, moist soils, but can tolerate light shade. Best of all, the plant requires little, if any, maintenance. Though the Arkansas amsonia was discovered in the wild in 1942 by Leslie Hubricht, a mollusk specialist and naturalist, it was first distributed commercially in the early 1980s by Woodlanders (Taylor 2000), which had obtained it from Ken Wurdack (Maryland), a collector of obscure native plants. The specific epithet honors Hubricht and is sometimes misspelled as *A. hubrectii* or *A. hubrictii*.

Amsonia hubrichtii, in bloom PHOTO BY ROBERT LYONS

Amsonia hubrichtii, fall color PHOTO BY ROBERT LYONS

The swamp jessamine, *Gelsemium rankinii* (Loganiaceae), is a perennial woody climber of the U.S. Southeast and is rare in the wild. Unlike the more widely grown spring-blooming Carolina jessamine (*G. sempervirens*), the swamp jessamine produces spectacular yellow, trumpet-shaped flowers (without any fragrance) both in the spring, usually March and April, *and* in the autumn, usually October and November. It even bears flowers in the winter when the weather is mild. Though native to swamps, it grows well in various types of soil, even in clay and light shade, in which it grows on my mailbox. I acquired my plant in the early 1990s from the North Carolina State University Arboretum and J. C. Raulston, who promoted it heavily. Woodlanders's original stock came from the campus of William and Mary College (Williamsburg, Virginia) from a collection by J. T. Baldwin in Mississippi. Other collections were later made in northwestern Florida by Woodlanders.

Another Woodlanders introduction is *Gelsemium sempervirens* 'Pale Yellow' (also called 'Woodlanders Pale Yellow'), which produces a flower with a much paler color than the typical yellow of *G. sempervirens*. Bob's friend, Chris Early, found it near Eglin Air Force Base (Florida) and passed it along to Woodlanders.

Illicium (Illiciaceae) consists of about forty species of shrubs and small trees. They grow in Southeast Asia with a complementary group in the U.S. Southeast, the West Indies, and in Mexico. The Florida anise tree, *I. floridanum*, has evergreen foliage that is olive green, and waxy flowers. It derives its common name

Gelsemium sempervirens 'Pale Yellow' PHOTO BY JULIA MACKINTOSH

from the anise-like fragrance of the foliage of some species, which is noticeable when you break or bruise the leaves.

The Mexican anise-tree, *Illicium mexicanum*, has lustrous dark leaves and cinnabar-red flowers about 2 inches (5 cm) across. The habit is pyramidal. Like most anise-trees, it has a long blooming season, from the spring till fall. Bob obtained his plant from the U.S. National Arboretum, which had gotten it through the efforts of Harold Hopkins (Maryland), a former president of the Magnolia Society.

Illicium 'Woodland Ruby', the pink anise-tree, is a chance hybrid that originated at Woodlanders between the red-flowered *I. mexicanum* and the white-flowered *I. floridanum* f. *album*, the Florida anise-tree. It is a vigorous, evergreen shrub with pink flowers, which are larger than either of the parents.

Virginia sweetspire or Virginia willow, *Itea virginica* (Escalloniaceae), is a deciduous to semi-evergreen shrub to about 5 feet (1.5 m) tall and up to 4 feet (1.2 m) across. In its native habitat, it is found primarily along streams and moist areas from the New Jersey pine barrens southward to Florida and Louisiana, bearing fragrant flowers in midspring. It grows best in full sun, but in the garden it will tolerate some shade and a variety of soil types.

A selection called 'Henry's Garnet' has a rich history and has been an award winner for its brilliant red-purple to garnet-burgundy autumn foliage and long, drooping racemes of white flowers, up to 6 inches (15 cm) long. Mary Gibson

Illicium mexicanum PHOTO BY JULIA MACKINTOSH

Itea virginica 'Henry's Garnet' PHOTO BY ROBERT LYONS

Itea virginica 'Henry's Garnet', fall color PHOTO BY ROBERT LYONS

Henry of the Henry Foundation for Botanical Research (Gladwyne, Pennsylvania) collected this form in 1954 in Coweta County, Georgia. She liked it and planted it along the driveway in Gladwyne. The Scott Arboretum at Swarthmore College (Pennsylvania) obtained cuttings of the plant and grew them. There the plant's autumn colors caught the attention of Michael Dirr in 1982 (Copeland and Armitage 2001). Woodlanders first distributed the plant as 'Selected Form' in 1985. Swarthmore College gave it the appellation 'Henry's Garnet' to honor Mrs. Henry, and Woodlanders offered it under its new name beginning in its fall 1986 catalog. Most gardeners consider the leaf color and flower spires superior to the species.

Other Woodlanders introductions of *Itea virginica* are 'Longspire', which Robert and Julia Mackintosh found while canoeing along the Savannah River near Augusta, Georgia. It has exceptionally long flower racemes. *Itea* 'Sarah Eve', selected by Nancy Bissett of the Natives Nursery in Polk County, Florida, is named for her daughter. Bissett gave the seedling to Bob who propagated it vegetatively. 'Sarah Eve' was the first known pink-flowered *Itea*.

Another Southeast native shrub that Woodlanders has promoted is the titi or leatherwood, *Cyrilla* (Cyrillaceae). *Cyrilla racemiflora* is a sprawling shrub typically found in low, wet areas in the U.S. Southeast's Coastal Plain. It produces white flowers on 6-inch (15-cm) racemes. The leaves are evergreen in the Deep South and deciduous farther north (Dirr 2002). One selection, 'Graniteville', is a short, low-spreading compact form that Bob found near Graniteville in Aiken County, South Carolina, growing on eroded kaolin-sand soils. It is hardy in USDA Zones 6 to 11.

Cyrilla arida is a smaller version of *C. racemiflora* in all respects. After a lot of detective work, Bob and plantsman Ken Wurdack re-discovered it in Highlands County, Florida, at Sebring, near the original site of the first known collection of the species by John K. Small, curator at the New York Botanical Garden and U.S. Southeast plant explorer who began collecting in the late nineteenth century. In its native dry, scrubby habitat, *C. arida* grows among *Nolina brittoniana*, *Pinus clausa*, *Quercus myrtifolia*, and *Q. chapmanii*. This evergreen grows to 6 feet (1.8 m) tall and has small leaves. *Cyrilla arida* does well in sandy, well-drained soils. It is hardy to USDA Zone 7. Woodlanders introduced it into cultivation. The original plant they collected is 11 feet (3.3 m) tall after twenty years of growth.

Thelypteris kunthii (Thelypteridaceae) is known both as the Southern shield fern and the abundant maiden fern. In the United States it is distributed from South Carolina to Florida and westward along the Gulf states to Texas. It is a deciduous fern with large pale green fronds. The plant spreads slowly from rhizomatous clumps, producing fronds about 3 to 5 feet (0.9–1.5 m) tall. *Thelypteris kunthii* does well in moist conditions, often growing around seasonal ponds and ditches in part sun to shade. It tolerates a bit more sun than most ferns and is hardy in USDA Zones 7 to 9. The Mackintoshes obtained the Southern shield fern from a roadside ditch near Savannah, Georgia. Now Bob gets his plants through tissue culture.

Thelypteris kunthii PHOTO BY TONY AVENT

The whorled sunflower, *Helianthus verticillatus* (Asteraceae), has limited distribution in four southern states. John K. Small described it as a new species in 1898. Since then it has been determined to be a natural hybrid of *H. angustifolius* and *H. grosseserratus*. After a hundred years, it was recollected in the mid-1990s in northwestern Georgia and northeastern Alabama and in 1998 in western Tennessee. Now new morphological descriptions and root-tip chromosome studies suggest it is not a hybrid but a fertile diploid species of sunflower (SERPIN 2003). It grows to about 10 feet (3 m) tall and has whorls of pale green, lanceolate leaves and terminal clusters of deep yellow ray flowers that are 3 inches (7.5 cm) across. It blooms in late August to October, typically growing in "moist, prairie-like openings in woodlands and along adjacent creeks . . . in sandy clays" (U.S. Fish and Wildlife Service 2000) in a community known as the tall grass prairie. The plant is designated as endangered in some listings. Bob obtained his plant from George Sanko at Georgia Perimeter College in Atlanta.

Aster carolinianus (syn. *Ampelaster carolinianus*), the climbing aster, is a Southeast native from North Carolina southward to Florida, primarily in the Coastal Plain around marshes, shores, and other open, wet areas. Woodlanders introduced it in 1984, probably the first time it was available to the gardening public. The main stem and principal branches of the climbing aster are woody, about 0.4 inch (1 cm) thick, from which new growth is produced each spring. In the wild

Aster carolinianus PHOTO BY TONY AVENT

the aster can clamber up to 20 feet (6 m) over bushes, sometimes upon itself, but in the garden 6–10 feet (1.8–3 m) is more common. It does not produce tendrils or other holdfasts, but rather clasps by its sprawling stems, launching itself upon a fence, trellis, or on surrounding vegetation. *Aster carolinianus* produces numerous rose-magenta flowers in late October, and in the Middle South is often still blooming at the end of November and occasionally at Christmas time. The climbing aster is a member of the Asteraceae and is hardy to USDA Zone 6.

Hypericum reductum (Clusiaceae, formerly Hypericaceae) is a small, semi-decumbent shrub growing to about 6 to 8 inches (15–20 cm) tall. Its leaves are tiny and needlelike, no more than 0.4 inch (1 cm) long. *Hypericum reductum* is somewhat stoloniferous, spreading perhaps to 3 feet (0.9 m) wide. It produces yellow, five-petaled flowers from June to September. Its range is the Coastal Plain from the Carolinas to the Florida Panhandle where it grows in flatwoods and sandy areas. In the garden it should be sited in a sunny location, in well-drained sandy soil.

A close relative of *Hypericum reductum*, *H. lloydii* grows in dry pine woods and among rocky outcrops; it tends to have a bit larger leaves (greater than 0.4 inch or 1 cm long). It is less common in its range from North Carolina to Georgia and produces golden-colored flowers in midsummer. It is also a smaller plant than *H. reductum*, shorter spreading to only about 1 foot (0.3 m) wide.

Woodlanders appears to be the first nursery to propagate and offer these and other Southern native *Hypericum* species.

Hypericum lloydii PHOTO BY JULIA MACKINTOSH

Woodlanders was one of the first nurseries to promote *Baptisia* species (Fabaceae) other than *B. australis*, the blue false indigo. One species that Woodlanders has promoted is the white false indigo, *B. alba*, a native of the southern United States. It grows up to 4 feet (1.2 m) tall and about 3 feet (0.9 m) wide, producing showy white, pealike flowers in late spring. The plant is suitable for well-drained soils in full sun to part shade. *Baptisia alba* is native to dry open woods and cleared areas from Virginia to Florida. The foliage is blue-gray and the stems are charcoal gray. The plant is hardy in USDA Zones 5 to 9.

Another one, first offered in 1987 from material collected in Chambers County, Texas, is *Baptisia sphaerocarpa*, the yellow false indigo. Still another, *B. megacarpa*, the streamside wild indigo from Florida, has creamy yellow flowers.

Mountain laurels are exclusively a North American genus, ranging from Alaska to Cuba. They belong to the genus *Kalmia* (Ericaceae) and all are low to medium-sized shrubs, rarely small trees, with leathery evergreen leaves (Jaynes 1997). *Kalmia latifolia*, the mountain laurel, ranges in the eastern United States

Kalmia latifolia 'Pristine' PHOTO BY JULIA MACKINTOSH

from Maine to Mississippi and flowers in late spring to early summer. The corolla is light pink with purple spots around the anther pockets, the small pouches on the corolla that hold the anthers attached to "elastic" filaments, which release pollen when disturbed by an insect. It is highly valued as an ornamental plant.

Most *Kalmia* varieties and ecotypes in cultivation came from nurseries in the North or from higher elevations of the southern Appalachians. Woodlanders began offering kalmias from the Deep South as these were presumed to be more heat tolerant.

Kalmia latifolia 'Pristine' has pure white buds and flowers and clean foliage that is resistant to most insects. It grows to about 4 feet (1.2 m) tall and wide. 'Pristine' was discovered by Ernestine Law, a gardener, in Aiken, South Carolina, in the mid-1980s. Ernestine told her friends, the Mackintoshes, who collected the plant and grew it in the garden at Woodlanders. The plant has now been tissue cultured by a lab in the state of Washington. Initially it was offered exclusively by Woodlanders in 1989. It is hardy in USDA Zones 5 to 9.

Dichondra sericea (Convolvulaceae), the silver dichondra, is a species new to me. Woodlanders introduced it from a collection Bob made in 1993 at Sierra de la Ventana, south of Buenos Aires (Argentina) in "gaucho country." He describes it as a "low, creeping ground cover with very silvery, rounded leaves about the size of a quarter." It is ideal for the sunny border or the rock garden, where it will not be trampled on. It is hardy in USDA Zones 7 to 9.

Concentrating on an area largely ignored since the days of John Bartram and André Michaux, Woodlanders has done an invaluable service in promoting plants of the southeastern United States. Many of its introductions are now firmly established in cultivation.

Bob McCartney PHOTO BY BOBBY J. WARD

Robert B. "Bob" McCartney
Woodlanders
1128 Colleton Avenue
Aiken, SC 29801
United States
www.woodlanders.net

26

Invasive Plants

What is a weed? A plant whose virtues
have not yet been discovered.

Ralph Waldo Emerson, *The Fortune of the Republic* (1878)

I grew up on a farm in eastern North Carolina, where agricultural crops such as cotton, peanuts, and corn frequently needed weeding by hoe or hand. "The peanuts need to be grassed," my father would say, meaning that the grass and other pestiferous weeds needed to be pulled out by hand. Grassing was a summer chore and one that never thrilled me. No wonder I always looked forward to late August when the school year would begin again. (I would learn there were other meanings for "grass" and "weed" during my college education in the 1960s.)

Now I have before me two books: one titled *Gardening by the Sea* (Foley 1998), the other, *Invasive Plants: Weeds of the Global Garden* (John M. Randall and Marinelli 1996). The former bears august endorsements on its dust jacket from *The New York Times* and *Boston Herald*; the latter furnishes no seals of approval, but its forty authors display an impressive list of credentials. An examination of the two books shows considerable contradiction. In the first book *Euonymus fortunei* (the shrub wintercreeper) is "valued for colorful fruits . . .[and] variegated foliage." It creates a "richly textured surface" and "it is most valuable" for the landscape. There is no admonition that it can run amuck and become rampant, or that you would even want to contain it. The other book notes that wintercreeper "smothers and kills wildflowers . . . and trees" and results in loss of landscape diversity, flowers, and shelter for butterflies "and many other creatures." The authors suggest ultimately eliminating *Euonymus* by application of a twenty-percent solution of glyphosate herbicide.

Note: *John M. Randall* is an invasive weed specialist for The Nature Conservancy and lives in California. *John L. (Johnny) Randall* is a conservationist with the North Carolina Botanical Garden and lives in North Carolina. They lecture and write extensively about invasive plants and, because of name similarities, are frequently confused and miscited in scientific and lay literature.

The two books contain other examples of dueling horticulturism. Both include *Buddleja* spp. (butterfly bush), *Digitalis purpurea* (common foxglove), *Ilex aquifolium* (English holly), *Nandina domestica* (heavenly bamboo), and *Taxus cuspidata* (Japanese yew)—one recommending to plant them and the other to nuke them. Depending on which book you consult, these plants, and many others they cite, either naturalize beautifully or spread vigorously out of control. *Invasive Plants* recommends that you can defend your property by increasing the potency of the chemical arsenal; all else failing, use a hand-held propane torch (honest to goodness—that is what it says). No toleration for hand-pulling, they.

What intrigues me most is that the plants in the six examples above are in my garden and behave themselves reasonably well (at least the last time I looked). What frightens me is that the books do not mention the two weediest plants in my garden, *Microstegium vimineum* (Japanese stilt-grass) and *Stellaria media* (chickweed) though I spend hours each year trying to eradicate them. The plants in the six examples given above are easily obtainable from nurseries, garden centers, and even through mail order, though not *Microstegium* or *Stellaria* as far as I know, unless they hitch a ride in a nursery pot.

Clearly there are strong differences of opinion at work here on *what* a weed is and *where* it is a weed. I single out these two books as examples, but there are many more on the shelves with dichotomous points of view. Ralph Waldo Emerson provided a definition of a weed, still appropriate today, in a speech in Boston in 1878. He said, "A weed is a plant whose virtues have not yet been discovered." So what is a flummoxed gardener or landscaper to do, and whose advice should one listen to when assaulted by a welter of information?

Invasive plants *are* a serious business in the United States. About three hundred species currently invade wildlands and are therefore weeds in Emerson's definition (John M. Randall and Marinelli 1996). We refer to them as *invasive exotics*, non-indigenous invasives, or alien invasives, the latter moniker sounding rather Hollywoodesque. They cause economic and environmental harm including damaging agricultural crops, displacing native plants, altering natural (as well as artificial) areas, invading local ecosystems, affecting water availability, and impacting native wildlife—to name just a few of these problems. Johnny L. Randall (pers. comm.) points out that many invasive exotic plants do not require soil disturbance for seed germination and growth as most annual weeds do; they frequently have fleshy fruits for dispersal by birds, can germinate in many different sites, and some propagate vegetatively.

Unfortunately, roughly half of the invader plants in the United States were imported for well-intentioned horticultural and agricultural reasons, but they muscled their way out of the garden and off the farm. Some species have become widespread, such as *Ailanthus altissima* (ailanthus or tree-of-heaven); it has book and Hollywood fame as the tree in Betty Smith's *A Tree Grows in Brooklyn*, where it is noted that "no matter where its seed fell, it made a tree . . . the only tree that grew out of cement . . . [and] neglected brush heaps." The roots of *Tamarix* species (tamarisk) seek groundwater and lower the level of water table in locales in the U.S. West. *Gypsophila paniculata* (baby's breath), innocent as it may appear, is wreaking havoc with native plants on freshwater dune habitats of the Great Lakes because "it has a 15-foot [4.5-m] taproot, about as big around as your thigh" (Raver 1999). In the U.S. Southeast, there are the legendary infestations of the climbing vine *Pueraria montana* var. *lobata* (kudzu), which one writer has dubbed "cathedrals of kudzu," smothering the landscape, including tall trees, but not live-stock and children as legends would have you believe. Interestingly, *Invasive Plants* does not list kudzu, probably because it is already considerably out of con-trol. Some plants are regional invasives such as *Melaleuca quinquenervia* (cajeput tree) from Australia, now invading South Florida's wetlands. In California, an 8000-acre (3200-ha) population of *Arundo donax* (giant cane) is strangling banks along the Santa Ana River, while the plant is being simultaneously sold in nurs-eries a few miles away. Surprisingly, the mainland U.S. state with the most inva-sive plants is not Florida or California; it is New York (John M. Randall and Marinelli 1996).

A rogues' gallery of other irksome plants is found; however, the problem does not limit itself to invasions only *into* the United States. American plants are frequent fliers to other continents. *Robinia pseudoacacia* (black locust), a native of the eastern United States, is a serious invasive problem in much of Europe and the United Kingdom, and *Solidago canadensis* (goldenrod) is taking over wetlands in Japan (Johnny L. Randall 1999). *Buddleja davidii* (butterfly bush), a plant from China introduced about 1900 into the West, is now a pest in the United Kingdom, particularly in disturbed areas such as railways. Take a midsummer train ride from London's Gatwick Airport southward to the coastal city of Eastbourne, for example, and you will see miles and miles of butterfly bush, brushing against speeding trains and lapping at oblivious passengers. Yet it is still avidly recom-mended to wildlife gardeners for its attraction to butterflies.

Invasive plant introductions are not just by mom-and-pop operations or from arrogant plantspeople, who should know better, and who secret seed, plants, or cuttings in dirty clothes hidden in their luggage as they breeze through agricul-tural inspections at airports. Some big-name heavyweights are also associated with invasive plants in the United States. *Sapium sebiferum* (Chinese tallow tree) was first introduced by Benjamin Franklin in 1776 as a potential seed oil crop; now the plant is invasive in wetlands on the Gulf Coast and along the Atlantic Coast northward to North Carolina. The celebrated David Fairchild, for whom the renowned Fairchild Tropical Garden in Miami is named, grew the afore-mentioned kudzu in Washington, D.C., near Rock Creek, though it was intro-duced into the United States in 1876 by others. He writes in *The World Was My Garden* (1938) that

> seedlings all took root with a vengeance, grew over the bushes and climbed the pines, smothering them with masses of vegetation which bent them to

the ground and became an awful, tangled nuisance. I spent over two hundred dollars in the years which followed trying to get rid of it, but when we sold the place there was still some kudzu behind the house and the new owner pastured his cow on it all summer

Fairchild introduced *Jasminum* species (Gold Coast and Brazilian jasmines). Brazilian jasmine now invades hardwood forests in Florida, where "dense concentrations of jasmine seedlings can be found sprouting from raccoon droppings" (John M. Randall and Marinelli 1996). The U.S. Department of Agriculture encouraged the use of kudzu for erosion control and many grasses that have become problematic have entered the country for benign reasons: *Arundo donax* (giant reed), *Cortaderia jubata* and *C. selloana* (pampas grasses), and *Miscanthus sinensis* (Chinese silver grass).

Panayoti Kelaidis (2002) of the Denver Botanic Gardens points out:

The general drift I get from those who claim to be anti-exoticists . . . is that we must somehow go back, restore or re-create an untrammeled, presettlement flora. Do we mean pre-European settlement, or prior to Amerindian settlement? America's "native peoples" (who were Eurasian transplants, incidentally) are now credited with vectoring more and more "native" plants: the ranges of Kentucky coffee trees in the East and *Datura wrightii* in the West are two of many plants that may in large part be thanks to prehistoric human distribution.

Panayoti goes on to say:

How far back do we go? Coast redwoods and cycads grew in Colorado in Cenozoic times: are you going to tell me that these are not native? If I were to plant my rock garden with a lush endemic Tertiary flora (it could be argued that's precisely what many woodland gardeners are doing), would I not be trumping [a] depauperate Pleistocene flora (horribly mucked up by mammoths and cave men)? You can see that things can get a bit slippery if you really want to get literal minded [when talking about native plants versus exotics].

This is an argument made frequently. I remember J. C. Raulston at North Carolina State University making this point and opening my eyes at a lecture in the early 1990s.

To set the record straight, there are American native plants that are also problematic even here in North America. One example is *Robinia pseudoacacia* (black locust), a weedy plant which frequents disturbed woodlands and urban landscapes. In 1996 Hurricane Fran toppled thirteen trees in my yard in Raleigh, North Carolina. I spent considerable time the next two summers whacking back the comely *Phytolacca americana* (pokeweed) whose seeds from bird droppings, I suppose, had lain dormant till there was sufficient sun and moisture to stimulate germination. In addition, *Toxicodendron radicans* (poison ivy) began spreading around in formerly shaded, but now disturbed, areas. In a purely ecological sense, pokeweed and poison ivy are opportunistic weeds, taking advantage of disturbance, and are not invasives, in the classical definition, as they do not disrupt whole ecosystems. Plants such as poison ivy specialize in colonizing or invading disturbed areas. Generally, no *native* plant is declared invasive even if it "invades" where it's not wanted. I now think the grasses and other weeds I pulled from crops on our farm years ago were native plants. Such disturbed areas are fruitful grounds for natives as well as non-native plants. Hurricanes, floods, fire, and tornadoes are constantly creating new disturbed areas and no one requires a passport or visa for entry.

The cost to contain invasive exotics is staggeringly expensive. The U.S. Department of the Interior estimated that "invasive plants are causing $123 billion a year in damage" and the acreage affected is expanding at a rate of 3 million acres (1.2 million ha) a year (Raver 1999). Another source, citing Cornell University, estimates a cost of $138 billion a year (Westbrooks 2001). Considerable finger-pointing goes around on who is to blame and who is responsible for controlling them. Johnny L. Randall and Rob Gardner (2000) explain that invasive, non-native plants are the current hot-button topic for the nursery industry, professional horticulturists, and the home gardener, whom many ecologists and botanists blame for the problem:

> Ecologists have, for example, labeled an entire species as invasive when it's actually only one variety that is causing the problem. Horticulturists, on the other hand, continue to propagate and market plants without realizing they are invasive plants.

That is the heart of the conflict and the source of the extreme viewpoints.

Plant scientists and nursery owners are working on the problem, particularly for new introductions, and U.S. government regulations are attempting to control invasive plants and prevent the introduction of new ones. Reputable plant hunters who find a marvelous new plant or horticultural variety test it thoroughly for invasiveness potential before offering it for sale to the public. (See, for example, the testing protocols for introduction of new plants on the Web sites of Plant Delights and Heronswood nurseries.) Sarah Reichard (University of Washington in Seattle) has developed a model for risk assessment that can predict the invasive potential for non-native woody species and help screen new introductions (Reichard 2000a). In January 1999, U.S. President Clinton issued an executive order charging several federal departments to develop a plan to solve the problem. For seed coming into the United States, the U.S. Department of Agriculture is requiring phytosanitary permits, but this deals only with diseases and does not apply to invasiveness issues.

The downside of such requirements is that they concern nursery owners who fear that new plant introductions, their life blood, will dry up (Raver 1999).

Further, the typical rock gardener who relies on seed from societies abroad (often distributed free to members) is likely to see the stock of harmless garden plants considerably diminished. A gardening friend told me once:

> Sometimes it is overlooked that all plants are native to this one planet and that wind, water, and birds and animals do a fairly decent job of spreading them about across political and geographical boundaries without the help of mankind, thank you.

So where are we? Backyard gardens, farmland, city parks, canals and drainage ditches, abandoned lots, cemeteries, and other ruderal areas are not natural landscapes; these areas are artificial and thus vulnerable to invasion by alien plants without controls by natural predators or competitors to keep them in check. Barry Yinger says, "Native plants did not evolve for our current disturbed landscapes, and it is romantic nonsense to claim that they are the answer to our landscape problems" (Raver 1999). Importantly, he points out that the plants that adapt best to our contemporary, unnatural landscapes are often the non-native or exotic plants. And that is often exactly what is happening. Some argue that "man-dispersed species actually increase biological diversity, benefit ecosystems . . . and that [they are] a potent driving force in evolution" (Theodoropoulos 2003).

Awareness about invasive plants is not entirely a recent phenomenon. Charles Darwin noticed invasive exotics in the 1830s and wrote about them in chapter three of *On the Origin of the Species* (1859):

> Several of the plants, such as the cardoon and a tall thistle, which are now the most commonest over the wide plains of La Plata [Argentina], clothing square leagues of surface almost to the exclusion of all other plants, have been introduced from Europe.

He also reported on plants "which have been imported from America" ranging in India from the Himalaya to Cape Comorin on the southernmost tip of the Indian subcontinent. The invasiveness Darwin witnessed has grown exponentially around the world; new plants are being constantly introduced and plants are escaping to uncontrolled areas. Thus, it is not a past tense thing. Getting consensus on which are the "good guys" and which the "bad guys" remains elusive. Dan Ward, a botanist retired from the University of Florida, says that plant "invasiveness is like pornography; I know it when I see it" (Ferriter 1999). Unfortunately, like pornography, everyone sees something different.

Bibliography

Ahlburg, Marlene S. 1993. *Hellebores: Christmas Rose, Lenten Rose*. London: B. T. Batsford.

Alpine Garden Society. 1993. Conservation and the Alpine Garden Society. *Quarterly Bulletin of the Alpine Garden Society* 61 (3): 236–237.

Anderson, Edward F. 2001. *The Cactus Family*. Portland, Oregon: Timber Press.

Anonymous. 1995. Mail-order explorer: Championing the Southeast. *American Horticulturist* (6 May).

Anonymous. 1996. Bill McNamara: Plant world explorer. *California Garden* (November–December): 1.

Archibald, James C. 1963a. Corsican spring. *Quarterly Bulletin of the Alpine Garden Society* 31 (3): 205–218.

Archibald, James C. 1963b. Among Moroccan mountains. *Quarterly Bulletin of the Alpine Garden Society* 31 (4): 314–340.

Archibald, James C. 1971. *Euphorbia niciciana*. *Journal of the Royal Horticultural Society* (May): 232–234.

Archibald, James C. 1982. The introduction and maintenance of new plants. In *Alpines '81. Report of the Fifth International Rock Garden Plant Conference and Show*, ed. A. Evans, 99–123. Nottingham, United Kingdom: Alpine Garden Society.

Archibald, James C. 1993. People and their plants: Hellebores at Buckshaw, 1964–1983. In *The Gardener's Guide to Growing Hellebores*, Graham Rice and Elizabeth Strangman, 115–118. Portland, Oregon: Timber Press.

Archibald, James C. 1999. Silken sad uncertain queens. *Quarterly Bulletin of the Alpine Garden Society* 67 (3): 245–264.

Archibald, James C. 2000. Raiser unknown: Eric Smith, a plantsman. *Hardy Plant Society* 22 (1): 94 ff.

Argus, G. W. 1973. The genus *Salix* in Alaska and Yukon. Canadian Museum of Nature. http://info.dec.state.ak.us/pdf/usfs/ARGUS_73/SALIXAK1.pdf (accessed 17 July 2003).

Argus, G. W., C. L. McJannet, and M. J. Dallwitz. 2000. Salicaceae of the Canadian arctic archipelago: Descriptions, illustrations, identification, and information retrieval. Memorial University of Newfoundland. http://www.mun.ca/biology/delta/arcticf/sal/www/wlsare.htm (accessed 17 July 2003).

Armitage, Allan M. 2001. *Manual of Annuals, Biennials, and Half-Hardy Perennials*. Portland, Oregon: Timber Press.

Avent, Tony. 1995. Cutting through the jungle: Native plant myths and realities. Raleigh *News & Observer* (North Carolina), 11 March.

Avent, Tony. 1997. Bizarre plants that only a mother could love. http://www. plantdelights.com/Tony/bizarre.html (accessed 28 February 2004).

Avent, Tony. 1999. The trademark myth: when is a name not a name. *Nursery Management Pro* (October).

Avent, Tony. 2000. Cool blue hostas. *Fine Gardening* (February): 46–50.

Avent, Tony. 2002. Revenge of the "redneck lupines." *Horticulture* (May–June): 70–75.

Bartholomew, Bruce. 1997. Asia: in search of horticultural treasure. *Leaflet and Calendar* (Newsletter of the Strybing Arboretum Society) 20 (4): 1–3.

Bartram, William. 1980. *Travels Through North and South Carolina, Georgia, East and West Florida*. Charlottesville: University of Virginia Press.

Basement Shaman. 2003. *Heimia salicifolia*. http://basementshaman.com/heimsal.html (accessed 6 November 2003).

Baumann, Adrienne. 1995. Stalking the threatened plant. *Sonoma Business* (October): 82–84.

Beckett, Kenneth, ed. 1993. *Encyclopaedia of Alpines*. 2 vols. Pershore, Worcestershire: Alpine Garden Society.

Bender, Steve, and Felder Rushing. 1993. *Passalong Plants*. Chapel Hill: University of North Carolina Press.

Bird, Richard, and John Kelly. 1994. *The Complete Book of Alpine Gardening*. London: Wardlock.

Bishop, Joshua. 2002. Markets for environmental services and rural developments. In *World Summit on Sustainable Development Parallel Event: Mainstreaming Biodiversity at the Bioregional Scale* (conference proceedings 30 September 2003). Roodespoort, South Africa: National Botanic Institute and Witwatersrand Botanical Gardens.

Boroughs, Don. 1999. Battle for a wild garden. *International Wildlife* (May–June): 12–21.

Bown, Deni. 2000. *Aroids: Plants of the Arum Family*. 2nd ed. Portland, Oregon: Timber Press.

Branney, Tim, and Adam Draper. 2000. New epimediums and ginger introductions. *Plants* 6 (1): 4–6.

Brody, Jane E. 1998. Rootin' shootin' raiders conquer new ground. *New York Times*, 9 June.

Brown, Jennifer. 2001. Plant hunting in China: An interview with Darrell Probst. Online Extra to *Fine Gardening Magazine*. http://www.taunton.com/finegardening/pages/g00092.asp (accessed 13 August 2001).

Buchan, Ursula. 2000. Heaps and hellebores. *The Garden* 125 (8): 18–21.

Campbell, Faith Thompson. 1989. The problem of wild-collected bulbs from the perspective of the natural resources defense council. *Herbertia* 45 (1–2): 1–5.

Carlock, Marty. 1998. Love on the rocks. *The American Gardener* (January–February): 33–37.

Cascorbi, Alice. 1995. The edge of the world revisited. *Bulletin of the University of California, Santa Cruz, Arboretum Associates* (Summer): 4.

Chadwell, Chris A. 1985. Kashmir botanical expedition 1983. *The Rock Garden* 19 (3): 290–293.

Chadwell, Chris A. 1986. Some notable high alpines introduced from the Kashmir Botanical Expedition 1983. *The Rock Garden* 19 (4): 354–356.

Chadwell, Chris A. 1993. Twelve seeded high-alpines. *The Rock Garden* 23 (2): 195–201.

Chadwell, Chris A. 1994a. A Himalayan plant hunter's foray into New Zealand. *The Rock Garden* 23 (4): 418–429.

Chadwell, Chris A. 1994b. Flowers fit for a Maharaja. *The Garden* 119 (3): 121–124.

Chadwell, Chris A. 2000a. Anatomical and chemical studies of Himalayan joint-pines: *Ephedra. Sino-Himalayan Plant Association Newsletter* 20 (1): 23–26.

Chadwell, Chris A. 2000b. Plant hunting in the Lumbasumba Himal, East Nepal. *The Rock Garden* 26 (4): 324–326.

Chadwell, Chris A. 2001a. Good Himalayan plant introductions. *Plants* 6 (3): 106–108.

Chadwell, Chris A. 2001b. In search of Himalayan lilies. *Rock Garden Quarterly* 59 (3): 165–170.

Chadwell, Chris A. 2002. The cultivation of some Himalayan lilies. *Rock Garden Quarterly* 60 (3): 179–186.

Challenger, Charlie. 1996. The pleasure of *Crocus. The New Zealand Garden Journal* (Journal of the Royal New Zealand Institute of Horticulture) 1 (1): 12–17.

Charlesworth, Geoffrey B. 1988. *The Opinionated Gardener*. Boston: David R. Godine.

Cheers, Gordon. 1999. *Botanica: The Illustrated A–Z of over 10,000 Garden Plants and How to Cultivate Them*. 3rd ed. New York: Ball Publishing.

Clabby, Catherine. 2002. Botanist's creed: Avoid kudzu, other aggressive plants. Raleigh *News & Observer* (North Carolina), 6 January.

Clark, Ethne. 1999. Peckerwood Garden. *Pacific Horticulture* 60 (4): 24–29.

Clebsch, Betsy. 1997. *Salvias*. Portland, Oregon: Timber Press.

Clebsch, Betsy. 2003. *The New Book of Salvias*. Portland, Oregon: Timber Press.

Clinton, William J. 1999. Executive Order 13112. Invasive species. *Code of Federal Regulations*. Title 3.

Coats, Alice M. 1964. *Garden Shrubs and Their Histories*. New York: E. P. Dutton and Company.

Coats, Alice M. 1969. *The Plant Hunters*. New York: McGraw-Hill.

Compton, James. 1985. Some worthwhile Mexican salvias. *The Garden* 110 (3): 122–124.

Compton, James. 1999. Heronswood. *Gardens Illustrated* (September): 92–97.

Copeland, Linda L., and Allan M. Armitage. 2001. *Legends in the Garden: Who in the World Is Nellie Stevens?* Atlanta: Wings Publishers.

Cowie, Denise. 2000. A globe-trotting gardener finds a cozy spot under Burpee's tree. *Philadelphia Inquirer*, 28 July.

Cowling, Richard, and Dave Richardson. 1995. *Fynbos: South Africa's Unique Floral Kingdom*. Vlaeberg, South Africa: Fernwood Press.

Creech, John L. 2000. Plant hunting: then and now. *The American Gardener* (July–August): 24.

Dallmann, Peter R. 1998. *Plant Life in the World's Mediterranean Climates*. Sacramento, California: California Native Plant Society.

Darke, Rick. 1999a. *The Color Encyclopedia of Ornamental Grasses*. Portland, Oregon: Timber Press.

Darke, Rick. 1999b. Fusion horticulture: Plant hunter Barry Yinger is bringing the best of the East to the West. *The American Gardener* (January–February): 48–53.

Darwin, Charles. 1967. *On the Origin of Species*. New York: Crowell-Collier.

Davidson, B. LeRoy. 1996. Some elegant eriogonums. In *Rock Garden Plants of North America*, ed. Jane McGary, 122–125.. Portland, Oregon: Timber Press.

Davidson, B. LeRoy. 2000. *Lewisias*. Portland, Oregon: Timber Press.

Davis, Peter. 1965–1988. *Flora of Turkey*. 10 vols. Edinburgh: University Press.

Del Tredici, Peter. 2000. Plant exploration: A historic overview. In *Plant Exploration: Protocols for the Present, Concerns for the Future* (symposium proceedings, 18–19 March 1999), ed. J. R. Ault, 1–5. Glencoe, Illinois: Chicago Botanic Garden.

Denman, Della. 1993. Slough's exotic climbers. *Independent* (London), 13 June.

Dirr, Michael A. 1990. *Manual of Woody Landscape Plants: Their Identification, Ornamental Characteristics, Culture, Propagation, and Uses*. Champaign, Illinois: Stipes Publishing.

Dirr, Michael A. 2002. *Dirr's Trees and Shrubs for Warm Climates*. Portland, Oregon: Timber Press.

Druse, Ken. 1996. *The Collector's Garden: Designing with Extraordinary Plants*. New York: Clarkson Potter.

Dufresne, Richard. 1999. Agastaches for the rock garden. *Rock Garden Quarterly* 57 (3): 184–189.

Dupree, A. Hunter. 1968. *Asa Gray: 1818–1888*. Cambridge, Massachusetts: Harvard University Press.

Easton, Valerie. 1999. Bring them back alive. *The Seattle Times*, 31 October.

Easton, Valerie. 2001. Burpeewood? Heronsburp. *The Seattle Times*, 4 March.

Easton, Valerie. 2002. Seeds of success. *The Seattle Times*, 29 September.

Edwards, Amelia B. 1892. *Pharaohs, Fellahs, and Explorers*. New York: Harper and Brothers.

Elizabeth, Mary. 2000. Steppe. Blue Planet Biomes. http://www.blueplanetbiomes.org/steppe.htm.

Fairchild, David. 1938. *The World Was My Garden*. New York: Charles Scribner's Sons.

Fairchild, David. 1948. *Garden Islands of the Great East*. New York: Charles Scribner's Sons.

Fairey, John G., and Carl M. Schoenfeld. 1993. Mexican magic. *American Nurseryman* 178 (12): 55–79.

Fairey, John G., and Carl M. Schoenfeld. 1994. Mexican dogwoods. *Pacific Horticulture* 55 (3): 42–46.

Fairey, John G., and Carl M. Schoenfeld. 1995. The mystery *Magnolia*: On the trail of *Magnolia tamaulipana* in Mexico. *Magnolia* 57:6–21.

Farrer, Reginald. 1919. *The English Rock Garden*. London: T. C. and E. C. Jack.

Fernandez, Peggy. 1996. Bill McNamara: The Indiana Jones of the plant world. *Aptos Times* (California), 15 August.

Ferriter, Amy. 1999. Editor's note. *Wildland Weeds* (Winter): 4.

Figlar, Richard B. 2001. A taxonomic history. American Magnolia Society. http://www.magnoliasociety.org/classifications_ndx.html (accessed 12 November 2003).

Fischer, Tom. 2003. Epimedium man. *Horticulture* (January–February): 46–53.

Fisher, Kathleen. 2002. Cold-hardy camellias. *The American Gardener* (November–December): 39–43.

Flook, Marnie. 1997. Plants of southern Patagonia. In *Southern Alpines '96* (conference proceedings, 5–10 January 1996), ed. John S. Sheppard, 145–150. Christchurch, New Zealand: Southern Alpines.

Flora of China Project. 2003. Flora of China. http://flora.huh.harvard.edu/china.

Flores, Anita, and John Watson. 2000. Notes on *Puya gilmartiniae* and *Puya coquimbensis*. *The New Plantsman* 7 (2): 87–94.

Foley, Daniel J. 1998. *Gardening by the Sea*. Hyannis, Massachusetts: Parnassus Imprints.

Foote, Leonard E., and Samuel B. Jones, Jr. 1989. *Native Shrubs and Woody Vines of the Southeast*. Portland, Oregon: Timber Press.

Foster, H. Lincoln, and Laura Louise Foster. 1990. *Cuttings from a Rock Garden*. New York: Atlantic Monthly Press.

Furse, Paul. 1963. Some Iranian and Turkish mountain plants. *Quarterly Bulletin of the Alpine Garden Society* 31 (4): 295–304.

The Garden Conservancy. 2000. The Garden Conservancy mourns. *The Garden Conservancy Newsletter* 11 (2): 4.

Gardner, Rob. 2000. Going native. *Wildlife in North Carolina* (April): 17–24.

Garvey, Edward J. 2000. Legal and ethical issues in introducing plants into the United States. In *Plant Exploration: Protocols for the Present, Concerns for the Future* (symposium proceedings, 18–19 March 1999), ed. J. R. Ault, 60–64. Glencoe, Illinois: Chicago Botanic Garden.

Gerard, John. 1975. *Herbal or General History of Plants*, ed. Thomas Johnson. New York: Dover.

Gittlen, William. 1998. *Discovered Alive: The Story of the Chinese Redwood*. Berkeley: Pierside Publications.

Goldblatt, Peter, and John Manning. 2000. *Wildflowers of the Fairest Cape*. Cape Town: Red Roof Design.

Goode, Patrick, and Michael Lancaster. 1986. *The Oxford Companion to Gardens*. Oxford: Oxford University Press.

Grey-Wilson, Christopher. 1999a. Editorial. *Quarterly Bulletin of the Alpine Garden Society* 67 (3): 206–207.

Grey-Wilson, Christopher. 1999b. Trading at a loss. *The Garden* 124 (9): 704–705.

Grey-Wilson, Christopher, ed. 2000. *Erigeron* 'Goat Rocks' award of merit. *Quarterly Bulletin of the Alpine Garden Society* 68 (4): 471–472.

Griffiths, Mark. 1994. *Index of Garden Plants*. Portland, Oregon: Timber Press.

Griffiths, Mark. 1995. *Manual of Bulbs*. Portland, Oregon: Timber Press.

Grimshaw, John. 1998. *The Gardener's Atlas: The Origins, Discovery, and Cultivation of the World's Most Popular Garden Plants*. Buffalo, New York: Firefly Books.

Grothaus, Molly M. 2001. The genus *Erythronium*. In *Bulbs of North America*, ed. Jane McGary, 139–150. Portland, Oregon: Timber Press.

Grounds, Roger. 1989. *Ornamental Grasses*. Bromley, Kent: Christopher Helm.

Gusman, Guy, and Liliane Gusman. 2002. *The Genus Arisaema: A Monograph for Botanists and Nature Lovers*. Ruggell, Lichtenstein: A. R. G. Gantner Verlag KG.

Gustafson, Phyllis. 1995. Marcel Le Piniec Award: Joseph Halda. *Rock Garden Quarterly* 53 (4): 329–330.

Halada, Milan, Josef J. Halda, and Josef Jurášek. 1997. In search of *Saxifraga columnaris* and *S. dinnikii*. *The Saxifrage Magazine* 5: 21–27.

Halda, Josef J. 1973. Plant hunting in the Bulgarian mountains. *Bulletin of the American Rock Garden Society* 31 (2): 54–61.

Halda, Josef J. 1975a. In the Caucasus mountains. *Bulletin of the American Rock Garden Society* 33 (1): 3–10.

Halda, Josef J. 1975b. Plants of Julian Alps and Karawanken Mountains. *Bulletin of the American Rock Garden Society* 33 (4): 195–199.

Halda, Josef J. 1976. King's rock. *Bulletin of the American Rock Garden Society* 34 (2): 66–73.

Halda, Josef J. 1984. The great Fatra. *Bulletin of the American Rock Garden Society* 42 (2): 63–72.

Halda, Josef J. 1991. Ten gems of the Tien Shan. *Bulletin of the American Rock Garden Society* 49 (3): 175–183.

Halda, Josef J. 1992a. *The Genus Primula in Cultivation and the Wild.* Englewood, Colorado: Tethys Books.

Halda, Josef J. 1992b. Ten Primulaceae of the Pamir. *Bulletin of the American Rock Garden Society* 50 (3): 171–176.

Halda, Josef J. 1996. *The Genus Gentiana.* Dobré, Czech Republic: SEN.

Halda, Josef J. 1999. Some taxonomic problems in the genus *Daphne* L. (II). *Acta Musei Richnoviensis* 6 (3): 195–233.

Halda, Josef J. 2001a. *The Genus Daphne.* Dobré, Czech Republic: SEN.

Halda, Josef J. 2001b. *Seeds 2001.* Catalog.

Halda, Josef J., and James W. Waddick. 2004. *The Genus Paeonia.* Portland, Oregon: Timber Press.

Halloy, Stephan. 1996. South American native ornamental begonias. New Zealand Institute for Crop and Food Research. http://www.crop.cri.nz/psp/broadshe/begonia.htm (accessed 12 October 2003).

Hammer, Roger L. 2000. The genus *Jasminum* in Florida. *Wildland Weeds* 4 (Winter): 13–15.

Hammond World Atlas Corporation. 2002. *Hammond Compact Peters World Atlas.* Union, New Jersey: Hammond World Atlas Corporation.

Hannon, Dylan P. 1997. What is a plant collector? *Herbertia* 52: 182–187.

Harkness, Jack. 1977. Breeding with *Hulthemia persica* (*Rosa persica*). From *American Rose Annual.* http://www.geocities.com/kingke.geo/Persica/PERSICA.HTM (accessed 30 August 2003).

Harkness, Jack. 1989. Breeding with *Hulthemia persica*—second report. From *Australian Rose Annual.* http://www.geocities.com/rosebreeder/articles/hulthemia.htm. (accessed 30 August 2003).

Harper, Pamela. 2000. *Time-Tested Plants: Thirty Years in a Four-Season Garden.* Portland, Oregon: Timber Press.

Heeger, Susan. 2003. The garden's sturdy little treasure: *Epimedium. Martha Stewart Living* (April): 103–111.

Hensler, Christy. 2003. Meet the breeder of 'Illumination'. PlantHaven. http://www.planthaven.com/vinca/breeder.html (accessed 13 August 2003).

Hepper, F. Nigel. 1989. *Plant Hunting for Kew.* London: HMSO Publications Centre.

Higgins, Adrian. 2000. Gardeners expand horizons: Horticulturist brings eastern
plants to western gardens. *The Springdale Morning News* (Arkansas), 4 December.

Hilliard, O. M., and B. L. Burtt. 1991. *Dierama: The Hairbells of Africa*. Randburg,
South Africa: Acorn Books.

Hinkley, Daniel J. 1997. A plant treasure hunt. *American Nurseryman* 186 (2): 56–61.

Hinkley, Daniel J. 1999a. *The Explorer's Garden: Rare and Unusual Perennials*.
Portland, Oregon: Timber Press.

Hinkley, Daniel J. 1999b. Nepetas. *Rock Garden Quarterly* 57 (3): 179–184.

Hinkley, Daniel J. 2002. *Gardens Illustrated* (April): 48–55.

Hinsley, Stewart R. 2003. The Fremontodendreae pages.
http://www.meden.demon.co.uk/Malvaceae/Fremontodendreae/
Fremontodendreae.html (accessed 10 October 2003).

Hirshfeld, Mary. 2003. Pretty peonies. Cornell Plantations. http://www.plantations.
cornell.edu/publications/IthacaJournalArticles/Pretty_Peonies.cfm (accessed 13
November 2003).

Hoffmann, Adriana E. 1982. *Flora Silvestre de Chile: Zona Araucana*. Santiago, Chile:
Fundación Claudio Gay.

Hogan, Sean. 1990. Lewisias, wild and cultivated. *Bulletin of the American Rock
Garden Society* 48 (1): 47–52.

Hogan, Sean. 1993. Argentinian plants you can grow. *Bulletin of the American Rock
Garden Society* 51 (4): 257–266.

Hogan, Sean, ed. 2003. *Flora: A Gardener's Encyclopedia*. 2 vols. Portland, Oregon:
Timber Press.

Holubec, Vojtěch. 2001. Occurrence of *Saxifraga columnaris*, *S. dinnikii*, and *S. scleropoda* hybrids in upper Balkaria (Russian Federation). *Journal of the National
Museum* (Prague) 170 (1–4): 111–115.

Hong De-Yuan, Pan Kai-Yu, and Xie Zhong-Wen. 1998. Yinpingmudan: The wild
relative of the king of flowers, *Paeonia suffruticosa* Andrews. From *Acta Phytotaxonomica Sinica* 36 (6): 515–520. http://www.paeon.de/h1/hon/98yin1.html
(accessed 3 November 2003).

Howard, Thad M. 1982. 1981 Mexican plant exploration trip. *Plant Life* 38: 112–116.

Howard, Thad M. 1983. 1982 plant collecting trip into Mexico. *Plant Life* 39: 118–122.

Howard, Thad M. 1986. Stalking the *Polianthes* of Mexico: Part Two, 1985. *Herbertia*
42: 84–86.

Howard, Thad M. 1996. Two new *Zephyranthes* species from Mexico. *Herbertia* 51:
38–41.

Howard, Thad M. 1999. Three new *Milla* species from Mexico. *Herbertia* 54: 232–237.

Howard, Thad M. 2001. *Bulbs for Warm Climates*. Austin: University of Texas Press.

Hudson, Marjorie. 1992. Review of *Among the Tuscarora: The Strange and Mysterious
Death of John Lawson, Gentleman, Explorer, and Writer*. *North Carolina Literary
Review* 1 (1): 62–82.

Hyam, Roger, and Richard Pankhurst. 1995. *Plants and Their Names*. New York:
Oxford University Press.

Ingwersen, Will. 1991. *Alpines*. Portland, Oregon: Timber Press.

Irish, Mary, and Gary Irish. 2000. *Agaves and Yuccas, and Related Plants*. Portland,
Oregon: Timber Press.

Jacobs, Don L. [n.d.]. *Iris* that bloom in shade. *Perennial Notes* (Journal of the Georgia Perennial Plant Association) 6 (2): 6.

Jacobs, Don L. 1982. An American perspective. *American Horticulturist* (December): 20–23, 38.

Jacobs, Don L. 1985. *Lysimachia congestiflora*: Another of Mount Emei's treasures. *Bulletin of the North American Rock Garden Society* 43 (3): 135–138.

Jacobs, Don L. 1993. From China with concern. *Bulletin of the American Rock Garden Society* 51 (2): 136–144.

Jacobs, Don L. 1995. *Pellaea viridis*: A hardy orphan or evolution at work? *Hardy Fern Foundation Newsletter* (Spring): 22–23.

Jaeger, Anne. 2003. Nonmaples are fools for flowering. Transcript. Portland, Oregon: KGW-TV. www.kgw.com/homegarden/stories (accessed 23 September 2003, page no longer available).

Jaynes, Richard A. 1997. *Kalmia: Mountain Laurel and Related Species*. Portland, Oregon: Timber Press.

Jefferson-Brown, Michael, and Harris Howland. 1995. *The Gardener's Guide to Growing Lilies*. Newton Abbot, Devon: David and Charles.

Jermyn, Jim. 2001. *The Himalayan Garden*. Portland, Oregon: Timber Press.

Jones, David L. 1995. *Palms Throughout the World*. Washington, D.C.: Smithsonian Institution Press.

Jones, James L. 1999. *Lychnis and Silene in the Garden*. Millwood, New York: North American Rock Garden Society.

Jones, Judith. 1996. Marcel Le Piniec Award: Sally Walker. *Rock Garden Quarterly* 54 (4): 330.

Jonsson, Roy. 1999. New nursery species excite plant fanciers. *North Shore News* (North Vancouver, British Columbia), 12 April.

Jonsson, Roy. 1999. New species available to add interest to yards. *North Shore News* (North Vancouver, British Columbia), 19 April.

Kay, Stratford H., William M. Lewis, and Kenneth A. Langeland. 1995. Integrated management of multiflora rose in North Carolina. Publication AG-536. Raleigh: North Carolina Cooperative Extensive Service.

Kelaidis, Panayoti. 1984. Fiery phloxes of Chihuahua. *Pacific Horticulture* 45 (4): 38–40.

Kelaidis, Panayoti. 2002. Invasives: My last word. Post from an internet discussion group of the North American Rock Garden Society. ALPINE-L@NIC.SURFNET.NL (accessed 8 September 2002).

Kettler, Bill. 1999. On the rocks: Czech botanist has traveled the world learning to design rock gardens. *The Medford Mail Tribune* (Oregon), 6 April.

Kincaid, Jamaica. 1999. The great plant hunt. *Travel and Leisure* (September): 215–220, 250–255.

Kingsbury, Noël. 1998. On the look-out for chances to grow. *Financial Times* (London), 9 May.

Klinkenborg, Verlyn. 1999. A perfect madness for plants. *The New York Times Magazine* (20 June): 44–49.

Ladendorf, Sandra. 1988. Stalking the rare wildflower. *The Christian Science Monitor*, 22 March.

Lancaster, Roy. 1987. *Garden Plants for Connoisseurs*. Portland, Oregon: Timber Press.

Lancaster, Roy. 1991. A brief history of plant hunting as it concerns woody plants. In *The Hillier Manual of Trees and Shrubs*, 31–36. Newton Abbot, United Kingdom: David and Charles.

Lancaster, Roy. 1993. *Travels in China: A Plantsman's Paradise*. Woodbridge, Suffolk: Antique Collectors' Club.

Lancaster, Roy. 1995. *A Plantsman in Nepal*. Woodbridge, Suffolk: Antique Collectors' Club.

Lancaster, Roy. 1997. *Syneilesis aconitifolia*. *The Garden* 122 (4): 262–263.

Lancaster, Roy. 2002. Rarities in Caernarfon. *The Garden* 127 (5): 350–353.

Laskin, David. 1998. Green enough for envy. *The New York Times*, 22 March.

Lasseigne, Todd. 2003. What is that plant? *JC Raulston Arboretum e-Update*. JC Raulston Arboretum. http://www.ncsu.edu/jcraulstonarboretum/index.html?page = /jcraulstonarboretum/jcra_updates/jcra_e-updates/2003/july/july_2003_e-update.html (accessed 1 July 2003).

Lawson, John. 1967. *A New Voyage to Carolina*. Chapel Hill: University of North Carolina Press.

Leapman, Michael. 2000. Orchid fever. *Times* (London), 19 July.

Lear, Linda, ed. 1998. *Lost Woods: The Discovered Writings of Rachel Carson*. Boston: Beacon Press.

Lefler, Hugh Talmage. 1967. Introduction to *A New Voyage to Carolina*, by John Lawson. Chapel Hill: University of North Carolina Press.

Lehmiller, David J. 1999. A new species of *Sprekelia* (Amaryllidaceae). *Herbertia* 54: 228–231.

Levine, Ketzel. 1997. Heronswood takes flight. *Horticulture* (November): 46–51.

Lewandowski, Rick J. 2000a. Embracing the future: Plant exploration in the new millennium. In *Plant Exploration: Protocols for the Present, Concerns for the Future* (symposium proceedings, 18–19 March 1999), ed. J. R. Ault, 32–38. Glencoe, Illinois: Chicago Botanic Garden.

Lewandowski, Rick J. 2000b. Plant exploration in the twenty-first century. *The American Gardener* (July–August): 18–23.

Li, Hui-Lin. 1971. Floristic relationship between eastern Asia and eastern North America. *Transactions of the American Philosophical Society* 42 (2): 371–429.

Lighty, Richard W. 2000. An assessment of ornamental plant introductions in the not-for-profit sector. In *Plant Exploration: Protocols for the Present, Concerns for the Future* (symposium proceedings, 18–19 March 1999), ed. J. R. Ault, 14–22. Glencoe, Illinois: Chicago Botanic Garden.

Lipington, Jane. 1998. Treasure seekers. *Gardens Illustrated* (January): 64–68.

Lipkin, R., and D. F. Murray. 1997. Bering Sea Wormwood *Artemisia senjavinensis* Bess. In *Alaska Rare Plant Field Guide*. U.S. Fish and Wildlife Service, National Park Service, Bureau of Land Management, Alaska Natural Heritage Program, and U.S. Forest Service. http://www.uaa.alaska.edu/enri/rareguide/pdfs/25-26as.pdf (accessed 17 July 2003).

Lucas, Jannette M. 1939. *Where Did Your Garden Grow?* New York: J. B. Lippincott Company.

Lupp, Rick. 1993. *Erigeron* 'Goat Rocks'. *Bulletin of the American Rock Garden Society* 51 (2): 134.

Lupp, Rick. 1995. Slug-proof campanulas for the rock garden. *Rock Garden Quarterly* 53 (3): 189–192.

Lupp, Rick. 1999. Strategies for growing choice alpines. *Rock Garden Quarterly* 57 (4): 249–257.

Lupp, Rick. 2003. The north side of Mt. Adams: An alpine paradise. *Northwestern Chapter Newsletter* (North American Rock Garden Society) (April): 3–4.

Maillet, Neal. 2000. Edgar T. Wherry Award: Sean Hogan. *Bulletin of the American Rock Garden Society* 58 (4): 309–310.

Mabberley, D. J. 1997. *The Plant-Book*. Cambridge, England: University of Cambridge Press.

Mariette, Auguste. 1877. *Deir el-Bahari*. Leipzig, Germany.

Maslin, T. Paul. 1996. The rediscovery of *Phlox lutea* and *Phlox purpurea*. In *Rock Garden Plants of North America*, ed. Jane McGary, 230–237. Portland, Oregon: Timber Press.

Mathew, Brian. 1982. *The Crocus*. Portland, Oregon: Timber Press.

Mathew, Brian. 1989a. *Hellebores*. Woking, United Kingdom: Alpine Garden Society.

Mathew, Brian. 1989b. *The Iris*. Portland, Oregon: Timber Press.

Mathew, Brian. 1992. Germinating *Helleborus thibetanus*. *The Garden* 117 (11): 518.

Mathew, Brian. 1993a. A botanist's view. In *The Gardener's Guide to Growing Hellebores*, Graham Rice and Elizabeth Strangman, 121–125. Portland, Oregon: Timber Press.

Mathew, Brian. 1993b. Bulb conservation and the grower. *Quarterly Bulletin of the Alpine Garden Society* 62 (3): 288–297.

Mathew, Brian. 1994. The spotted hellebore: *Helleborus orientalis* subsp. *guttatus*. *The New Plantsman* 1 (3): 181–183.

Mathew, Brian. 2002. William Stearn: The monographer. *The Linnean* 18 (4): 32–34.

Matthews, Lewis J. 1993. *Proteas of the World*. Portland, Oregon: Timber Press.

McCormick, Kathleen, and Michael Leccese. 1995. A rock garden grows, eclectically, in the Rockies. *The New York Times*, 26 March.

McDonough, Mark, Jim Robinett, and Georgie Robinett. 2001. The genus *Allium*. In *Bulbs of North America*, ed. Jane McGary, 21–65. Portland, Oregon: Timber Press.

McGary, Jane, ed. *Rock Garden Plants of North America*. Portland, Oregon: Timber Press.

McLewin, Will. 1992. Hunting for red *Helleborus niger*. *Bulletin of the American Rock Garden Society* 50 (4): 294–298.

McLewin, Will. 1993. Confessions of a hellebore addict. In *The Gardener's Guide to Growing Hellebores*, Graham Rice and Elizabeth Strangman, 125–130. Portland, Oregon: Timber Press.

McLewin, Will. 1994. Hellebore *notes*. Stockport, Cheshire: Phedar Nursery.

McLewin, Will. 1996. Colour variations in *Helleborus niger*. *The Garden* 121 (1): 38–39.

McLewin, Will. 1999. Hellebore *notes*. Stockport, Cheshire: Phedar Nursery.

McLewin, Will, and Brian Mathew. 1995. Hellebores: The first of a series of articles discussing the genus *Helleborus*. *The New Plantsman* 2 (2): 112–121.

McLewin, Will, and Brian Mathew. 1996a. Hellebores 2: *Helleborus dumetorum*. *The New Plantsman* 3 (1): 50–60.

McLewin, Will, and Brian Mathew. 1996b. Hellebores 3: *Helleborus atrorubens*. *The New Plantsman* 3 (3): 170–177.

McLewin, Will, and Brian Mathew. 1997a. Hellebores 4: *Helleborus multifidus* subsp. *hercegovinus*. *The New Plantsman* 4 (1): 44–50.

McLewin, Will, and Brian Mathew. 1997b. Hellebores 5: *Helleborus purpurascens*. *The New Plantsman* 4 (3): 175–177.

McLewin, Will, and Brian Mathew. 1998. Hellebores 6: *Helleborus orientalis* and *Helleborus ×hybridus*. *The New Plantsman* 5 (2): 117–124.

McLewin, Will, and Brian Mathew. 1999. Hellebores 7: *Helleborus vesicarius* and *Helleborus thibetanus*. *The New Plantsman* 6 (3): 139–147.

McLewin, Will, and Brian Mathew. 2000. Hellebores 8: *Helleborus argutifolius*, *Helleborus lividus*, and *Helleborus ×sternii*. *The New Plantsman* 7 (2): 95–102.

McLewin, Will, and Brian Mathew. 2002. *Helleborus viridis*. *The Plantsman* 1 (3): 150–153.

McNamara, William A. 1999. *Schima*. Unpublished article. Glen Ellen, California: Quarryhill Botanical Garden.

McNamara, William A. 2000. All in a day's work: China, 1990. *The American Gardener* (July–August): 25.

McNamara, William A. 2001. *Illicium simonsii*. Quarryhill Botanical Garden. http://www.quarryhillbg.org/Articles/IlliciumSim/IlliciumSimonsii.htm (accessed 10 November 2003).

McNamara, William A. 2002. Making a last stand: *Acer pentaphyllum*. *Pacific Horticulture* 63 (2): 35–39.

McNough, Noel. 1993. Alpine plants and conservation legislation. *Quarterly Bulletin of the Alpine Garden Society* 61 (3): 238–253.

Meyer, Paul W. 2000. Plant collecting expeditions: A modern perspective. In *Plant Exploration: Protocols for the Present, Concerns for the Future* (symposium proceedings, 18–19 March 1999), ed. J. R. Ault, 7–13. Glencoe, Illinois: Chicago Botanic Garden.

Mineo, Baldassare. 1999. *Rock Garden Plants: A Color Encyclopedia*. Portland, Oregon: Timber Press.

Morin, Nancy R. 2000. Botanists seek to stop loss of plant diversity. *Newsletter* (American Association of Botanical Gardens and Arboreta) (June): 1–2.

Musgrave, Toby, Chris Gardner, and Will Musgrave. 1998. *The Plant Hunters*. London: Ward Lock.

Nicholls, Graham. 2001. Five choice European campanulas. From *Rock Garden Quarterly* 59 (2). http://members.aol.com/graplant/Articles.html (accessed 9 June).

Nicholls, Graham. 2002. *Alpine Plants of North America*. Portland, Oregon: Timber Press.

Nold, Robert. 2003. *Columbines: Aquilegia, Paraquilegia, and Semiaquilegia*. Portland, Oregon: Timber Press.

Northern Prairie Wildlife Research Center. Wyoming rare plant field guide. http://www.npwrc.usgs.gov/resource/distr/others/wyplant/SPEC/aquilara.htm (accessed 19 August 2002).

Nyberg, Jonathan. 1997. Plant News: J. C. Raulston selection program. *Friends of the JC Raulston Arboretum Newsletter* 1 (Fall): 3–5.

O'Brien, Joan. 1999. Botanist travels the globe to study and save rare plants. *The Salt Lake City Tribune*, 9 April.

Ogden, Scott. 1994. *Garden Bulbs for the South*. Dallas: Taylor Publishing Company.

Ohwi, Jisaburo. 1965. *Flora of Japan*. Washington, D.C.: Smithsonian Institution Press.

Oldfield, Sara. 1999. Collected wisdom. *The Garden* 124 (9): 700–703.

Panich, Paula. 2000. Tiger leaping man: Dan Hinkley in China (and Massachusetts). The Armchair Gardener. *Dirt: A Garden Journal from the Connecticut River Valley* 2 (1). http://www.dirtagardenjournal.com/articles/tigerleapingman.htm (accessed 16 September 2002).

Parks, Clifford R. 2002. The acquisition, maintenance, and breeding potential of *Camellia* germplasm. *Landscape Plant Symposium: Plant Development and Utilization* (symposium proceedings, 23–25 May). Asheville, North Carolina: Metropolitan Tree Improvement Alliance.

Philippo, Martin. 2003. *Muscari mcbeathianum*. Muscari pages. http://home.tiscali.nl/~hennessy/mcbeathianum.htm (accessed 30 August 2003).

Phillips, Roger, and Martyn Rix. 1989. *Bulbs*. New York: Random House.

Phillips, Roger, and Martyn Rix. 1997. *Indoor and Greenhouse Plants*. Vol. 2. New York: Random House.

Polo, Marco. 1958. *The Travels*, trans. Roland Latham. New York: Penguin.

Polunin, Oleg, and Anthony Huxley. 1965. *Flowers of the Mediterranean*. London: Chatto and Windus.

Polunin, Oleg, and Adam Stainton. 1997. *Flowers of the Himalaya*. New Delhi: Oxford University Press.

Pooley, Elsa. 1998. *A Field Guide to Wild Flowers of KwaZulu-Natal and the Eastern Region*. Durban, South Africa: Natal Floral Publications Trust.

Pradhan, U. C. 1997. *Himalayan Cobra-lilies*. Kalimpong, West Bengal: Primulaceae Books.

Prior, Richard. 1864. *On the Proper Names of British Plants*. In *Oxford English Dictionary* (CD-ROM). 1993 ed. Oxford: Oxford University Press.

Probst, Darrell R. 1997. New epimediums from China. *Rock Garden Quarterly* 55 (3): 174–176.

Probst, Darrell R. 2003. Up-and-coming epimediums. *Fine Gardening* (July–August): 44–47.

Quarrie, Joyce, ed. 1992. *Earth Summit 1992: The United Nations Conference on Environment and Development, Rio de Janeiro*. London: Regency Press.

Randall, John L. 1999. Botanical gardens, arboreta, and invasive exotic plants. *Wildland Weeds* (Winter): 4–12.

Randall, John L. 2000. The effects of invasive exotic plant species on the reproductive ecology of natives. In *Invasive Exotic Species: Truth and Consequences* (symposium proceedings, 16–18 March 2000). Chapel Hill: University of North Carolina and North Carolina Botanical Garden.

Randall, John L. 2001. This grass isn't greener: Help control invasive menace. Raleigh *News & Observer* (North Carolina), 8 September.

Randall, John L., and Rob Gardner. 2000. Pretty is as pretty does. *Carolina Gardener* (July–August): 38–41.

Randall, John M., and Janet Marinelli. 1996. *Invasive Plants: Weeds of the Global Garden*. Brooklyn: Brooklyn Botanic Garden.

Raver, Anne. 1999. What's eating America? Weeds. *The New York Times*, 16 September.

Raver, Anne. 2001. An intrepid voyager broadens America's garden repertory. *The New York Times*, 1 February.

Read, Mike. 1989. Overexploitation of wild bulbs by the horticultural trade. *Herbertia* 45 (1–2): 6–12.

Reichard, Sarah H. 2000a. Risk assessment: In principle and in practice. Abstract. In *Invasive Exotic Species: Truth and Consequences* (symposium proceedings, 16–18 March 2000). Chapel Hill: University of North Carolina and North Carolina Botanical Garden.

Reichard, Sarah H. 2000b. Screening and monitoring for invasive ability. In *Plant Exploration: Protocols for the Present, Concerns for the Future* (symposium proceedings, 18–19 March 1999), ed. J. R. Ault, 23–31. Glencoe, Illinois: Chicago Botanic Garden.

Reid, Mayne. 1884. *The Plant Hunters: Adventures Among the Himalaya Mountains*. New York: Thomas S. Knox.

Reveal, James L. 1992. *Gentle Conquest: The Botanical Discovery of North America*. Washington, D.C.: Starwood Publishing.

Rice, Graham, and Elizabeth Strangman. 1993. *The Gardener's Guide to Growing Hellebores*. Portland, Oregon: Timber Press.

Richards, Richard. 1993. *Primula*. Portland, Oregon: Timber Press.

Riffle, Robert Lee. 1998. *The Tropical Look*. Portland, Oregon: Timber Press.

Rolfe, Robert. 2000. Plant Awards 1999–2000: *Erigeron* 'Goat Rocks'. *Quarterly Bulletin of the Alpine Garden Society* 68 (4): 471–472.

Rooney, Derrick. 1991. A Himalayan plant-hunter's foray into New Zealand. *The Press* (Christchurch City, New Zealand), 23 March.

Royal Horticulture Society. 2003. *RHS Plant Finder 2003–2004*. London: Dorling Kindersley.

Ruíz, Hipólito. 1998. *The Journals of Hipólito Ruíz*, trans. Richard Evans Schultes and María José Nemry von Thenen de Jaramillo-Arango. Portland, Oregon: Timber Press.

Russell, Loren. 2000. Marcel Le Piniec Award: Rick Lupp. *Rock Garden Quarterly* 58 (4): 307–308.

Sanchez, Janet H. 1998. Where East meets West. *Horticulture* (March–April): 56–60.

Sargent, Charles Sprague. 1969. *Scientific Papers of Asa Gray*. Vol. 1. New York: Kraus Reprint Company.

Saunders, Rachel. 2000. South Africa new: Two new species discovered at Nieuwoudtville, South Africa. *Bulbs* (International Bulb Society) 2 (2): 8.

Schmid, George W. 1991. *The Genus Hosta*. Portland, Oregon: Timber Press.

Schmid, George W. 2002. *An Encyclopedia of Shade Perennials*. Portland, Oregon: Timber Press.

Schmiemann, Gisela, and Josh Westrich. 1997. *Helen Ballard: The Hellebore Queen*. Cologne, Germany: Edition Art and Nature.

Schoenfeld, Carl M. 1998. *The Yucca Do Log: Emphasis on Rain Lilies*. Hempstead, Texas: Yucca Do Nursery.

Schoenfeld, Carl M. 2001. Finding *Sabal* sp. "Tamaulipas" in northeastern Mexico. *Rhapidophyllum* (Fall): 8–11.

SERPIN. 2003. *Helianthus verticillatus*. Southeastern Rare Plant Information Network. http://www.serpin.org/cfm/pllitsearch.cfm?Genus1 = Helianthusand SpecificEpithet1 = verticillatusandplantID = 270 (accessed 23 September 2003).

Sheley, Roger L., Bret E. Olson, and Carla Hoopes. 1998. *What Is So Dangerous about the Impacts of Noxious Weeds on the Ecology and Economy of Montana?* Publication EB 152. Bozeman: Montana State University.

Shulman, Nicola. 2002. *A Rage for Rock Gardening.* London: Short Books.

Silk, Steve. 1999. Tracking down terrific plants. *Fine Gardening* (November–December): 30–35.

Smith, A. W. 1963. *A Gardener's Book of Plant Names.* New York: Harper and Row.

Smith, Betty. 1989. *A Tree Grows in Brooklyn.* Pleasantville, New York: Reader's Digest Association.

Smith, Gideon F., et al. 1998. *Mesembs of the World.* Pretoria, South Africa: Briza Publications.

Spongberg, Stephen A. 1990. *A Reunion of Trees: The Discovery of Exotic Plants and Their Introduction into North American and European Landscapes.* Cambridge, Massachusetts: Harvard University Press.

Springer, Lauren. 2002. A rare plantsman. *Horticulture* (September–October): 56–59.

Stearn, William T. 1992. *Stearn's Dictionary of Plant Names for Gardeners.* London: Cassell Publishers.

Stearn, William T. 2002. *The Genus Epimedium.* Portland, Oregon: Timber Press.

Stuart, David. 2002. *The Plants That Shaped Our Gardens.* Cambridge, Massachusetts: Harvard University Press.

Sullivan, Barbara J. 2003. *Garden Perennials for the Coastal South.* Chapel Hill: University of North Carolina Press.

Sun, Hang, Will McLewin, and Michael F. Fay. 2001. Molecular phylogeny of *Helleborus* (Ranunculaceae), with an emphasis on the East Asia–Mediterranean disjunction. *Taxon* 50:1001–1018.

Taylor, Patricia A. 2000. Perennial combinations that add to fall colors. *The New York Times*, 8 October.

Taylor, Patricia A. 2002. A ho-hum plant proves exciting after all. *The New York Times*, 1 December.

Theodoropoulos, David I. 2003. *Invasion Biology: Critique of a Pseudoscience.* Blythe, California: Avvar Books.

Thomas, Catherine. 1990. Woodlanders caters to the exotic plant lover. *Aiken Standard* (South Carolina), 18 February.

Thornton, Linda. 1998. Lone star super star. *The American Gardener* (March–April): 46–52.

Tripp, Kim E., and J. C. Raulston. 1995. *The Year in Trees: Superb Woody Plants for Four-Season Gardens.* Portland, Oregon: Timber Press.

Upson, Tim. 2001. Beautiful bergenias. *The Garden* 126 (3): 174–177.

U.S. Fish and Wildlife Service. 2000. Candidate and listing priority assignment form for *Helianthus verticillatus.* http://southeast.fws.gov/es/pdf/WSF.PDF (accessed 23 September 2003).

U.S. Fish and Wildlife Service. 2003.. Invasive plants in our backyards. http://southeast.fws.gov/ea/Fun_Facts/pubbck9.pdf (accessed 1 September 2003).

Walker, Sally. 1981a. Three skyrockets. *Bulletin of the American Rock Garden Society* 39 (1): 43–44.

Walker, Sally. 1981b. Two southwestern primroses. *Bulletin of the American Rock Garden Society* 39 (3): 127–129.

Walker, Sally. 1987. The hypothetical convention of southeast Arizona. *Bulletin of the American Rock Garden Society* 45 (2): 88–92.

Walker, Sally. 1999. Rainy-season plants of the Southwest. *Rock Garden Quarterly* 57 (3): 191–210.

Walton, Craig. 1998. Preventing the introduction of potential weeds as ornamental plants. *The Nursery Papers* (Nursery Industry Association of Australia) 10: 1–2.

Watson, John M. 1974–1977. Andes, 1971 and 1972. *Quarterly Bulletin of the Alpine Garden Society* 42 (2): 123–124; 42 (3): 227–234; 42 (4): 290–301; 43 (1): 78–83; 43 (2): 139–149; 43 (3): 230–239; 43 (4): 282–290; 44 (1): 34–38; 44 (2): 98–108; 44 (3): 202–212; 44 (4): 310–318; 45 (1): 74–81; 45 (2): 154–159; 45 (3): 221–231; 45 (4): 292–296.

Watson, John M. 1994. South American alpines. *Quarterly Bulletin of the Alpine Garden Society* 62 (3): 293–355.

Watson, John M. 1997. Collecting and introducing alpines from Chile, Argentina, Bolivia, and Peru. In *Southern Alpines '96* (conference proceedings, 5–10 January 1996), ed. John S. Sheppard, 129–144. Christchurch, New Zealand: Southern Alpines.

Watson, John M., and C. von Bohlen. 2000. *Mimulus naiandinus* (Scrophulariaceae). *Curtis's Botanical Magazine* 17 (4): 195–201.

Weakley, Alan S. 1997. *Flora of the Carolinas and Virginia*. Working draft. Chapel Hill, North Carolina: The Nature Conservancy.

Wen-Pei Fang. 1959. Notes on Chinese peonies: An abstract. From *Acta Phytotaxonomica Sinica* 6: 313–323. http://www.paeon.de/h1/fang/fang.html (accessed 3 November 2003).

van der Werff, Dirk. 1999. *Bergenia emeiensis*. *Plants*. http://www.plants-magazine.com/newplants/newplant12.shtml (accessed 28 October 2003).

Westbrooks, Randy C. 2001. Invasive species, coming to America. *Wildland Weeds* (Winter): 5–11.

Wheeler, David. 1994. Crûg Farm. *The Garden* 119 (5): 206–209.

Wherry, Edgar T. 1955. *The Genus Phlox*. Morris Arboretum Monographs 3. Philadelphia: University of Pennsylvania.

Whittle, Tyler. 1997. *The Plant Hunters*. New York: Lyons and Burford.

Williams, Jean, ed. 1986. *Rocky Mountain Alpines*. Portland, Oregon: Timber Press.

Wilson, Ernest H. 1927. *Plant Hunting*. 2 vols. Boston: Stratford Company.

Wilson, Ernest H. 1985. *Smoke That Thunders*. London: Waterstone and Company.

Worthington, Francis. 1993. The temperate temptations of Woodlanders. *Carolina Gardener* (July–August): 18–19.

Wrightman, Harvey, and Phyllis Gustafson. 2003. Crevice gardens. In *Rock Garden Design and Construction*, ed. Jane McGary, 96–111. Portland, Oregon: Timber Press.

Wu, Quanan. 1999. *Wild Flowers of Yunnan in China*. Beijing: China Forestry Publishing House.

van Wyk, Ben-Erik, and Gideon Smith. 1996. *Guide to the Aloes of South Africa*. Pretoria, South Africa: Briza Publications.

Wynn-Jones, Bleddyn. 2001. Solomon's seal. *Gardens Illustrated* (October): 54–61.

Wynn-Jones, Bleddyn, and Sue Wynn-Jones. 1998. Korean kaleidoscope. *The Hardy Plant* 20 (1): 11–22.

Wynn-Jones, Bleddyn, and Sue Wynn-Jones. 2001. New wild seed introductions from the Far East. *Plants* 6 (2): 56–58.

Wynn-Jones, Bleddyn, and Sue Wynn-Jones. 2002. Collections in the Far East. *Plants* 7 (1): 6–9.

Yinger, Barry. 1993. Asarums. *Bulletin of the American Rock Garden Society* 51 (2): 83–91.

Yinger, Barry. 2000a. All in a day's work: the North Korea border. *The American Gardener* (July–August): 24–25.

Yinger, Barry. 2000b. Challenges in plant exploration: Building and maintaining relationships in host countries. In *Plant Exploration: Protocols for the Present, Concerns for the Future* (symposium proceedings, 18–19 March 1999), ed. J. R. Ault, 47–51. Glencoe, Illinois: Chicago Botanic Garden.

Yoshida, Toshio. 2002. *Portraits of Himalayan Flowers*. Portland, Oregon: Timber Press.

Zhang, Donglin, and F. Todd Lasseigne. 1998. A survey of Chinese native plants of potential ornamental and economic value for the southeastern United States. *Friends of the JC Raulston Arboretum Newsletter* 3 (Spring): 3–6, 27–35.

Index